Beloved
and
Chosen

Women of faith

by
JILL EVANS

The Canterbury Press
Norwich

*Typeset by Datix International Limited, Bungay, Suffolk
and printed in Great Britain by
St Edmundsbury Press Limited
Bury St Edmunds, Suffolk*

Foreword

IT IS IMPOSSIBLE to deny that, on first reading, the history of the Christian Church makes a depressing study for women. In the last few years, countless scholars and writers have collected instances of ludicrous and shameful rhetoric directed against women by some of the most influential figures in the Church's spiritual and intellectual life over the centuries; and continuing debates over the position of women in the ordained ministry and over the admissibility of female imagery in talking about God have brought to light some startling attitudes still deeply entrenched in the Christian psyche.

Dealing with such a long record of hurt and humiliation for women is not just a matter of reforming structures, vital as that is, nor even of admitting responsibility for errors. It must also be a reclaiming of what Christian women themselves have made of the gospel of Jesus Christ in the midst of an ecclesiastical environment that must so often have seemed to be out to make the gospel inaccessible or repulsive to women.

That Christian women have heard it as good news, as something giving them strength and joy, says something about both the resources of the gospel itself and the resources, in imagination and courage, of women. It encourages Christians to think that the Christian tradition can meet the challenge of women claiming their dignity; that feminism and Christianity are not after all enemies.

So we need to learn a new depth of familiarity with *women's* Christian history – which is by no means the same as the textbook version of the Church's past. Necessarily, it is a history of persons rather than institutions, since the public institutional face of the Church has been so largely male. *Persons*, notice, rather than individuals: we are not talking about a history of dramatic and isolated heroines, but about people serving visions of the Christian community, the Christian commonwealth, even when these are not the visions that they are instructed to have. In recent years, research in this area has begun to flourish in remarkable ways.

What we have not yet seen is a bold overview, a survey that enables us to see something of the immense variety of ways in which Christian women in very diverse cultures have answered the gospel. This is what Jill Evans provides, in a book of exceptionally wide range. We encounter here those who found a secure place in the life of their churches by developing 'conventional' roles – wives and mothers and nuns – in fresh ways, without simply colluding with existing power systems; and also those who have had a calling to be uncomfortable and thoroughly unconventional, thorns in the ample flesh of the Church.

This is, then, a book that will encourage readers of very different backgrounds and gifts. All, male or female, will have their assumptions about what has been and could be possible for Christian women challenged; all will have their sense of the potential richness of the Church's life enlarged – a richness we have hardly yet begun to recognize and feed upon, so long as we are stuck with clichés and stereotypes about what women can give to the life of Christ's Body.

ROWAN WILLIAMS, *Bishop of Monmouth*

Contents

Acknowledgements

The author wishes to thank those publishers listed for permission to use extracts from the following copyright works:

Basil Blackwell, *Maude Royden: A Life* by Sheila Fletcher; Bible Society, *Word in Action* report; David Bolt Associates, *Helen Waddell* by Dame Felicitas Corrigan; Cassell, *Harlots in the Desert* by Benedicta Ward SLG, also *The Light of Christ* by Roger L. Roberts; The Central Board of Finance of the Church of England, *Deacons in The Ministry of the Church*; Church Times, *obit on Emma Hawkins*, by the Revd. R. Hunt and Canon M. Parsons 7 Dec. 1990; Darton, Longman & Todd Ltd, *The Mirror of Love* by Gillian Hawker, also *Iulia de Beausobre: A Russian Christian in the West* by C. Babington-Smith; Andre Deutsch Ltd, *Emily Davies and Liberation of Women, 1830–1921* by Daphne Bennett; Doubleday, a division of Bantam, Doubleday, Dell Publishing Group, Inc, *A Dictionary of Catholic Biography* © by John J. Delaney and James Edward Tobin; Eagle, *Gladys Aylward – A London Sparrow* by Phyllis Thompson; The Ecumenical Forum of European Christian Women (EFECW), material provided by delegates from the nations of the women concerned for the Forum's Assembly in York, July 1990; the author and The Watkins/Loomis Agency (Eerdmans), *Are Women Human?* by Dorothy L. Sayers; Hamish Hamilton, *Women in Medieval Life* by © Margaret Wade Labarge (pp. xiii, 108, 127) 1986; Harper Collins Publishers Ltd, *Something Beautiful for God* by Malcolm Muggeridge; David Higham Associates, *The Joy of The Snow*, by Elizabeth Goudge; Hodder & Stoughton *Open to God* by © Joyce Huggett 1989; Lion Publishing plc, *Christian Classics* compiled by Veronica Zundel; The Dean of Liverpool Cathedral (windows commentary); Longmans Group UK Ltd, *A People's Book of Saints* by J. Alick Bouquet © 1930; Oxford University Press, *Oxford Illustrated History of Christianity: Eastern Christendom* by Kallistos Ware and *North America* by Martin Marty; Paulist Press, *Francis de Sales; Jane de Chantal: Letters of Spiritual Direction*, Wendy M. Wright and Joseph Power © the authors, 1988; Penguin Books, 'On Mary Magdalene' by Cassia, tr. by Constantine A. Trypanis from *The Penguin Book of Greek Verse* (Penguin Books 1971) © 1971; *A History of the English Church and People* by Bede tr. by Leo Shirley-Price, (Penguin Classics, revised ed. 1968) © 1955, 1968; *Revelations of Divine Love* by Julian of Norwich, tr. by Clifton Walters (Penguin Classics 1966), © 1966; *The Penguin Dictionary of Saints* by Donald Attwater, revised and updated by Catherine Rachel John, (Penguin Books, 2nd Edit 1983), © the Estate of D. Attwater, 1965, © C. R. John, 1983; People to Lourdes Trust, *Have you heard of Akita?*; Powage Press (Faith Press), *Joseph Butler – The Forgotten Saint* by Joseph Williamson; Charles Preece, (The Mother Shepherd Project) *Women of the Valleys*; Routledge, Kegan & Paul, *Waiting for God* by Simone Weil, tr. Emma Crauford; St Vladimir's Seminary Press, Crestwood, NY 10707, *The Meaning of Icons* by Ouspensky L. & Ossky V., © 1982; SCM Press, *The Book of Christian Martyrs* by Chenu, Prud'homme, Quéré & Thomas, 1990; Sheed & Ward, *The Comforting of Christ* by Carryl Houselander, 1947; SPCK, London, *The Silence of the Heart* edited by Kathryn Spink; also *The Russians and Their Church* by Nicholas Zernov and *The Hidden Tradition* by Lavinia Byrne; Thames & Hudson, *The Book of Kells*, 1980 by P. Brown; also *The Christian World* by Margaret Aston, ed. Geoffrey Barraclough, © 1981; University of California Press, *Christian Century in Japan, 1549–1650* by Charles Boxer, © 1951, 1979 Charles Boxer; Virgin Publishing, *She for God* by Katherine Moore; Weidenfeld & Nicholson, *A History of Christianity* by Paul Johnson. Scripture Quotations are from the Revised Standard Version of the Bible, © 1946, 1952, 1971 by the Division of Christian Education of the National Council of Churches of Christ in the USA, also from Holy Bible, New International Version, © 1973, 1978, 1984 by International Bible Society.

The author has made every endeavour to trace and obtain permission for the use of copyright material, but in cases of oversight or error, offers sincere apologies and undertakes to acknowledge in a future edition.

THE MINISTRY OF WOMEN

IN THE

SERVICE OF CHRIST

Mark me this portent! strange beyond all telling!
How this despoiled Kingdom stricken lay,
And no man raised his hand to guard his dwelling,
Until a Woman came to show the way.
Until a Woman (since no man dare try)
Rallied the land and bade the traitors fly.
Honour to Womankind! It needs must be
That God loves Woman, since He fashioned Thee!

(Verse from a poem about Joan of Arc
by Christine de Pisan, 1363–1429)

Preface

THIS BOOK has been in the making for some time. It was Ruth
Epting from Switzerland who first gave me the idea, when she
drew up a list of women of faith divided into different eras for
the Ecumenical Forum of European Christian Women
(EFECW), of which she was a founder member and Honorary
President. I found this exciting and Jean Mayland, the President of EFECW in 1990, encouraged me to gather more
material. When the Forum met for their third Assembly in
York that year, Jean asked me to collect the stories of women
of faith, one from each country. They came in different forms,
and I quite frequently had to rearrange them or have them
translated. I am grateful to those women from across Europe
who sent me stories from their countries, and to others who
helped me in my task of collecting and translating stories,
particularly Stephanie Coutts, a language teacher in Monmouth, and her pupils, and Gisela M'Caw.

Although I had no particular knowledge of social or religious history, I have learnt a great deal in the writing of this
book about Roman and European history. However the book
is not solely confined to Europe and I have tried to include
stories from as broad an area as possible. The subject matter
has been one close to my heart and despite my initial lack of
knowledge, I increasingly felt that my own position of being a
deacon in the Church at this time was a useful place from
which to start.

The work has been a labour of love, but it has also been
hard and exacting work and I am grateful, therefore, for
the support and encouragement of many, particularly my
husband, Gary, and children, Mandy, Christopher and
Elizabeth.

Many of the stories are inspiring but many also are tales of
women struggling against the odds in a male dominated
society. (I have used the word women for the sake of tidiness

although some of the women mentioned were young girls.) They were often the encouragement for me to continue as they touched a wound in me which reflected some of the difficulties which women still experience in the Church. However it is so often from wounds that creativity arises.

There are many, I know, who have supported me in prayer and in other ways and for their encouragement and support I am most grateful. Equally there are many other stories I could tell, but if every one of them were written down the whole world would not have room for the books that would be written. So for those who have helped create this book in the way they led their lives or otherwise, I can only say a humble *Deo Gratias*

Monmouth   JILL EVANS
February 1993

Introduction

WHEN MARY said 'I am the Lord's servant. Be it unto me according to your word', she was initiating a whole new way of life and the opportunity for women to share in God's mission to the world. For Christianity could be said to have started with a young girl's obedience to God. No doubt Mary's acquiescence in God's great plan was not absolutely necessary, either he could have found another young woman, or Jesus could have begun his human life in a different way from us, as indeed his conception was different. How strange that it was in fact the man's part in his birth which was usurped! It is as if, right from the start, Jesus was giving women a new and much greater part in his kingdom. From before the Christian era can be said to have begun, God chose a woman to be the prime bearer of His Word to the world, and from that point on women have been among the foremost in bearing his Word, taking his message of salvation, witnessing even to death of their faith in his love.

When theological or history books or the stained glass windows of our churches are studied, however, it would appear instead that women have taken little part in the Church's life. The women who are portrayed in stained glass are most often Mary in a Nativity scene or at the Annunciation, or occasionally Mary Magdalene. The cloister windows in Chester Cathedral are a typical representation of the women recognized in the Church, where only one in every three or four are women. Liverpool Anglican Cathedral, however, has many women of faith in its staircase windows. In the Welsh Calendar, there are seventeen female saints and ninety-one male saints, which is a ratio of approximately two women to eleven men.

The question which has to be asked, therefore, is whether these figures are representative of the contribution that women and men have made in the service of God, or whether the contribution of women has been consistently undervalued.

Although it has not been possible to include even a small part of the contribution of women through the ages, the research which has gone into the contents of this book suggests that far from being representative, Christian women have been virtually ignored in the way in which their service has been acknowledged.

Leaving aside the better known names, such as Teresa of Avila, Julian of Norwich, Joan of Arc, Florence Nightingale and Mother Teresa, there have been millions of wives, mothers and sisters who have influenced their husbands, children and brothers. For often the first understanding of the Christian faith comes at the mother's knee, the first prayers are taught by those who suckle the infant at their breast and the self-denying love of a women is very close to that of God himself.

However when we consider the history of the spread of Christianity, we also find the influence of Christian women in bringing their faith to pagan countries, so that many parts of Europe, for example, can thank women for their Christian heritage.

After the Anglo-Saxons had conquered England, pushing the Celtic church towards the western boundaries of Britain, a young Frankish bride, Bertha, brought her faith to Canterbury where she restored the tiny church of St Martin's, still to be seen today by those who search. When Pope Gregory wanted to send his emissary, Augustine, to the land of the Angles, where better to send him than to where the faith was already established and Queen Bertha had already prepared the way, so that the King was now a convert. Through her missionary work, Canterbury was to become the first province of England, and it was from Canterbury that Bertha's daughter, Ethelberga, took her faith to York, when she went to marry and eventually convert the pagan King Edwin and his family. So both provinces in England have the faith of women to thank for their foundation.

Much later on, it was a woman, again a queen, who was determined that the national Church in England should be the Anglican Church. Mary, who was eventually to marry William of Orange, had spent much of her life studying the theology of the Christian faith, and though her father had been a Roman Catholic, and her husband was a staunch Calvinist, Mary knew that as far as her realm was concerned, there could only be one Church, a church which was neither Roman nor Calvinist but was both Catholic and Protestant. Without Mary's firm insistence, the whole Anglican Communion might not exist today.

Other women who brought the Christian faith to new lands include Olga of Russia, who was so attracted to the Orthodox Church on a visit to Constantinople that she took the faith back to her own country, and Nino or Nina who converted Georgia in the fourth century. The final part of the European Church jigsaw was completed in 1387 when Jadwiga, or Hedwig, brought Christianity to the country of Lithuania, over which she and her husband ruled.

These major conversions of whole countries to the Christian faith through the steadfast belief of many women and their insistence that there was only one true way to God does not take away from the missionary work of many other women. It is necessary to remember particularly the women who went to join Boniface in Germany in the eighth century and the many missionaries and hymn-writers of the nineteenth century.

However, missionary work is but one part of the work that women have contributed in God's service. 'By their fruits, ye shall know them', and the fruits which have grown from the sufferings and deaths of many martyrs throughout the centuries were seen in the strength they gave to the rest of the Church to increase and spread. From the very first, women were among the martyrs, diamonds of light in the desert of the pagan world and their stories need to be told again and again to remind us what they had to suffer in order for the truth of the Gospel to be told. The social revolution of the eighteenth and nineteenth centuries saw women very much in the forefront of the fight against injustice, a fight in which women still play an important part today. The Ignatian spirituality which is having such a revival in the Church at this present time depends upon the inspiration which Iñigo received from reading the stories of saints. It is to be hoped that in reading this book many women, and men also, will be both affirmed and inspired as they share in the struggles and the joys which are told in these pages. Women have a history which has so often been neglected in previous books of Christian history, books which have more often been written by men. In the Middle Ages, the greatest stories were those about the great deeds of kings and heroism in battles. These were the stories which were told in the Great Halls and the Courts and were eventually written down. Learning and study was not for women, indeed women were considered incapable of such matters, and the only opportunity available was often to enter a religious community which some preferred to the restrictive life of the dutiful wife often bearing children until death or old age spared them. It is all the more surprising, therefore, that women did have such an influence in the Christian world.

'Just as many a flower blooms and dies unseen, so many a woman must have lived her life, serviceable to her special environment, but wholly unrecorded. Just as, in the course of ages, the seeds of some humble plant have been carried by wind or water from some lonely region to one less remote, and made to serve a purpose by adding to the sum total of beauty and usefulness, so the thoughts and deeds of many an unremembered woman have doubtless passed into the great ocean of thought, encircling us to-day, and influencing us as a living force.'[1]

It has been asked why we need to know the stories of these women. The answer is that it is part of our identity, an identity which has been denied to women for the most part. But it is not only part of the identity of the women of today, it is also part of the identity of the men, for if we reject one portion of the whole, then the story is incomplete, and we fail to recognize the totality of that history.

Also, in acknowledging the great contribution that women have given to the development of Christianity, we are following the lead which God himself gave and Jesus took up in affirming the place of women as members of his family, servants in his household, chosen and beloved. The women mentioned in this study are mere representatives of a far greater body who have been instrumental in spreading the Gospel and witnessing to their faith. Many of the better known have been given less space than others who are little known. Some, who might have been included, have not been mentioned. At best these stories can only be appetisers for the reader to seek further.

Wherever possible, the authenticity of the lives has been checked, although at times these have been derived from legends, hopefully based on fact. All history is a biased account of what has happened, as can be seen by the discrepancies between the Gospels, and more particularly between newspapers when recording the day's events. If there is a bias in this book, where it exists it will perhaps do something towards balancing the previous bias of history. The book does not pretend to be an academic or purely historical study, but it is a fascinating and exciting insight into the contribution of Christian women to God's service.

Within the confines of one book it is not possible to include all the life-stories of all the women of faith. Particularly during the last two hundred years, there has been such a large known contribution that the names included have had to be very limited. However, it is to be hoped that this book will stir the imagination of many to discover for themselves that God not only loves women, but he chose them to be his apostles, members of his Body, living stones in the building of his Church in the world of their day.

CHAPTER ONE

Honour to Womankind

'Fear not, for I have redeemed you. I have called you by name, you are mine. When you pass through the waters, I will be with you; and when you pass through the rivers they will not sweep over you. When you walk through the fire, you will not be burned; the flames will not set you ablaze. For I am the Lord your God, the Holy one of Israel, your Saviour.

Since you are precious and honoured in my sight, and because I love you, I will give men in exchange for you, and people in exchange for your life. Do not be afraid for I am with you.'
(Isaiah 43.1–5 NIV)

'Then the woman, seeing that she could not go unnoticed, came trembling and fell at his feet. In the presence of all the people, she told why she had touched him and how she had been instantly healed. Then he said to her, "Daughter, your faith has healed you. Go in peace."' (Luke 8.47–48 NIV)

★ ★

THAT WOMEN were to take a not inconsiderable part in both the life and ministry of Jesus demonstrates his true humanity. Born of a woman, recognized whilst still in his mother's womb by another woman and her unborn child, Jesus was welcomed into the temple as a six week old child by yet another woman. Although men were also present in the Nativity stories, this comparatively high profile of women in the narratives of his infancy show that they were to play a fairly major part in Jesus' life, and that from the first it was his intention to give honour to womankind.

Jesus acknowledged women, even when they were unclean or immoral, and he welcomed their attentions as they brought their children to him or anointed him with costly spices. No doubt there were many women whom he healed, talked with, welcomed and just loved and whom we shall never hear

about. They would come out from their homes to watch as he
passed by and receive a loving glance as he saw them standing
on the edge of the crowd. They were present when the five
thousand were fed on the hillside, present when Jesus brought
Lazarus and Jairus' daughter back to life and present when
he died on the cross. Among the names of the women mentioned as being present at the cross were some who were
described as having been caring for Jesus as he travelled
about Galilee. No doubt there were many more who had
opened their homes and prepared meals and a bed for Jesus
and his band of followers.

However, it was not only humble service of the domestic
kind to which Jesus called his womenfolk. The first apostle of
the Resurrection was a woman and she was commanded by
Jesus to take the Good News to the other apostles. '"Go to my
brothers and tell them, 'I am returning to my Father and
your Father, to my God and your God'"'. Mary of Magdala
went to the disciples with the news.' (John 20.17, 18 NIV)

The women in Jesus' family

It is with Mary, the mother of Our Lord, that we must begin.
For were it not for **Mary of Nazareth**, then perhaps it could
be said that Christianity might not exist at all. It was her '*Yes*'
in obedience to God that gave Jesus Christ to humanity.
Mary was a young country girl from Nazareth, a small town
in the north of Judaea. While she was engaged to be married
to a carpenter called Joseph, she was visited by the Archangel
Gabriel, who told her she had been chosen to be the mother of
the Son of God. She agreed without hesitation, although it
must have been difficult for her to understand what this
would mean to her and she may well have been fearful of the
consequences of becoming an unmarried mother. However
Joseph, guided by a dream, stood by the betrothal and went
ahead with the marriage although Mary remained a virgin
until her son, the Son of God, was born. This took place in
the town of Bethlehem, where she and her husband had
travelled because of the Roman census, which demanded that
all the Jews should return to the place of their family roots for
taxation purposes. Because the town was crowded, the baby
was born in an outhouse where the animals were kept, and

the young mother gave birth to her first-born in one of the lowliest earthly homes imaginable.

Bringing up her son in Nazareth, Mary took him to Jerusalem when he was twelve, and must have felt the anxiety of any mother, when she discovered him missing on their return home. We do not know her feelings about bringing up such a son. She was a woman who cherished the things which were said to her as she no doubt cherished her son. There would have been much love, much wonder and anxiety, yet obviously that same deep faith which had been present in her when she accepted such a task at the Annunciation.

Mary had been present at the first recorded miracle of Jesus at Cana in Galilee, where he appeared to have spoken somewhat roughly to her. She was probably not with him for most of his ministry, but perhaps went to see him frequently especially when he was in the neighbourhood. For instance Mark mentions her presence in Galilee with her sons, the brothers of Jesus, when he tells how all are now his sisters and brothers and mother. She was present at his death, where she was committed to the charge of his beloved disciple, John, and he to her, as mother and son. It is believed that they both went to live in Ephesus afterwards, where there is a church existing on what is believed to be the site of her home. It remains a place of peace and serenity, despite the crowds who come to visit.

Mary is highly honoured in the Church as befits someone who was chosen to be the mother of God, and who was no doubt greatly loved by her son. She is known also by the titles of Our Lady, the Blessed Virgin Mary, and the Theotokos, or Mother of God.

Not much is known about her mother, **Anne**, the wife of Joachim and grandmother of Jesus, although no doubt she was, in true Jewish tradition, a great influence on her grandson and loved him dearly. Believed to be very devout, she was venerated greatly in Egypt and is the patron saint of Brittany.

We hear more about **Elizabeth** who was a kinswoman of Mary and would have seen Jesus as a child at least on family occasions. A descendant of Aaron and wife of the priest, Zechariah, she was 'upright in the sight of God, observing all God's commandments and regulations blamelessly' (Luke 1.6 NIV). The first mention of her in Luke's Gospel tells us that both Elizabeth and her husband were advanced in years but had not been able to bear children. It now appeared to be impossible that they would ever have any children of their own. However while her husband was serving in the Temple he had a vision in which an angel appeared to him, prophesying that Elizabeth would become pregnant and that their son should be called John.

Elizabeth did conceive and then went into seclusion for five months. She was visited in the sixth month of her pregnancy by Mary, after she too had become pregnant. When Mary entered Elizabeth's home, Elizabeth's baby had jumped in her womb and Elizabeth herself became filled with the Holy Spirit. Recognizing the importance of Mary and the babe which she carried within her, Elizabeth then greeted Mary saying 'Blessed are you among women, and blessed is the child you will bear! Blessed is she who has believed that what the Lord has said to her will be accomplished!' As her son, John the Baptist, was later to proclaim the coming of Jesus by the River Jordan, so Elizabeth proclaimed the blessing of his coming before he was born.

Meanwhile, her husband, Zechariah, had been struck dumb by the incident in the Temple, and when their son was born, it was Elizabeth who told their family what his name was to be, according to what the angel had told her husband in the Temple. When she said that he was to be called John, her relatives would not believe her and made signs to Zechariah to get his opinion. Much to their surprise he agreed with what his wife had told them and so, in this way, Elizabeth became the first among many in the history of Christianity who had their word doubted and ignored because they were women.

Other women in the Gospels

Anna was a prophetess, the daughter of Phanuel, of the tribe of Asher. She had been widowed after she and her husband had been married only seven years, and she had remained a widow. When Luke tells her story Anna was an eighty-four year old who made prayer and worship her priority in life, never leaving the temple precincts and worshipping night and day in fasting and prayer. 'She was one of the "quiet of the land" – a group of people who lived in Jerusalem at the time when Jesus was born who were rather like the contemplative monks and nuns of our own day; people who had such a burden for God's needy world that they give their entire lives to pray for the coming of the Messiah.'[1]

She must have watched the young couple, Mary and Joseph, as they came into the Temple and seen their joy at Simeon's words. With a thrill of recognition she would have known that this child was to be the Messiah, and after Simeon had blessed the baby, she would have gone forward, shyly and yet full of joy to greet the parents, to give thanks and to proclaim the baby's role for the future of all people, women as well as men. In fact, her presence at the presentation of Christ is seen by many to demonstrate this very fact, that Jesus came for the salvation of *all* believers. As Simeon in his words made it known that Jesus was coming to the Gentiles, so Anna's presence did the same for women. She spoke about the child to all who were looking forward to the redemption of Jerusalem.

There were other important pointers in Anna's story. She was of the tribe of Asher, and a prophetess. The tribe of Asher was from Galilee, and as the Pharisees later said about Jesus, no prophet ever came from Galilee. Not only that, the spirit of prophecy had died out in Israel some three hundred years earlier, and the official view was that the gift of prophecy would only return when the Messiah came in the new age. By calling Anna a prophetess, and one also from Galilee, Luke was emphasising that a new age had arrived.

Anna being the daughter of Phanuel becomes interesting when we hark back to the story in Genesis where Jacob has been wrestling with God. He decides to call the place Penuel, (the same word as Phanuel,) 'for I have seen God face to face' (Genesis 32.30). Now the daughter of Phanuel has also seen God face to face.

By her actions of prayer and fasting, and in welcoming the Baby Jesus on behalf of all womankind, Anna rightly becomes the first woman outside the immediate family of Jesus to have her story told in this history of women in the service of Christ. For in Luke's story, Anna becomes the first woman to proclaim to the world the good news of the Incarnation after the birth of Jesus.

After her come many other women in the Gospels, some

mentioned by name who eventually were to be among Jesus' closest friends. Others were known for the part they played in the Gospel stories or the message their story told to the early Church.

One whose name we know was **Mary Magdalene**, so called because she was born in Magdala, on the western side of the sea of Galilee. She was one of the many disciples of Jesus who followed him in his ministry and may have been the woman who was a sinner and anointed his feet and also the sister of Martha and Lazarus, all close friends of Jesus. According to St Luke, seven demons had been cast out of her, and she becomes an example of one who loves much because she has sinned much. She was present at the crucifixion and at the empty tomb and she became the first witness of the risen Christ when he met her in the garden. Mary Magdalene has often been called the 'Apostle to the Apostles' and the Eastern Church recognizes her as equal to the Apostles in veneration. Early tradition suggests that she accompanied Mary, the mother of Jesus, and John to Ephesus, where she later died, although her body was afterwards taken to Constantinople.

Mary and Martha were the sisters of Lazarus living in Bethany. They were great friends of Jesus who often used to stay with them. Early on Mary had anointed the feet of Jesus with costly ointment and wiped them with her hair. When she was rebuked by the disciples for wasting money Jesus defended her action as he did on other occasions.

It is possible that she was in fact the same sinful woman who had anointed the feet of Jesus, wetting them with her tears of repentance and wiping them with her hair. Again this story appears very similar to another in which a woman anointed the head of Jesus with a very expensive perfume at the house of Simon the Leper, and whom Jesus said had done a very beautiful thing for him. Certainly the anointing with oil or perfume was recognized by Jesus as a sacramental act by the woman or women concerned and welcomed as such by him.

Mary tended to have a more contemplative nature whereas Martha was more active and down to earth, one who cared first for the bodily needs of Jesus, his food and refreshment, before settling down to listen to him. Martha often is taken as reflecting the more practical side of women and Mary the mystical side, different parts of a woman's personality which may often clash within the whole. Martha was the sister who went to look for Jesus when Lazarus died, while Mary sat in the house and waited until Martha told her that Jesus was calling for her. Tradition is that they both died in the year AD 80.

The story of other women in the Gospels often has a wider message in that they represent a type of women or person who receives a particular healing or acceptance from Jesus. Amongst these are the **mothers who bring their children to Jesus**.

Although it does not actually say that those bringing the children to Jesus were their mothers, it is natural to think that this was so. They were rebuked by the disciples for daring to bring them to Jesus as so often at later times women have been rebuked by men of authority for daring to offer their gifts to the Church. However once again Jesus reacts against the lack of understanding of the disciples by indignantly demanding that the women should not be hindered from coming with their children and the disciples realize that everyone is welcome in God's sight. (Mark 10.13–16)

Jesus and the unacceptable

Two women who also might have wondered how Jesus would react to them were the Canaanite woman and the woman of Samaria.

The Canaanite woman was Greek and Syrophoenician by birth and came from the region of Tyre and Sidon. She was therefore a Gentile and when she asked Jesus for help for her daughter, who was possessed by demons, he appeared to be reluctant to give it because of her race. His response was 'I was sent only to the lost sheep of the house of Israel.' When she pleaded with him, he replied that it was not right to take the children's bread and toss it to their dogs, a reference to the children of Israel and their attitude to the Gentiles. However the woman remained insistent arguing 'Yes, Lord, but even the dogs eat from the crumbs that fall from their master's table.'

Jesus, hearing this recognized her great faith in him, and granted her request. *And her daughter was healed from that very hour*. But in that healing, Jesus was also opening the way for all women and Gentiles to be included in his healing, and therefore in the salvation he had to bring to all who had faith. By her response, the Canaanite woman demonstrates how persistence in the face of difficulties can bring salvation, an example which must have sustained many another woman later on. (Matthew 15.21–28)

The woman of Samaria came to the well where Jesus was sitting at Sychar in Samaria. She must have been surprised when Jesus spoke to her asking for a drink, because not only was he a stranger but also a Jew and Jews did not converse with Samaritans. Jesus continued by telling the woman that he was able to give her what he called 'living water', a phrase she misunderstood at first and then puzzled her especially when he told her this living water would give her eternal life. Jesus then asked her to call her husband, knowing that she had been married five times already and was now living with a man who was not her husband. She realised then that he must be some sort of a prophet, and questioned him about the differences which the Jews have with the Samaritans. When she declared that she knew the Messiah would come and he would reveal all, Jesus declared to her that he was himself the Messiah.

Just then the disciples turned up, astonished that Jesus was once again talking with a woman, alone and a Samaritan of dubious background. The woman did not stay to hear their comments but leaving her water jar at the well rushed to her town nearby to tell the people there about this man who could tell her everything and had declared himself to be the Messiah. Through her witness to them, many came to believe that Jesus was the true Messiah.

In this story Jesus meets and talks with this most unlikely woman even though, in the eyes of Jewish society, she would not have merited an acknowledgement. She is an example of a woman who is despised because of her race and her immoral life, and whom Jesus, far from rejecting, accepts and even uses in his service. It was to such a person that he openly declared he was the Messiah, something of which only the disciples had previously been aware. In doing so, Jesus is again demonstrating his love and willingness to care for all, both men and women, and use them in his service regardless of their circumstances or background. (John 4.1–42)

Another woman who would not expect to be welcomed by Jesus was the **woman with a haemorrhage**. This woman had been bleeding from her womb for twelve years which meant that according to Jewish law she had been unclean for all that time. All women who are menstruating or 'having an issue of blood', for example after childbirth, were considered unclean. She was therefore both too embarrassed and too ashamed to ask Jesus for help. Hoping to receive healing quietly, she gathered up her courage and touched the hem of his garment believing his healing power would be so strong it would pass through his clothing. Immediately she did so, Jesus felt that power go out from him. Much to the women's shame, Jesus asked who had touched him and she realised with great fear that she had to own up. When she did he bid her go in peace, healed because of her great faith.

This woman is an example of one who experienced shame not for having done wrong, but because of rules made by men. By his acceptance of her touching him, Jesus showed that an issue of blood whether in menstruation, childbirth or otherwise, did not make a woman unclean, and his bidding was a bidding of peace to all women who were made to feel that this bleeding was something sinful. As the old Adam had died with the coming of Jesus, so the old Eve and the feeling of guilt associated with the Genesis story which had been attached to women ever since had also died. The new woman was cleansed by Jesus and given his peace. As if to verify this giving of new life to women, the story about the woman with a haemorrhage is intermingled with that of the raising to life of the daughter of Jairus. **Jairus' daughter**, who was only twelve years old, was very ill when her father asked Jesus for help in healing her. By the time Jesus was ready to go to see her, after the delay of the incident with the woman, word came that the young girl had died. However Jesus still went to her and taking her by the hand he asked her to rise and she immediately got up and walked. The twelve years of the little girl's life were the same length of time that the woman had been suffering from the issue of blood, and the girl herself would have been beginning her menstruation at that time. 'Little girl, arise.' Words of invitation, an offering of new life to all women. (Mark 5.21–43)

Many women were amongst those healed by Jesus including

one who was **crippled**. This time it was not so much the
woman who was unacceptable, but the fact that her healing
took place on the Sabbath and therefore, in the eyes of the
ruler of the synagogue, was against the law. The woman
herself had been crippled 'by a spirit' for eighteen years, was
bent over and could not straighten her back. Probably the
cares of the world and her own guilt about something had
made her so bent, for Jesus said that Satan had kept her
bound for eighteen long years. Jesus called her forward saying
'Woman, you are set free from your infirmity'. He then laid
hands on her, and immediately she straightened up and
praised God. So often women are bound by spirits of desolation
or depression which cripple their ability to live properly. In
this story, Jesus releases the woman from the spirit which has
bound her for so long, and through her healing shows his
willingness to release all women (and men) from such spirits.

Jesus' concern for women is also shown when he visits the
town of Nain, where he meets a widow (**the widow of
Nain**), whose only son has just died. Although surrounded by
a large crowd, she was no doubt, like any bereaved person
whose most dearly loved close relative has died, alone in her
grief. 'When the Lord saw her, his heart went out to her and
he said, "Don't cry."' (Luke 7.13 NIV). Jesus could feel her
pain and answered it with healing by bringing the young man
back to life and returning him to his mother.

Those who ministered to Jesus

Among the followers of Jesus were a number of women including some who were mentioned as having ministered to him.
Two of these were relatives of his closest disciples. The
mother-in-law of Simon Peter was not well when Jesus
came with his disciples to the home of Simon and Andrew
where she lived. She was sick in bed with a fever and could
not serve Jesus as she would have wished. It was only natural
therefore for Jesus to minister to her by healing the fever. As
soon as he had helped her she again began to wait on him.
Many women have been restricted in their ministry by sickness
or poor health, but have been healed by Our Lord in order to
minister to others.

Mary, the mother of James and John, was another who

came to know Jesus through her sons. Mary was the wife of
Zebedee and often described as the mother of the sons of
Zebedee, a common way of describing a woman in that part
of the world. (Many other women in this study are described
according to the situations of their fathers or husbands, because often this is the only information known with which to
place them in history.) Mary was, like any loving mother
might be, ambitious for her sons, asking that they should sit
beside Jesus in his new kingdom. According to Matthew, she
was one of the women present at the cross (Matthew 27.56).

Luke describes how many of the women who had been
healed travelled with Jesus as he proclaimed the good news.
Joanna, the wife of Chuza, Herod's steward was one of these
and she was with **Mary Magdalene** and Mary, the mother
of James, when the women went to the tomb to anoint the
body of Jesus. Susanna also joined with Joanna, Mary
Magdalene and others in ministering to Jesus, helping to
support the disciples and Jesus out of their own means.

The names of the women present at the crucifixion and
who went to the empty tomb vary according to the evangelist. According to John, **Mary, the wife of Clopas** was
standing at the cross with Mary, the mother of Jesus, her
sister and Mary Magdalene. Mark tells us that, besides these,
there was also **Mary, the mother of James and Joses**
and **Salome** at the cross, all of whom had been following
Jesus and caring for his needs in Galilee whilst Matthew
includes the mother of the disciples, James and John. James'
mother, Salome and Mary Magdalene were the ones who,
according to Mark, took the spices to go to anoint Jesus'
body very early on the first day of the week, just after
sunrise. Luke includes Joanna and in Matthew's Gospel it
was the other Mary who watched with Mary Magdalene
when Jesus' body was placed in the tomb and went to anoint
his body on the morning of the Resurrection and found the
tomb empty.

Whoever was actually present at the cross, and at the
empty tomb, there is no doubt that there were a number of
women who had been caring for Jesus as he travelled about
Galilee, who remained with him as far as possible while he
was crucified and who came to anoint his body as it lay, or so
they thought, in the tomb. These women ministered to Jesus

and his followers as he had ministered to them. They can be seen to be among the first to have followed his call to serve because of their great love for Our Lord.

Veronica is one of those women whose existence is legendary. It is believed that she was a woman who was in the crowd watching Jesus as he passed on his way to be crucified. She was distressed to see him as he staggered under the weight of the cross, his face covered in dirt and sweat, and ran forward to wipe it with a cloth. On the cloth there remained an image of his face, and a cloth said to be the original has been preserved in St Peter's in Rome, probably since the beginning of the eighth century.

The name, Veronica, is derived from the words *vera icon* meaning true image and a 'vernicle' is a veil with the image of Christ's face which is often carried by pilgrims.

Many stories have been told about Veronica, that she was the wife of the Roman officer in charge of the execution of Jesus; that she cured the Emperor Tiberias of disease by wiping his face with the cloth; that perhaps she was the wife of Zaccheus, who climbed a tree to see Jesus, and that she brought Christianity to France. It was also said that she may have been the woman cured of a haemmorhage by touching the clothes of Jesus.

Veronica, who is remembered in the Stations of the Cross, is a woman who, even if she did not exist, stands for all those women whose compassion for the suffering makes them stand out, bearing the image of Jesus in their hearts.

In his relationships with the women in this chapter Jesus was expressing his love and concern for them. He treated them in a way which was unusual for their time, meeting and speaking with those who were sinners, those who were unclean and those who were not even Jewish. His acceptance and even affirmation of them as human beings is an example of his attitude to all people, and comes from his own act of atonement for the sin, not just of the Jewish people, but of the whole world. Jesus called women to be his messengers and his servants, as he has continued to call them throughout the ages. Whenever they showed their faith, he returned it with a healing love, and they out of their love for God would perhaps re-echo Mary's words, 'My soul glorifies the Lord and my spirit rejoices in God my Saviour, for he has been mindful of the humble state of his servant. From now on all generations will call me blessed, for the Mighty One has done great things for me – holy is his name.' (Luke 1.46–49 NIV)

CHAPTER TWO

Living
Stones

'Come to him, to that living stone, rejected by men but in God's sight chosen and precious; and like living stones be yourselves built into a spiritual house, to be a holy priesthood, to offer spiritual sacrifices acceptable to God through Jesus Christ.'(1 Peter 2.4, 5 RSV)

'Now you are the body of Christ and individually members of it.'
(1 Corinthians 12.27 RSV)

★ ★

AFTER THE death and resurrection of Jesus, the small band of his followers met together frequently, and when Jesus had ascended to heaven, they returned to Jerusalem, to stay near the Mount of Olives. According to Luke, this group consisted of the eleven apostles, the women, (probably many of those mentioned in the last chapter), Mary, the mother of Jesus and the brothers of Jesus.

There was also a larger group of about one hundred and twenty men and women, from whom they chose a man to be the twelfth apostle to replace Judas. It would not have occurred to them to choose a woman, although Mary Magdalene would have been an obvious choice.

It is not clear whether the Holy Spirit descended on the apostles only, or on the larger group, but in his sermon which followed this event Peter quotes a passage from Joel which most definitely sees women as receiving the gifts of the Holy Spirit. 'I will pour out my Spirit upon all flesh, and your sons and your daughters shall prophesy, and your young men shall see visions, and your old men shall dream dreams; yea, and on my menservants and my maidservants in those days I will pour out my Spirit; and they shall prophesy' (Acts 2.17, 18

RSV). This passage is clearly treating men and women as equal in God's service and gifts.

It is no wonder then that, in the first century, fired by the affirmation which Jesus had given to women, the early Church, though not giving them equality, at least recognized their calling as leaders within the Church and servants of God. Though this must have created difficulties within Jewish sections of the Church, (but not so much in the Graeco-Roman parts), Paul certainly valued the women among his fellow workers and the women must be included as living stones in the foundations laid by the Church at this time.

Widows, deacons, deaconesses and virgins

One of the first women to be mentioned by name as a member of the new church was Dorcas. **Dorcas**, in Greek, or Tabitha in Aramaic, meaning Gazelle, was an early Christian who lived at Joppa, was well known for her good works and acts of charity and therefore called a disciple by Luke (Acts 9.36). She was well loved by her friends and was probably a widow who may have lived with other widows whilst making clothes to provide herself with an income. When she became sick and died, Peter was called to her death bed, where she was lying washed and ready for burial. He asked everyone to leave her room while he knelt down and prayed. He then followed his Master's act of raising a young girl from the dead by taking her hand and asking her to rise. This act of Peter's was the first time that he was instrumental in raising the dead, and through his bringing Dorcas back from the dead, many believed in the Lord.

There has been much discussion recently as to the exact nature of **Phoebe**'s ministry, but it is generally agreed that, as her title in the original Greek is *diakonos* which translates to deacon and is no different from the word used about men deacons, Phoebe was indeed a deacon at Cenchrae. In fact 'the feminine form *diakonissa* is not found before the fourth century and even then, as well as later, we meet the form "woman deacon" (*gune diakonos*).'[1]

Paul commends Phoebe to the Romans, describing her as a saint and a helper to many including himself and she is believed to have been the one who took Paul's letter to the

Romans (Romans 16.1–2). In fact the word translated 'helper' is more often translated as chief, president or patron, and it has been used of bishops, angels and God.[2]

Though Clement of Alexandria and Origen refer to the ministry of women and mention Phoebe in Paul's time, they do not mention deacons existing in their own time which was a century later. However there is evidence of the existence of deaconesses from the fourth to the eleventh century. In the ordination service for deaconesses in the fifth century, the Greek Euchologion refers to Phoebe and includes the laying on of hands. At this time, the deaconesses were referred to as 'most reverend' or 'venerable' as were Bishops and other clergy and appeared to rank equally with deacons.[3]

In the first four centuries of the Church, women served officially in three different ways. There were the **widows** who had no family and were over sixty. These women spent their time in prayer often in small communities such as the one in which Dorcas was living. Deaconesses were also appointed, women such as Flavia Arcas who was also a widow. The woman-deacon, or deaconess as she became known, originally had the same functions as a man-deacon, but as the authority of male deacons increased so that of female **deacons** decreased. A female deacon would have been present at the baptism of a woman to perform the anointing and would also have been involved in visiting the sick and washing them and in instructing women in the faith. Deaconesses had to be either widows or virgins.

Then there were **virgins** such as Nicarete of Constantinople, who did not want to become a deaconess, but was nevertheless a great support to St John Chrysostom at the time of his exile and was herself exiled.

The four unmarried daughters of Philip the deacon were also virgins who were said to have the gift of prophecy. Not much is known about these four women except that they lived with their father in Caeserea and may have been buried with him in Hierapolis in what is now Turkey. Other women are also known to have prophesied in the church at Corinth, and a woman who prophesied there was instructed to make sure that she had her head covered, a sign of respectability at that time (1 Corinthians 11.5).

Workers for the Lord

In his letters to the various churches, Paul mentions many women who were busy working for the Lord. He kept in touch with the leaders of many different groups including one run by a woman called **Chloe**. Paul tells the Corinthians how her people had reported to him that there were difficulties among the different factions in Corinth. They were obviously concerned that the dubious behaviour of some of the members there was bringing the church into disrepute, and judging from Paul's letters to them they had good reason.

Frequently it was the women who became converts first and they brought the members of their families into the church, a foretaste of what was to happen often in the future. Timothy was one person who became a Christian because of the influence of his womenfolk. His grandmother, **Lois**, was the first to become a Christian, and then her daughter **Eunice**, who was Jewish, was also converted to the new faith. The husband of Eunice was Greek and not Jewish so their son, Timothy, was not circumcised, although Paul later felt it necessary to have him circumcised before taking him to work with him among the Jews. Paul writes how he has been reminded of Timothy's sincere faith which occurred first in his grandmother and his mother.

While Paul was in Athens waiting for Timothy and Silas to join him, he began telling the philosophers about his beliefs and the good news about Jesus, so they took him to the Areopagus, the high place in the centre of Athens where the philosophers met. There Paul proclaimed the gospel about the living God and the Resurrection. Amongst those who heard him there and who became one of his followers was a woman named **Damaris**, presumably someone of importance either in the life of the city or of the Church for Luke to mention her by name.

After this incident, Paul left Athens and went to Corinth where he met **Priscilla** or **Prisca** and her husband, Aquila, who was probably one Manius Acilius Glabrio. Because they were Jewish they had moved from Rome to Corinth, after Claudius ordered all Jews to leave Rome. Priscilla and Aquila earned their living by tentmaking and Paul stayed with them when he arrived in Corinth, helping them in their business, being a tentmaker himself. When Paul moved on, first to Syria and then to Ephesus, Priscilla and her husband went with him. They were also friendly with Timothy. The fact that Priscilla's name sometimes appears first is unusual when referring to a married couple, and would tend to imply that Priscilla was the more active one of the partnership in the work of the Church.

The couple are believed to have been martyred possibly in the year 98. Priscilla may have been host to St Peter at her villa in Rome, beneath which is a catacomb named after her. Paul describes them as fellow-workers in Christ in the greetings he sends to the Church in Rome.

There were many woman members of the churches in these early days who were active in the service of Christ. Amongst those included in Paul's greeting to the **women of the Church in Rome** in addition to Phoebe and Priscilla are Mary, Tryphena and Tryphosa and his dear friend Persis, all women who are described as having been working hard for the Church or for the Lord; the mother of Rufus, who is probably also the wife of Simon of Cyrene; Julia; the sister of Nereus; Olympas and others.

Junia and Andronicus are described as being outstanding among the apostles. Although Junia is sometimes translated as a masculine name, 'John Chrysostom recognized Junia as female when he wrote: "To be apostles is something great. But to be outstanding among them – just think what a wonderful encomium that is!" How great this woman's devotion to learning (philosophia) must have been that she was deemed worthy of the title apostle.' Origen, Jerome and Abelard among others also thought of Junia as a woman, and it was not until the thirteenth century that it was suggested Junia was a man.[4]

Junia (and Andronicus) are described as kinsfolk of Paul and his fellow prisoners, notable among the apostles and having been in Christ before Paul. They were obviously greatly esteemed by Paul. The whole of the passage in the letter to the Romans where Paul sends greetings to his fellow workers in Christ confirms the involvement of women in the work of the Lord in building up the new Church.

Other women mentioned in Paul's letters to the churches include **Euodia** and **Syntyche** who were members of the Philippian church, and were apparently having a disagreement. Paul writes in his letter asking the members of the Church to help them as they have laboured with him in the Gospel together with Clement and others.

Nympha, too, is mentioned in Paul's letter to the Colossians as having a church in her house. It is believed that many of the Roman matrons who were converted encouraged the growth of Christianity by holding the gatherings in their homes. For these women the new faith of Christianity clearly had its advantages, for it was a religion which appeared to be giving women a new equality with men. 'There is neither Jew nor Greek, there is neither slave nor free, there is neither male nor female; for you are all one in Christ Jesus' (Galatians 3.28). And it was these women converts who 'began the Christian penetration of the upper-classes and then brought their children up as Christians; sometimes they ended by converting their husbands.'[5]

The influence of women on their menfolk is shown in the example of **Claudia** who was mentioned by Paul in his second letter to Timothy. Possibly the daughter of a British king, Claudia was the wife of Aulus Pudens, a Roman senator, and mother of Linus, who was to be the second Pope, 67–76, after Peter. Her influence as mother to the young Linus would have been very important especially as Linus was Pope at such a crucial time in the history of the infant Church.

Other names which are known from this period include **Anastasia**, **Basilissa** and **Iphigenia**. Anastasia and Basilissa were two noblewomen who lived in Rome. They were Christian converts who were believed to have buried both Peter and Paul in Rome and were said to have themselves been tortured and beheaded on the orders of Nero in the year 68. Iphigenia is believed to be an Ethiopian who was converted by Matthew the apostle. It was not only in the Graeco-Roman church that women had their influence, but wherever the Christian message went, including the African continent.

Bringing the Gospel to Britain

However, it was throughout the Roman Empire that Christianity spread most rapidly, and one of the bearers of the Good News to these shores was a young girl called **Eurgain**.

Though Llantwit Major, in South Gamorgan, now bears the name of Illtyd, he was not the original founder of this llan or settlement, for the place had been at least partly cleared and settled by the Romans. The remains of a Roman station still exist nearby which, while being part of the Roman system of occupation may also be regarded as a tribute to the character of the Silures, who inhabited these parts. For in their leader Caractacus, who is reputed to have lived on the site on which St Donat's Castle now stands, the Romans found a brave opponent whom they took to Rome as a hostage, together with members of his family, in order to control the Silures.

Some time after the arrival of Caractacus and his family in Rome, Paul the apostle also arrived there as a prisoner. 'He abode two whole years, in his own hired dwelling, and received all that went unto him, preaching the kingdom of God' (Acts 28.30), and preaching that the salvation of God is also for the Gentiles.

To the Roman intelligentsia this preaching was but a proclamation of a new superstition; and one of their writers states that a certain British lady had taken up this superstition. It is quite probable that this British lady was a member of the family of Caractacus, and traditionally she is said to have been his daughter, Eurgain.

Having been converted by Paul, the natural thing was to attempt to return to Britain to teach the faith to those at home, or to send other teachers to do so. Bran, the father of Caractacus is said to have returned to preach the Gospel here; and Eurgain, too, must have been keenly interested in the work of teaching the faith to her own people in her old home, for the church first founded here bore her name, Bangor Eurgain.

If the name Eurgain associated this place with the family of Caractacus, and with Paul, the prisoner of the Lord, the word 'Bangor' associates it with the earliest type of Christian architecture. At that time, the first thing that a builder of a Christian church did was to provide a place for the altar and for those who ministered at it. This place was given height and pre-eminence, that of the congregation being of a lower nature. Hence the Christian church often became known as the 'high place'. This translated into Welsh as 'Bangor', a high place or principal quire, from 'ban' meaning 'high' and 'cor' meaning 'quire'. 'The word quire in Christian architecture refers to that part of the church where the altar is placed, and the room provided for those who serve at it.' This early architectural association would confirm that Eurgain was amongst the very first to bring the new religion of Christianity to Britain in the first century.

By the end of the first century therefore, we have a picture of a Christian Church which is rapidly expanding in all directions. We do not know how much of this expansion is due to the women of the Church, but we do know that their influence was not inconsiderable. They were acting as hosts in the house churches and spreading the Word, converting not only their own households but many others also, both directly and indirectly. Young girls like Eurgain were taking the Gospel to new lands and older matrons like Priscilla were providing support for the church leaders, both financially and as fellow workers, whilst some such as Phoebe became ordained ministers of the Gospel. It was an exciting age and a difficult one, but women shared in this growth period with a faithfulness which cannot be denied.

CHAPTER THREE

Diamonds in the Desert

'God chose what is foolish in the world to shame the wise, God chose what is weak in the world to shame the strong.' (1 Corinthians 1.27)

AFTER THE initial period when the new found Jewish sect was looked upon with a certain amount of tolerance by the authorities, the Christians began to find that not only was the second coming of Christ not as imminent as expected, but that the authorities were not inclined to be as kindly disposed towards them now that they were beginning to make their mark. They were a challenge to the emperors' own supposed divinity and when they would not agree to sacrifice to the Roman gods, or acknowledge the divinity of the emperor it became clear that the Christian sect must be taken more seriously and dealt with in a manner which demonstrated that a new and non-Roman God would not be tolerated. It could easily lead to insurrection, which was a dangerous thing in a Roman Empire already beginning to show signs of strain.

Unfortunately difficulties were also arising for women within the Church itself. The early promise of accepting women as equals within the Church had begun to fade and many who sought to promote this were themselves discredited. 'In 170, Montanus, a successful charismatic personality who had many followers in Asia Minor, was declared to be an enemy of the Church. He had given women a prominent role in his congregations, as had some of the Pauline congregations, but he was attacked for breaking up marriages and giving women ecclesiastical offices. This gave the more orthodox in the Church the opportunity to ban women from the ministry. Tertullian in his treatise, *On Baptism and the Veiling of Virgins*, emphatically denied that women could exercise any ministry within the Church.'¹ But in these early years, the women were offering themselves on the altar of martyrdom as ministers in Christ's Church and as witnesses of his sacrificial love.

The early martyrs

The names of all those who died in the persecutions which took place over the next two and a half centuries will never be known, for there were so many, but among the many whose names we do know the women feature just as strongly as the men. Indeed, three of the best known are Blandina, Perpetua and Felicity whose stories were written down at the time. In recent years, Hassan Dehqani, Bishop of Iran, has said that having two modern martyrs in the tiny Church of Iran, one of them being his own son, gave the Church an ˙identity for which they give thanks.

The fact that, in the early Church, women were counted among the martyrs, as they continued to be throughout the ages, gave women a definite place in the sanctity of the Church. They were not just hangers-on, following the lead of the men, they were there in the heart of the Church, sparkling with their new found faith yet willing to give their lives in the service of the Christian God. By doing so they gave witness to their love for God and inspiration to others.

Many of these women were to die unknown and the names of all included here cannot always be confirmed, but the stories appear to be based on accounts of events which were known to have happened. Occasionally stories may have been copied, as perhaps with Felicity and Symphorosa in the second century, although these two women may well have lead similar lives and deaths.

Amongst the first of these many martyrs whose names we know are **Theodora**, sister of Hermes, who is believed to have been put to death in the year 132 in Rome and **Symphorosa** who died in 135. Symphorosa was ordered to sacrifice to the gods by the Emperor Hadrian, but refused and so was tortured by being hung up by her hair and drowned in the Anio River. She is alleged to have had seven sons, also Christians, who died with her each in a different way. Another women called Felicity is also supposed to have died in a similar way a few years later.

One of the best known early martyrs was **Blandina** who died with her mistress and forty-seven others at Lyons in 177. Their story was written down by a chronicler, who was obviously impressed by the outstanding martyrdom of Blandina. In that year, the Emperor Marcus Aurelius began a fierce anti-Christian persecution. It began by prohibiting Christians from entering private houses, the baths or the markets. Soon it built up to stoning, jeering and looting their homes. Accusations were made against them of incest, cannibalism and other terrible deeds.

Amongst the Christians was a slave, Blandina. 'Through her, Christ showed that those who in the eyes of men appear cheap, ugly and contemptible, are treated by God with great honour because of their love for him.'[2] Blandina and the other Christians began to be tortured to make them confess that the Christians did actually behave as their enemies suggested. Her friends were concerned that the slave women would give way under the relentless torture she was forced to suffer, but she was filled with strength so that even though the torturers followed each other in relays with every sort of torture, they could not break her faith. 'I am a Christian' repeated Blandina 'and we do nothing wrong amongst us.' Others too endured much torture and very few broke down. The Emperor ordered that those who remained defiant in their faith should be executed.

Blandina was then fastened to a stake, her cross, and there she prayed aloud, giving strength to those around who saw their Saviour working through the slave tied to the stake. The beasts were let loose but they would not touch Blandina and she was taken back to her prison. In prison, she was forced to watch the torturing of other Christians until eventually Blandina and a young boy, Ponticus, were brought back at the end of the spectacle. She gave encouragement to Ponticus as he was killed and then she was whipped, tied in a net and thrown to a savage bull which gored her to death. Together with the other bodies, hers remained unburied for a week, then the bodies were burnt and thrown into the river Rhone, so that there would be nothing left for their friends to keep and venerate.

The chronicler of the community of Lyons writes that 'Blandina shone with joy, as if she had been summoned to a

wedding banquet and not to be delivered over to the beasts.'
Though old, she 'entered the arena like a young beauty whom
a prince comes to escort to a seat at his side at the eternal
feast.'

About that time also in France a young Christian woman,
Regina, who was believed to have been the daughter of a
pagan was tortured and beheaded in Autun for refusing to
marry a proconsul. Blandina had been martyred in Lyons and
Regina in Autun, and wherever there were Christians in the
Roman Empire, they were likely to be martyred for their
faith.

Cecilia, who is the patron saint of music, is believed to
have lived in the second or third century and founded a
church in the Trastevee quarter of Rome. Cecilia was brought
up as a Christian, married a pagan and converted him, but
after their marriage they continued to live a life of celibacy.
Her brother-in-law was also converted but both brothers were
put to death for refusing to sacrifice to the gods. When she
went to bury their bodies, Cecilia, too, was arrested, tortured
and sentenced to death by being stifled by the steam and heat
in her own bathroom. Because this did not kill her, a guard
was sent to behead her, but the blows again were not sufficient
to kill her outright and she took three days to die. This story
was written down before the sixth century and although it
may not be true in detail, Cecilia's existence is not in doubt.
Among the catacombs in Rome there is a statue of Cecilia
which vividly depicts her martyrdom.

Flavia Domitilla, who also lived in the second century,
was the niece of two Roman emperors and after she married
she became a Christian. Her husband was martyred but
Domitilla escaped death, possibly because of her relationship
to the emperors, and was banished to an island in the Tyrrhe-
nian Sea.

The form of martyrdom was often particularly cruel. **Potamiaena** and her mother, **Marcella**, lived in Alexandria and
were sentenced to death in 202 by burning or scalding. It is
believed that attempts were made on Potamiaena's chastity.
The officer who was to execute them, Basilides, treated them
kindly and Potamiaena thanked him for this, saying that she
would continue to pray for him after her death. Basilides was
converted and shortly afterwards arrested as a Christian. He

was baptized in prison just before being beheaded for his faith. It was by their witness to the grace of God within them that the martyrs brought others to know their Saviour, Christ.

There were many women amongst the martyrs at this time, including young girls such as Herais who was burned to death, but perhaps the best known were **Perpetua** and **Felicity** who died around 203. Much of what we know about them came from the hand of Perpetua herself. She saw her suffering as a struggle with Satan, and her writings were therefore to be a declaration of the working of the Holy Spirit and a reminder of the glory of God.

Vibia Perpetua was well born, well educated and had married well. She lived in Carthage and was about twenty-two with an infant son, when she was taken prisoner with her slave, Felicity, and some of her companions. The experience was horrifying, and she was anxious for her baby, whom she was still nursing, but who had been left with her family. Yet her faith sustained her and when her baby was restored to her, she declared that the prison now appeared like a palace. During this time she had visions which gave her some idea of what lay ahead of her and how her fight was against the devil himself. Her father constantly entreated her to turn back from her faith, begging her to have pity on her family and baby, but she refused to offer a sacrifice to the Emperor, declaring that because she was a Christian she could not.

Perpetua's slave, Felicity, was eight months pregnant at the time of her arrest, and as she wished to die with the others at the games which were being arranged, she prayed for an early delivery, for it was against the law for a pregnant woman to be punished in this way and she did not want to die alone later amongst criminals. Shortly after her prayers had been offered, the baby was born.

The day before the prisoners were to be taken to the games, they had their last meal together which they celebrated as an Agape. As they travelled towards the amphitheatre, their faces shone with a radiant joy. The guards demanded that Perpetua and Felicity be forced to wear the robes of a priestess, but they steadfastly refused and were eventually allowed to remain dressed as they were as they entered the arena.

The two young women were then stripped and enclosed in nets, and a mad heifer was let loose on them. However the crowd took pity on the innocent women and they were given tunics to wear to cover their nakedness. Bearing themselves bravely in the first attacks, they were taken out of the arena and led back to prison. There Perpetua encouraged the others with the words, 'Stand fast in the faith, all of you, and love one another; and do not be offended by our sufferings.' When Perpetua eventually came to die she exchanged the kiss of peace with her fellow martyrs and as she was not killed immediately by the gladiator, she guided his sword to her throat.

The persecutions continued throughout the Roman Empire, and in 250 **Sabina** was put to death. She came from Smyrna, now Izmir in Turkey, where she suffered under the persecutions of the Emperor Decius. She was arrested together with the priest, Pionius, Ascleias and others. They were not prepared to eat food which was sacrificed to the gods, despite many pleas to them to do so in order that they might be saved from punishment for disobeying the emperor. When Sabina was told that for her punishment she would be sent to a public brothel, she replied, 'The Holy God will watch over me.'

Sabina had earlier escaped from the hands of her mistress, Politta, who had tried to make her give up her Christianity and had thrown her into a dungeon from where she had been rescued by the others. She took the name Theodota to avoid being captured again by her mistress. When asked who it was she worshipped, she answered 'The omnipotent God who made heaven, earth and all of us, and whom Jesus Christ, his word, has made known to us.' Whilst in prison, Sabina and her companions encouraged and ministered to each other with praise and prayers.

Martyrdom often came after a long period in prison during which time the Christians were allowed visitors. One such visitor was **Mustiola** who died in 275. She was a noblewoman from Chiusi in Tuscany who cared for Irenaeus and other Christians in prison. The Roman officer who had imprisoned them tried to force his attentions on her and when she resisted and her friends made objection, Irenaeus was tortured to death. When Mustiola protested at this injustice, she was herself beaten to death.

Often the quiet witness of the women martyrs made a great

impression on their captors or their executioners. **Dorothy** was martyred probably in Cappadocia in 303 during the Diocletian persecution for refusing to sacrifice to idols. A lawyer named Theophilus jeered at her as she was on her way to die, asking her to send him flowers when she reached the 'garden of heaven'. Stories tell of his subsequent conversion and martyrdom.

Among the many women tortured and beheaded for their faith during the persecutions of Diocletian and Maximinian were **Archelais**, **Susanna** and **Thecla** who died in 293 at Salerno in Italy. In 304, the sisters **Menodora**, **Metrodora** and **Nymphodora** were tortured and killed in Bythinia for refusing to sacrifice to the pagan gods. That same year a thirteen year old girl was also put to death.

Agnes had a deep devotion and courage, according to St Ambrose, and her charm and beauty attracted a young man who sought to marry her. She refused because he was not a Christian, and he took vengeance by denouncing her as a follower of Christ. She was imprisoned, exposed to great cruelty and degradation. She was put in chains, tortured, and finally dragged to a house of ill-repute where she was stripped. There she prayed to God to protect her from her shame, at which her long hair grew even longer to help cover her nakedness, and an angel brought her a robe made white in the Blood of the Lamb to cover her. She was then dragged out by her guards and flung on a fire to die, but the flames did not harm her. Those around saw her standing in the midst of the flames and heard her thanking and blessing God.

At this, one of her guards who was standing nearby climbed on to the fire and beheaded her. Her little body was then taken by her Christian friends to a cemetery, where they knelt beside the grave to pray for her. Agnes, as if in answer to their prayers, then appeared to the mourners in a shining white bridal robe, comforting her friends and asking them to rejoice, for Christ had given her a place close beside his throne in heaven.

In the list of saints, Agnes is remembered particularly for her purity, and Jerome writes a few years later about how many were still praising her memory then. Her feast day, 21 January, was later kept for many years as a women's holiday in Britain.

Martyrs came from many countries at this time and not all were killed as a deliberate act of persecution by the Roman authorities. **Ursula** is believed to have been the daughter of a Christian British king who lived in the fourth century. Making a pilgrimage to Rome to escape marriage with a pagan, she took other young women with her. Whilst they were returning through Germany, they were captured by the Huns and killed at Cologne because of their Christian faith. The only proof of this story comes with the discovery of their bones around the year 400 at Cologne and an inscription on a stone nearby which read 'XI MM VV' meaning eleven virgin martyrs. Later on, others interpreted the inscription as meaning eleven thousand virgins, leading to the idea that this greater number had been murdered.

Amongst those killed during the persecution of Diocletian were many from Greece and some from Asia Minor. **Paraskeva** was a native of Iconia in Asia Minor although her name is Greek and means Friday. She is also known in Russia as Piatnitza, the Russian for Friday. Paraskeva was known for her strong preaching of the Gospel and her desire to place Christ first in her life. On one occasion when asked her name, she refused to tell it until she had first given the 'name of eternal life'.[3]

The personality of Paraskeva shines through the icons in which she is shown holding 'the cross in her upraised hand, the austere and concentrated expression of the face expressing the daring and unyielding firmness with which she preached and endured her tortures. The face and the whole figure of St Paraskeva breathes that calm and firm faith which neither tortures nor the sword could break . . . She was a person who crowned her life by the act of confession of truth, sealed with her blood.'[4]

Paraskeva is the patron saint of the work of women and also, because her name, Friday, was often market day, she became patron saint of trade. In some icons she is shown with **Irene** who was one of three sisters from Thessalonica in Greece who also died at this time.

Irene, Agape and Chionia were all put to death for possessing scriptures and refusing to eat food sacrificed to the gods. Agape and Chionia were burned to death, and Irene was shot later with arrows after having been exposed naked and then left chained in a brothel, where she was left unmolested until taken out to die.

Two others known to have given their lives while they were still young in these persecutions were **Theodosia** who died in 308 and **Pelagia** who died in 311. Theodosia was born in Tyre and when she was eighteen, she was put to death by drowning for inspiring other Christians who had refused to sacrifice to idols in Caesarea. Pelagia, one of several martyrs with that name, lived in Antioch until, at the age of fifteen, a group of soldiers came to her house to arrest her for being a Christian. Rather than lose her virginity to them, she threw herself from the roof top and died. Some time later her sacrificial action was praised by John Chrysostom.

Easy enough as it is to read and write of these horrific deaths, it may sometimes be necessary to stop and reflect quite how horrific this sort of treatment must have been for these young girls and how strong their faith must have been. Times were violent then as they still are in some countries, but the treatment and punishment received by some of these early Christian martyrs was terrible even for those times. So many women and men, both young and old, had been prepared to give their lives literally as a witness to their love for the Christian God. His importance to them was such that they were prepared to die a cruel death rather than forego their beliefs.

However at long last the persecution of the Christians was, at least for a while, drawing to a close. Among the later women martyrs from this period about whom much is known was **Crispina** who came from a very noble family living in Theveste in Numidia, which was part of Africa. Married with several children, when she was asked to sacrifice to the gods for the safety of the emperors, she declined saying, 'I have never sacrificed and I never will except to the one true God and to our saviour Jesus Christ, his Son, who was born and suffered.'[5] Asked why she persisted in this superstition and would not worship the Roman gods, she responded 'I worship every day, but to the true and living God; he is my Lord and I know none other than him.'[6] Reminded that people all over Africa had been willing to sacrifice to the gods, her answer came back 'Nothing will ever make me sacrifice to demons. I sacrifice to the Lord who made heaven and earth, the sea and all that is in them. He is the true God who is to be feared. He made the sea, the green fields, the sand of the desert. What have I to fear from those who are only his creatures?'[7]

When threatened with death for her obstinate refusal, Crispina said she would give thanks to God for such an end. As she died, Crispina blessed God and offered thanks for releasing her from her persecutors, then making the sign of the cross on her forehead, she bent down to be beheaded in the name of her Saviour Jesus Christ.

Catherine of Alexandria, also living at this time, was one who also was quite capable of arguing for her beliefs. She was believed to have been converted by a vision after which she rebuked the Emperor, Maxentius, for forcing Christians to worship idols. In a debate with fifty philosophers about her faith, none could get the better of her. As she refused to deny this faith, she was sentenced to death by execution on a spiked wheel. The wheel used broke up, and so she was beheaded instead. It is said that her body was transported to Mount Sinai where a monastery built in her honour still stands. Although there is some doubt about parts of her story, her martyrdom was real and witnesses to her strong faith.

Almost the last of our martyrs of this period to be mentioned are the members of a group of young women who lived in a community of dedicated virgins in Rome. **Rhipsime** and **Gaiana** were members of this community of which Gaiana was the leader. Rhipsime however attracted the attention of the Emperor Diocletian with her beauty, and so they fled first to Alexandria and then to Armenia.

There the same thing happened with the King Tiridates, and again Rhipsime refused his attentions. Angrily, Tiridates had Rhipsime burnt alive and the rest of the community were put to the sword in 312. It is possible that Nina (see p. 33) was the only one to escape and she either fled or was taken as slave to Georgia.

Great beauty was once again the cause of the martyrdom of a young Christian woman, **Markella**, who was born around 300 on the island of Chios in the eastern Aegean. She came from a wealthy family who lived in the village of Volissos, but her mother died when she was young and her father was left to bring her up himself. Modest and pious, Markella desired only to be a true Christian and to become a bride of Christ.

All her time was devoted to worshipping God, to caring for others and spreading the Gospel. She loved her father very much and also helped him in his work whenever she could.

As the young Markella grew up, her father became increasingly aware of this beautiful young woman at his side, and within him a savage and lustful passion developed towards his daughter. Markella, realizing what was happening, left her home and fled into the countryside. Her father followed and when he found where she was living, he chased her, shooting arrows to stop her running away. Markella fled along the seashore, her blood dripping on the pebbles, where it can still be seen as marks on the stones. As she ran, Markella prayed to God for help and immediately a rock opened up. Markella rushed in to escape, but her father caught up with her before she could hide completely. Unable to pull her from the rock, he struck off her head which was still exposed and threw it into the sea.

The place where this took place became a centre of pilgrimage and healing, and it is said that whenever a priest says a special prayer, the waters by this rock begin to warm up and eventually will boil.

The end of the persecutions

At this time Greece was part of the Roman Empire, but while it was a single entity when Markella was born, by the year 311 the Roman Empire had become divided into two parts, Eastern and Western. In that year, Galerius, who had become Emperor of the Eastern Empire signed an edict which ended the persecution just six days before he died. That same year, both Constantine and Maxentius were proclaimed Emperor in different places, and both decided to end their persecution of the Christians. By 313, Constantine, who united the Empire again briefly from 324–337, had declared himself to be Christian, no doubt greatly due to the influence of his mother, Helena.

Helena, who was believed to have been born of poor parents in Asia Minor in about 255, became the wife of Constantius Chlorus who followed Maxentius as Emperor of the Western Roman Empire, but he sent her away in 292. Constantine, however, treated his mother well, and when

Christianity was fully accepted in the Empire, Helena did her best to encourage its development. She went on a long visit to the Holy Land when she was old and spent much of her wealth on helping the poor, building churches on Mount Olivet and at Bethlehem. Helena was believed to have found pieces of the true cross while excavating holy sites about the year 326. She died around the year 330, after her son Constantine had become Emperor of both the Eastern and Western Roman Empire.

It was during the reign of the pagan Emperor, Julian, some years later, when once again the Church began to be persecuted and many were again put to death including a young woman called Susanna. **Susanna** was the daughter of a pagan priest and his Jewish wife, who became converted to Christianity after her parents had died. She was a deacon at Eleutheropolis, but was martyred in 362, about the same time as three other women, **Bibiana**, **Dafrosa** and **Demetria** are known to have been martyred. Dafrosa was the wife of a Roman ex-prefect Flavian, and the whole family had become Christians, but she and her daughter, Bibiana, were put to death for their faith. Dafrosa was beheaded and Bibiana lashed to death on the orders of Julian the apostate, while Demetria dropped dead when she was brought before the judge.

The word travels

Despite this relapse during the reign of Julian, the Christian Church had become respectable and its influence began to spread. **Nina**, Nino or Christiana was believed to have come from Cappadocia, where she was captured and taken to Georgia as a slave. She may have belonged to the small group of virgins run by Gaiana, but she was certainly a Christian, whose goodness and devotion to God impressed those who met her. She cured many people in the name of Christ, and eventually the Queen of Georgia who was very ill came to hear of this. She sought out Nina who first cured her but then refused any reward except that the King and Queen should become Christians. After the King had become lost in a forest while hunting, and found his way home only after calling on the Christian God, he asked Nina to teach him more about

her God. He then sent to the Emperor Constantine for missionaries so that all his people could become Christians. Through
the witness of one slave girl, therefore, a whole country became
Christian. It is believed that Nina lived the last years of her
life as a recluse in Bodbe, Kakhetia in Georgia and died
around the year 340.

The desert mothers

In the early centuries and beyond, Christianity offered women
new interests and vocations outside their domestic life. It was
recognized that a woman's capacity for holiness and spiritual
service was as great as a man's. The monastic vocation became
open to women as well as men, and possibly women pioneered
the way in this life. Though Antony was regarded as one of
the founders of Christian monasticism, long before he decided
to become an ascetic, there existed communities of women
living together in Egypt. So it was that when 'as a young man
in the 270s Antony wished to become an ascetic after the
death of his parents, he was able to entrust his younger sister
to the care of a *"parthenon"* or convent of virgins.'[8]

Again, although Basil is seen as a father of monasticism in
the Orthodox Church, it was the influence of his elder sister,
Macrina, already living a contemplative life in a community,
that brought Basil to a life of prayer and eventually to join the
monastic life.

There were two Macrinas in Basil's life, his grandmother
and his sister. Macrina the elder suffered with her husband
during two separate persecutions, in which they lost their
home and all their possessions. They fled to a forest near their
home in Neo-Caesarea, Pontus, where she died in the year
340. Her granddaughter, Macrina the younger, had several
brothers including Basil the Great, Peter of Sebastea and
Gregory of Nyssa. She was born in Caesarea in 327 and was
betrothed to a young lawyer, but when he died, she helped to
teach her young brothers, over whom she continued to have a
great influence all her life. When her father also died, Macrina
and her mother, Emmelia, founded a convent on the family
estate by the river Iris in Pontus. Eventually, after her mother
died, Macrina gave away her wealth and lived a life of
poverty and prayer until her death in 379.

The Church fathers were undecided as to how to cope with Christian women at this time. 'As Christians, the Fathers could not deny that women possessed souls, however mistakenly it seemed to them that God had arranged matters thus, so that though they were looked upon as enemies, highly dangerous from Eve onwards to all men, they were never denied membership of the Church.'[9] There appeared to be two contrasting trains of thought. According to Ambrose, Bishop of Milan, 373–397, the best course for a woman was virginity, for in this role she could redeem the sin of her parents in conceiving her. A virgin was married to Christ, expected to remain perpetually silent, and need not even go to church often. If a virgin was suspected of having had sexual intercourse, she 'should not *normally* be medically examined by force, and if so, it should be on the authority and *under the supervision of a bishop*'.[10] If she was found guilty then head shaving and penance for life would suffice.

Ambrose's virgins were to be spotless, whilst for Jerome, virgins were sometimes 'squalid with dirt', because they stirred up emotions in him which he considered evil. Despite his opinion of them, Jerome gave encouragement to many of the desert mothers and the Roman matrons.

The desert mothers and fathers were women and men who withdrew themselves from the manipulations of a power-hungry society to fight against evil and to grow closer to God in the barrenness of the desert. The world they left behind was lukewarm in its spirituality and full of compromise, much as the world is today. They humbly dedicated themselves as witnesses of the crucified and risen Lord in a life of silent prayer, manual work, solitude and fasting. Whilst others saw possessions as all important, they gave up all to become daughters of God. Desert mothers were often reformed prostitutes who took up extreme asceticism. They were often mistaken for men because they wore male dress to protect themselves against attack.

Shining with a faith which contrasted with the wilderness in which they lived they were widely known as spiritual guides. Many people, bishops and priests as well as the laity, would go to receive direction from them. It is believed that there were approximately twenty thousand desert mothers and about half this number of desert fathers.

One of the best known of the Ammas, as the mothers were known, was **Amma Syncletica** who was the daughter of wealthy Macedonian parents living in Alexandria, in Egypt. Her sister was blind, and she and her sister became desert mothers after the rest of the family had died. Born in 316, she was widely revered for her teaching, humility and patience. After she died around the year 400, Amma Syncletica lived on in her many clear and homely writings.

'In the beginning there is a struggle and a lot of work for those who come near to God. But after that there is an indescribable joy. It's just like building a fire – at first it's smoking and your eyes water, but later you get the desired result. Thus we ought to light the divine fire in ourselves with tears and effort.

Why hate a person who hurts you, for it's not the person who is unjust but the devil. Hate the sickness not the real person.

Just as the most bitter medicine drives out poisonous creatures so prayer joined to fasting drives evil thoughts away.

Just as one cannot build a ship without nails, it is impossible to be saved without humility.

'Just as wax melts when it is near fire, so the soul is destroyed by praise and loses all the results of its labour.'[11]

At the same time, **Amma Sarah** lived on her own by the Nile for sixty years. For the first thirteen years, she had to struggle against lustful desires, praying that the inner warfare should not cease and that God would give her the strength to continue fighting. Fornication became personified as a demon who tempted her by saying that she had overcome him. She replied that it was not her but Christ who had overcome him.

When two men anchorites came to visit her, they thought they would humiliate her. So they said 'Be careful not to become conceited, thinking to yourself: "Look how these anchorites are coming to see me, a mere woman".'[12] But Amma Sarah, who considered that men and women in monastic life were equals anyway, replied that though she was a woman according to nature, she was defined no differently from the men in her thoughts and was not particularly impressed that they should condescend to visit 'a mere woman'.

Another woman who was believed to live in the desert at this time was **Thaïs**. According to a story retold by Roswitha (see p. 71), Thaïs was a wealthy prostitute whom one of the desert fathers, Abba Paphnutius, went to see because of the great scandal she caused. He gave her money and started to talk to her about God. She admitted that she knew about God and the eternal kingdom and the future torments of sinners. When Paphnutius asked her why she caused others to sin so much, she burst into tears and asked for a penance. She agreed to do whatever he asked, and he took her to a monastery of virgins where she was shut up in a sealed room for three years. Paphnutius told her that all she was to pray was 'You who have made me, have mercy on me.'

After three years, Paphnutius went to discuss with Antony and his disciples what was to be done with her. A disciple of Antony, Paul, had a dream in which a rich bed, guarded by three virgins, appeared in the sky, and he thought that it must be showing a glory for his saintly father, Antony. However a voice told him that the glory was actually for the woman who had been an harlot, Thaïs. Startled by this, the three men made their way to the monastery where Thaïs was and opened the door. Thaïs was reluctant to leave at first, but after Paphnutius told her that her sins had already been forgiven she came out, only to die fifteen days later.

Like Sarah and Thaïs, many of the desert mothers may have originally led immoral lives. **Maria** lived a moral life before turning to prostitution because of her own shame and fear at being corrupted by a man. She was the niece of Abba Abraham, a desert father, and from the age of seven when her father died she lived in a cell next to Abraham.

When she was twenty-seven, she was seduced by a monk who lusted after her, and ashamed of her behaviour and fearful of her uncle, she ran away and became a prostitute. Two years later, Abraham set out to find her and located her in a brothel where he arranged to see her, disguised as a customer. She did not recognize him and took him to her room where he then spoke to her and persuaded her to return by reminding her about how Jesus himself forgave a prostitute. Wearing a hair shirt and with the strictest asceticism, she returned to her cell where she prayed constantly, asking for a sign of forgiveness from God. After three years and many prayers, she was rewarded with the gift of healing.

Many people came to see her for spiritual direction and

many other desert mothers would also give spiritual guidance, but some, such as **Mary of Egypt** in the fifth century, lived completely solitary lives.

Mary dwelt in a cave in the Jordanian desert and had been an entertainer and probably a prostitute before becoming converted. According to a history of her written by Sophronius, bishop of Jerusalem, Mary left home when she was twelve and went to Alexandria full of lustful desires. She lost her virginity not for money, but for the enjoyment of sex and was happy to indulge in any form of sexual act.

One day, she saw large numbers of men walking down to the sea, and asked them what was happening. They said that they were all going to Jerusalem for the Exaltation of the Holy Cross. She was not certain what that would involve, but thought that she might as well go too, because, with such a large number of men, she could use her body to pay for her fare and food. She prostituted her body shamelessly, seducing as many men as possible, travelling with them all the way to Jerusalem. When the festival came round, she joined the others at the Cathedral, wanting to stay with the crowd, but still having no idea what it was all about. As she pushed to go into the Cathedral with the rest of the crowd, she was prevented by an invisible presence. Standing back, she watched while everyone else went in and, left alone in the forecourt, she suddenly became aware of her great sinfulness.

Mary then began to weep with a very deep sorrow, until looking up she appeared to see the Virgin Mary. The purity of Our Lady contrasted so much with her own impurity that she begged for help, forgiveness and the opportunity to enter the church so that she could gaze at the cross and the wounds which Jesus bore for her.

With great temerity she again approached the door. This time Mary found herself able to enter and, seeing the cross, for the first time she began to understand the promises of God as shown by the death and Resurrection of his Son. With humility and repentance, she threw herself down on the floor to kiss the dust at the foot of the cross.

Mary then returned to where she had seen the Virgin Mary and pledged herself to follow where she was led, 'Lead me wherever you please; lead me to salvation, teach me what is true, and go before me in the way of repentance.' A voice then told her to go across the Jordan where she would find rest. She was given three pennies by a stranger with which she bought three loaves. These Mary took with her into the desert and they never became any smaller even though she ate from them for the rest of her life. She received communion at the church of St John the Baptist by the Jordan and then crossed over and went to live as a solitary in the desert.

Some forty-seven years later, she met the monk, Zossima, to whom she told her tale. After begging his cloak to cover her nakedness, she described how for seventeen years she had experienced great temptations, particularly concerning lust, but after that she began to feel at peace. She had lost her clothing after a while, so that she went naked and her body had burnt black. Mary told Zossima, 'When I think from what evils the Lord has freed me, I am nourished by incorruptible food, and I cover my shoulders with the hope of my salvation. I feed upon and cover myself with the Word of God, who contains all things.'[13]

It is not known from where she received spiritual guidance, for despite not having read any books, she appeared to know and understand all that was in the Bible.

Mary asked the monk not to tell her story until she had died, but asked him to bring her the Holy Body and Blood of Christ a year later. When he did so, Mary made the sign of the cross then walked over the waters of the Jordan to receive it. Again, Zossima returned to visit her one year later as she had asked him, but this time Mary lay dead. A lion then came out of the desert and stood by her body, the sign of the Prince of Peace. Zossima found the lion guarding her dead body and was very afraid. However he summoned up his courage and asked the lion to dig the grave as he was not strong enough. This incident is used to indicate that Mary was a woman who was at peace with all creation.

Her story is also used to show 'the contrast of the self-satisfied monk who relies for salvation in his own works with Mary, the sinful woman who receives the simple gift of salvation from Christ without any acts, self-exploration, sacraments or prayers, but only because of her great need.'[14]

'The power of Thy Cross, O Christ, has worked wonders, for even the woman who was once a harlot chose to follow the ascetic way. Casting aside her weakness, bravely she opposed the devil and having gained the prize of victory, she intercedes for our souls.'[15]

Around this time an actress called **Pelagia**, living in Antioch, was noticed one day by Nonnus, a monk bishop, who found her very beautiful. Rather than lusting after her as other men might, Nonnus prayed for Pelagia. The following day, though she had never been in a church before, Pelagia found herself entering the church where Nonnus was preaching. Listening to him, she became aware of how sinful her life was and became overwhelmed with such a fear of God that she burst into tears. She repented of her sinful life and sent her servants to find out where Nonnus lived, begging for Baptism at his hands. 'My Lord,' she said, 'I am an ocean of sin, a deep pit of iniquity and I ask to be baptized.' She then confessed her sins before Nonnus, and was baptized with the lady Romana, (the first of the deaconesses in Antioch), being her sponsor.

Twice after her baptism the devil is said to have appeared to her, crying out to her for having deserted him. Nonnus taught her to banish the devil by making the sign of the Cross in the name of Christ. Pelagia was widely known for her costly jewels, but gave them all away because she saw them as riches with which the devil tried to ensnare her. She then dressed herself in men's clothing to protect herself from attack and went to Jerusalem where she built herself a cell on the Mount of Olives and became a hermit.

The story of Pelagia was written down by James the Deacon, a monk who accompanied Bishop Nonnus.

The Roman matrons

Meanwhile the Church had spread throughout North Africa, where in the year 332, **Monica** was born into a Christian family. Monica had married a pagan, by whom she had seven children, including a son, Augustine. She prayed constantly for this son, after he had rejected the Christian faith, and eventually her prayers were answered when he had a conversion experience. Although he lived to become a great Bishop, Augustine of Hippo, his mother died in the year 387, not long after he was baptized. Monica displayed not only a persistence in her prayers for her son, but an example that all is not lost to all those mothers whose sons go astray.

Family troubles also affected **Fabiola**, a member of the noble Roman family of Fabii, whose husband led such a dissolute life even after their marriage that she eventually divorced him. Fabiola then married again, much to the consternation of her fellow Christians but eventually, after both husbands had died, she did public penance for her remarriage, was readmitted to the Church and gave up her wealth to help the poor. She founded the first known Christian hospital in the western world at Rome.

In 395, she travelled to Bethlehem, where she met Jerome and tried to settle there helping him in his work. However she was not happy there and returned to Rome, after having fled from Bethlehem together with Jerome and others when the Huns threatened to invade. She died in 399. At this time many communities were beginning to spring up within the Christian world. **Asella** was a devout young woman who formed a community of Anchoresses at Rome which Palladius mentions in his writings. She became a nun when she was ten and a recluse when she was twelve eventually dying sometime around the year 406.

Many communities of women were formed including several by **Marcella**, a Roman matron. On the death of her husband, she set up sister communities in Rome following the Eastern ways. Born in 325, she was, like Fabiola, a friend of Jerome and welcomed him to Rome where he came to know many influential Roman ladies. A woman of wealth and intellect, Marcella gave away much of her money to the poor. However when the Goths sacked Rome in 410, they did not believe she was no longer wealthy and in trying to find out where her riches were they beat her so badly that she eventually died.

Paula was another wealthy Roman, connected with both the Scipios and the Gracchi. Born in 347, she married a senator, but was left a widow at thirty-three with five children. She came to know Jerome through her friend, Marcella, and in 385 she went to live in the desert under the spiritual direction of Jerome, near Bethlehem. Paula built a convent for women and a monastery for men, both of which were self-supporting and devoted to solitary contemplation, as well as serving as a hospice for pilgrims.

Paula was another of the many women who helped Jerome, and he writes about her excessive self-imposed mortifications and gifts to charity. She died in Jerusalem in 404 and was buried close to the birthplace of Jesus, beneath the Church of the Nativity.

Her daughter, **Eustochium**, went to Jerusalem with her mother also to receive direction from Jerome and was the first woman of noble Roman birth to make a vow of perpetual virginity. Both Eustochium and her mother helped Jerome with his translation of the Bible when his eyesight was failing. After her mother died, Eustochium became the superior of the monastery where they lived, until it was burned down in 417. She died in Bethlehem two years later.

Another woman who came to meet with Jerome in Jerusalem was **Melania**. She was born in 383, a Romano-Spanish heiress, the granddaughter of another Melania, also a Christian, who had lived from 345 to 410. The younger Melania married a Roman senator, Pinian, had two children who both died, and then made her villa the centre of a religious group. She gave much of her wealth to the poor and founded many churches and monasteries. When the Goths invaded Rome in 410, she and her husband fled to Thagaste in Africa, where they founded two monasteries. In 417, they moved to Jerusalem where they met with Jerome and where her husband died. Melania became abbess at the Mount of Olives after the death of her husband. She was well known for her spiritual direction, guiding amongst others the young Evagrius, an influential writer of the time, towards the monastic life. She died in 439.

At the same time as these women were spreading Christianity outwards from Rome, a young woman was appointed deaconess at Constantinople. **Olympias** was born in 366 and married when she was eighteen but was widowed two years later. She was very wealthy but although her hand was again sought in marriage by a nobleman, she rejected him and instead gave much of her wealth to charity, dressing herself in rags. She finally decided to become a deaconess at the age of twenty-five. Olympias not only advised Nectarius on ecclestiastical matters, she also exchanged letters with John Chrysostom. When he was expelled from Constantinople in 404, she and the forty other deaconesses, (including one Pentadia), who were attached to the Church of Constantinople were also persecuted for supporting him.

From then on Olympias experienced trials and bad health with which John Chrysostom sympathizes in his letters to her. He constantly praises her and encourages her, describing her patience and her dignity despite oppression, her wisdom and love even towards those who persecute her. He writes that these qualities 'have won a glory and reward which will later on make your sufferings seem light and passing'. She died in exile in Nicodemia in 408.

Euphrasia came from the Imperial family but after her father died she went with her mother to an hermitage in Egypt. Her mother died when she was twelve and she then asked that her inheritance should be given to the poor, her slaves freed and that she be released from a marriage contract arranged by the Emperor. She then remained as a desert mother until her death around 420.

The last of the influential Christian women to be included in this chapter are **Galla Placidia** and **Pulcheria**. These two were both devout women in the courts of the Roman Emperors of the early fifth century. At this time, the Roman Empire was again divided, part of it being at Constantinople under an Eastern emperor. Both women had a great deal of influence in the courts, Galla Placidia being in Milan and Ravenna, and Pulcheria at Constantinople.

Galla Placida, born in 390, was the sister of the Emperor Honorius and married first King Ataulf in 414 and then after his death, Constantius, who became Emperor Constantius III in 421. She became regent for her son, Valentinian III and virtually ruled the Western Roman Empire after the death of Honorius in 423 until her own death in 450. She built two churches and restored many others in Ravenna, the capital of the Empire at that time.

Pulcheria was born in 399 and was niece to Galla Placida, sister and regent to Theodosius II, and encouraged a monastic piety at the court in Constantinople. In 421, she arranged for the Emperor to marry Eudocia, a beautiful and intelligent young lady, who wrote some religious poetry and became involved in theological argument with her sister-in-law, Pulcheria. Eudocia moved to Jerusalem after being (unjustly?) accused of committing adultery. Between them, Pulcheria, Eudocia and her daughter, Eudoxia, visited Antioch and Jerusalem, built monasteries in Palestine, established shelters for the sick and homeless and also arranged for the relics of saints to be taken to Constantinople. After Theodosius died, Pulcheria was proclaimed Empress, and she and her husband sponsored the Council of Chalcedon in 451. She died two years later, after having helped to build many churches and establish a university at Constantinople.

The pagan invasion of the Huns and Goths

The Roman Empire was starting to crumble as both the Huns and the Goths began to invade Rome at the beginning of the fifth century. It seemed as if the Christians had only just convinced the Roman authorities at the beginning of the fourth century of the truth of Christianity, and again after the upset with the Emperor Justin in the 360s, when once again they were being persecuted, this time by the Huns and the Goths. As Fabiola and Melania fled from the invaders in the Mediterranean areas, so in far away Paris the people were becoming aware of the dangers of these wild pagans. One of those caught up with the pagan invasion was **Geneviève** who was born at Nanterre in 421. When she was a small girl, she met St Germanus of Auxerre, to whom she declared her longing to offer herself to God. At the age of fifteen, she became consecrated to the religious life, and after her parents died, Geneviève moved to Paris, where she was involved in many good works. She lived in partial seclusion, and was known for her sanctity and for her ministry of healing, particularly of those who were possessed.

In 451, when Attilla the Hun was advancing towards the city of Paris, Geneviève not only prophesied that the Huns would not take Paris, but she also arranged for food to be taken up the River Seine into the beseiged city for the starving people. She predicted that the Huns would pass by the city, without invading, and this prediction, like many others she made, came true. Highly respected by both Childeric, the Frankish leader, and the King, Clovis, she succeeded in persuading them to release prisoners who were about to be executed.

Many stories are told concerning Geneviève, both about events which took place during her lifetime and through her influence after her death. There is no doubt that she was a very saintly woman, who had a good influence over many others.

So as we come to the end of the first post-scriptural period, it can be seen how much women had contributed to the spread of Christianity at this time. There is no doubt that the faith in the face of martyrdom of the early Christians helped to build up the Church faster than the persecutors could kill. The prayerful life of those who had often turned from impure lives to devote themselves to a life of ascetic or monastic dedication and the spiritual guidance they gave to others also had its effect on the growth of the Church. And finally the influence of women in court circles who were willing to devote their lives to the service of God not only affected others in their families but also helped to spread the Gospel throughout the Roman world. The action of Geneviève in saving the starving people from the invading hordes was symbolic of how the Western world was being saved for Christianity by these women and their menfolk.

If the women of the New Testament began the establishment of the Church, these women by giving their lives, at times literally in following the example of their Saviour, helped to ensure that the Church would have a sure foundation and would stand firm against any enemy in the future.

CHAPTER FOUR

Beacons in the Darkness

'I will bring my daughters from the end of the earth, every one who is called by my name, whom I created for my glory, whom I formed and made.' (Isaiah 43.6,7)

W HILE THE Church had been experiencing growing pains in the Mediterranean areas and on the European continent, the Celtic Church had been passing through a quiet period. Many of the Christian settlements had grown into small communities, each with its own abbot or abbess and often a bishop attached. There was movement around the western shores of Britain by sea travel and the Celtic countries were developing a distinctive culture, which was increased by the Anglo-Saxon invasion which cut off the Celtic Church to a great extent from Rome. Although from the same roots as the Roman Church, the Celtic Church had limited contact with Rome and was becoming a separate part of Western Christendom.

The Celtic Church and women

Born in 389, Patrick was not against women participating in the ministry of the Church as the Church Fathers of the Roman Church had been. At this time, Christian legislators in Ireland were advocating chastity and monogamy as being the true way of life. As a result, Irish women and men were being encouraged to enter communities. This resulted in a great many communities, each having an abbot or abbess and bishop. In addition, a cult began in which those who did become nuns were considered to be particularly holy women.

An organization or order of 350 bishops with an orthodox basis in the Latin Roman Christianity was established by Patrick in the middle of the fifth century. This order 'did not disapprove the assistance and participation of women since, founded on the rock of Christ, they feared not the wind of temptation'.[1] In fact, special protection was given for women, and abbesses were allowed to own property both in Ireland and Wales. This gave Celtic women considerable opportunities to be free of marital and family constraints. So while the Roman Church was ensuring that women had very little influence in the Church, the women on the western fringes of Brittanny, Britain and Ireland were beginning to develop a strong role in the ministry of the Church.

Welsh princesses

Life was not easy at this time with many petty chieftains wanting to establish their own kingdoms. **Tydfil** is believed to have lived in the Taff valley in South Wales with her children, her brothers and other members of their family at this time. She was the daughter of Brychan, who was a ruler in that part of Wales and sister to another saint, **Morwenna**, who may have moved to Cornwall. A Christian, she cared for her family and had established a monastic community in the valley above Aberfan. When a gang of armed men began moving up the valley, she led her children and followers up the valley, towards her father's court at Brecon. However the invaders caught up with her group and massacred them in 480 at a place where later a shrine was to be built in her memory. The church of St Tydfil still stands at this place in a town which is known throughout the world as Merthyr (martyr) Tydfil. Tydfil died protecting her children, showing great courage in the face of danger, and, knowing that her Christian faith would bring no mercy from her attackers, she held fast, strong in the faith of Jesus Christ who had conquered death. Keyne, who was believed to have lived as a hermit and is associated with South Wales and Herefordshire, may have been her sister.

Further north at this time lived the Welsh princess, **Dwynwen**, who fell in love with a prince who did not love her in return. She prayed to be cured of her love, and in a dream learnt that not only would she receive healing, but Maelon, the prince, would be turned into a block of ice. On waking she prayed that Maelon would be normal, that she should never be tempted to marry, and that God would answer any prayers she offered for all true lovers. Eventually, Dwynwen moved to an island off Anglesey, known as Llanddwyn in her memory, and founded an abbey. The well there became known as a holy well at which lovers could make their vows. If their love was true as they made their vows, the waters there would boil, and so Dwynwen became the patron saint of Welsh lovers.

One of the best known saints of the Celtic Church was David, patron saint of Wales. His mother, **Non**, was the wife of Sant, King of Ceredigion. She is believed to have been educated by Maucan, who had himself been taught by Patrick. One day just as Non entered the church of Gildas at Caer Morfa, Gildas found he had lost his speech, and this event led him to prophesy about David, her son who was yet to be born. Legend has it that she gave birth to David in 500, at the site of the chapel dedicated to her near St David's in Pembroke-shire in Wales. There is a holy well near St David's, where pilgrims have visited throughout the centuries, and from these waters and prayer the author has herself received healing.

Like many of the Celtic saints, Non travelled to other neighbouring countries. She visited Brittany where there is another chapel and well dedicated to her at Dirnon and at the site of her tomb. Other Welsh women saints from this period include the martyr **Tegfedd**, the mother of David's friend, Teilo, killed by the Saxons; **Gwladys**, wife of Woolos and mother of Cadoc; **Cenedlon** who was aunt to Cadoc and was believed to have lived in a solitary cell and **Ciwa**, all of whom have associations with Gwent.

Many of the Celtic Christians crossed back and forth over the Irish sea, from Ireland to Scotland, Cumbria, Wales and Cornwall and Brittany. As a result there are churches dedi-cated to the same saints scattered throughout this region. One saint who travelled from Ireland to live in the seclusion of the hills of Pennant in Powys, Wales in the sixth century was **Melangell**, the daughter of an Irish nobleman.

A legend describes how one day she gave shelter to a hare which was being hunted, and the hounds would not approach her, nor could the huntsman blow his horn. The prince who was leading the hunt was impressed by her godliness and granted her the valley. She lived on her own for 37 years, and her retreat became a refuge for the oppressed. Eventually she founded a community of nuns, of which she became abbess.

Brigid and the Irish saints

Back across the seas in Ireland, a young girl was growing up. **Bride**, **Brigid** or **Bridget** was born in 451, supposedly the daughter of a peasant milkmaid and an Irish Prince, a fairy-tale beginning which shows itself again in a story of how she hung out her washing to dry on a sunbeam! Despite a certain amount of legend which has gathered around Bridget as around all Celtic saints, Bridget was a real woman of deep spirituality, who identified with the poor and the weak, including those of the created world of animals and birds.

Bridget was founder and abbess of a community which probably included men as well as women at Kildare in Leinster. She considered that men and women should be partners in worship as well as in life. It is thought that she may have married her own abbot, for there was no law enforcing celibacy in the Celtic Church even in communities. It is also said that she was consecrated bishop instead of abbess by the Bishop of Kildare, her consecration being no different from that of any male bishop and therefore completely valid. This may have been due to the forgetfulness of the Bishop who forgot to change the words, but it raises interesting questions, especially as it was from this time that many of the great abbesses began to hear confessions, baptize, preach and administer communion, both on the continent as well as in Britain. Some even wore mitres and carried croziers.

Bridget had the gift of being able to see the spiritual in the ordinary things of life, and she used these ordinary things to speak to others of God. Her familiar cross is said to have been made from the straws she picked up from the floor as she tended a sick man, using them to tell him of the saving love of God, so that the man became a Christian just before he died. On one occasion, she is said to have given her father's jewelled sword to a poor man to buy food for his children. In a land full of warring and violence, she witnessed constantly to her belief in the Prince of Peace.

Amongst many Celtic saints of this period, including some whose reputation is dubious, Bridget stands out as a woman of unity, peace and vision who used the gifts of God for the service of God, and brought the ways of God to his people and creation.

Bridget travelled widely and there are churches dedicated to her throughout the Celtic areas, including, of course, the famous St Bride's in Fleet Street in London. She is believed to have died around 523.

There were many other women saints in Ireland at this time including Foila and Briga. **Ita**, who died a little later in 570, was descended from a High King of Ireland and had a vision at an early age calling her to a life of celibacy. She dedicated her life to God and went to live in a place near Limerick which came to be called Killeedy, or the Cell of Ida. It is probable that she also founded communities in Cornwall and Devon, as St Issey, Mevagissey and St Ide are all believed to be named after her.

Amongst her other work, Ita was responsible for running a school for small children. One of those who went to this school was a young boy called Brendan who himself became a saint. Among the things that Ita taught Brendan was the need for 'faith in God with purity of heart, simplicity of life with religion, and generosity with love'.

As with many other Celtic saints of this period, there are many stories about the miracles that Ita is said to have performed, but there is no doubt that she was a very devout, loving yet ascetic person, who preferred the food of heaven to riches from earth. Her prayers and meditation gave her a spiritual strength which was widely known, so that many came to her for guidance.

One of the later Celtic saints was **Kentigerna** who was the daughter of Cellach, the prince of Leinster, and mother of St Fillan. When her husband died, she became a nun at an island retreat at Loch Lomond until she herself died in 734.

Women on the Continent

While the Celtic Church was developing its monastic settlements along the western shores of Europe, monasticism was also growing in continental Europe. In Umbria, a brother and sister, possibly twins were born around 480 and given the names of **Scholastica** and Benedict. Benedict was to become the founder of the Benedictine rule but very little is known about his sister, Scholastica, except what is written in the *Dialogues* of Gregory the Great. She dedicated herself to God from an early age, and when her brother went to live in a monastery at Monte Cassino, she moved nearby, possibly living in a community herself. Scholastica and her brother used to meet once a year in a house near the monastery to talk and spend time in prayer and the praise of God.

The last time they met in this way, in 543, Scholastica, perhaps sensing that it would be their last meeting asked her brother to stay the night. She wanted to have more time with him, but Benedict felt that this would be breaking one of his rules and would not stay. Scholastica was disappointed and began to pray, and immediately a great thunderstorm arose which was so fierce that Benedict was forced to remain. When her brother asked Scholastica what she had done, she replied, 'I asked a favour of you, and you refused, so I asked a favour of God and he granted it'.

They spent the night talking about the joys of serving God and His Church and when Benedict left in the morning it was the last time that he was to see her. Three days later, while he was at prayer, Benedict had a vision of a dove, rising to heaven and realized that it was the spirit of his sister. He arranged for her burial in the tomb that he had prepared for himself in the monastery, so that not even death would divide the brother and sister who had been so united in the service of their Lord.

No doubt Benedict was influenced on occasion by Scholastica as they talked together, in the same way as many women influenced those closest to them. Further north, in France, lived one who was both successful and unsuccessful in the conversion of her family.

Clothilde was born around 474, the daughter of the King of Burgundy. She married Clovis, the King of the Salian Franks when she was eighteen, and within four years had converted her husband to Christianity by her prayers and example. However, after her husband died she did not succeed quite so well with her sons who deeply saddened her with their quarrelling. She eventually died in 545, some thirty years or more after her husband.

One of their sons was Clotaire, who captured the princess **Radegund** of Thuringia when she was twelve years old. Born in 518, Radegund spent the six years after she had been taken prisoner being educated in a convent before she was forced to marry Clotaire, who was both cruel and unfaithful to her. Eventually he murdered her brother and she fled from the court to become a nun which rendered her safe from his pursuit. She became a deaconess in 544. Thirty-three years later, she founded a double monastery at Poitiers, and this monastery, that of Ste Croix, became well known as a centre of learning.

Radegund refused to be its abbess, but she did encourage Venantius Fortunatus to write there, and his works include not only a biography of Radegund, but the great Passiontide hymn *Vexilla Regis prodeunt*, ('The Royal Banners forward go') and the processional hymn, 'Hail thee, Festival Day!' (*Salve Festa Dies*). Baudonivia, who was one of her nuns, wrote a biography of Radegund, telling of the motherly care she showed for her nuns, her attempts at reconciliation amongst her husband's family and her efforts to make the monastery a centre of intercession. Whenever the kings began to wage war against each other, she would redouble her efforts to bring peace both through sending emissaries and through the prayer life of the monastery. She remained there until her death in 587 and the church she founded still stands in Poitiers.

Christianity returns to the English

Another Christian princess living in France at this time was **Bertha**, daughter of the Frankish King Charibert. The pagan King Ethelbert of Kent had asked for her hand in marriage but she would agree only on condition that she could bring her chaplain, Liudhard, with her.

Most of England had been conquered by the pagan Anglo-Saxons, who had pushed the native inhabitants west, and with them the Christian faith. Some of the churches, however, still remained in one form or another and when Bertha came with her chaplain, she worshipped at the tiny church of St Martin in Canterbury, believed to be the oldest church in Britain, which she had restored when she arrived in Kent. As with many other kings who married Christian women, Ethelbert eventually became a Christian encouraging his subjects to follow in his footsteps. When Pope Gregory sent Augustine to convert the English, she persuaded her husband to receive him in a friendly way, allowing him to preach freely. Canterbury, where Bertha worshipped, then became the political and religious centre of the Kingdom, and a cathedral was built there. Through Bertha's influence, Canterbury thus became the source and centre of the Roman Church in England, just as it is now the centre of the Anglican Church.

Having set the seal on Christianity in Kent, and opened the way for Augustine to continue the conversion of the Anglo-Saxons there, Bertha's influence spread further still. When Edwin, King of Northumbria asked for the hand of **Ethelberga**, Bertha and Ethelbert's daughter, in marriage, he 'received the reply that it was not permissible for a Christian maiden to be given in marriage to a heathen husband, lest the Christian faith and sacraments be profaned by her association with a King who was wholly ignorant of the worship of the true God'.[2]

When Edwin assured the messengers that he would place no obstacles in the way of her faith and would allow Ethelberga and her followers complete freedom to live and worship according to Christian belief and practice, Ethelberga, known as Tata, agreed to marry him following the example set by her mother. Edwin also said he was willing to accept the faith himself if on examination it appeared to be more holy and acceptable than his own.

Ethelberga had, like her mother, brought her priest, Paulinus, with her as spiritual counsellor and to be bishop, and she was urged by the Pope to exert her influence to obtain the King's salvation, so that, as in the scriptures, the unbelieving husband should be saved by the believing wife.

Because of his wife's influence, once again a king was converted and baptized as were many of his subjects. However in 633 when Edwin and his army were destroyed, Ethelberga went with Paulinus and her two children back to Kent, where Paulinus became Bishop of Rochester and where she died in 647. It was less than a century later, in 735, that the archbishopric of York was founded. Through the insistence of these two queens on bringing their faith with them as they travelled to new areas to marry heathen kings, the two English provinces of Canterbury and York were founded.

At the time the king, Edwin, was converted to Christianity, many others in his household also became Christians, including his young protegée, **Hilda**. Hilda's father, Hereric, had

been killed while she was still young, and her mother, Beorts-
with, fled abroad, leaving the young child in the care of her
great-uncle, King Edwin and his wife.

From then on, Hilda was brought up in a Christian home,
and was baptized in 627, at the age of thirteen, together with
Edwin and his family by Paulinus, the bishop whom Ethelburga had brought with her from Kent. From the early
Church onwards the opportunities for women to exercise
influence was increased by entering a religious community
which gave them freedom from 'the control of fathers or
husbands and an opportunity to live in cultured and disci-
plined independence'.[3] For a woman of deep intellect and
spirituality such as Hilda therefore, it was often more preferable to enter a religious community than to be restricted by
the confines of marriage.

Hilda had no doubt thought of the possibility of entering a
community, but her life was interrupted by the murder of
Edwin in a battle against Penda, the pagan king of Mercia,
after which both Ethelburga and Hilda were forced to flee
south. Despite this Hilda did become a nun when she was
thirty-three and two years later, Bishop Aidan called her to
take charge of a monastery at Hartlepool, which had been
founded by Hein, the first Northumbrian woman to become a
nun.

Some years later, after reviving the faith at Hartlepool, she
moved to Whitby where the king, Oswy, gave her land to
found a double monastery, one where monks and nuns lived
in adjoining quarters, giving each other support in their work
and prayer.

'She established the same regular life there as in her former
monastery, and taught the observance of justice, devotion,
purity and other virtues, but especially peace and charity.
After the example of the primitive Church, no one there was
rich or poor, for everything was held in common, and none
possessed any personal property. So great was her prudence
that not only ordinary folk, but kings and princes used to
come and ask her advice in their difficulties. Those under her
direction were required to make a thorough study of the
Scriptures and occupy themselves in good works, in order that
many might be found fitted for Holy Orders and the service of
God's altar.'[4] Five of the monks in her community eventually

became bishops, and Whitby was seen as a centre of excellence for Christianity in Britain.

Within the British Isles at this time the two distinct Churches had, at least in some part, overlapped by now. Though living in Anglo-Saxon England, Aidan, the Bishop of Lindisfarne, had come from Ireland and through his influence Hilda had been attracted to Celtic spirituality. It was natural, therefore, when the dispute arose between the Celtic and the Roman Churches over the date for celebrating Easter, that it was Whitby that was chosen to be the meeting place for the special Synod to decide the matter. The dispute had come to a head and Hilda, who was asked to preside over the Synod, which took place in 664, favoured the Celtic Church customs. However she had the spiritual insight to realize that the unity of the Church was the most important thing at this time, and despite her own preferences, the Roman custom was accepted. Amongst others whom she encouraged was Caedmon, a herds-man, who became a great writer of songs and poetry.

She brought peace and charity into the lives of those who knew her, and was a wonderful example of godliness and grace. Her dying message to her community in 680 was 'to maintain the Gospel peace among yourselves and with others. All who knew her called her Mother because of her wonderful devotion and grace. Such was her wisdom that not only ordinary folk but also kings and princes sought her counsel.'[5]

When Oswy, the king of Northumbria, gave Hilda land he also asked her to look after his little daughter, **Aelflaed** or Elflida, and it was Aelflaed who became co-abbess at Whitby together with her mother, Eanfleda, after the death of Hilda. Aelflaed was described as a great comforter and the best counsellor in the area and was a close friend and counsellor to Cuthbert, arranging for his body to be taken to Durham after his death. Aelflaed also brought about peace between Theodore of Canterbury and Wilfred of York before she died in 714 and her story is mentioned in the writings of the Venerable Bede and William of Malmesbury amongst others.

Forced marriages

While Aelflaed was placed in a convent at a young age and remained there, many of the women in this book from powerful families were forced into marriages by fathers or brothers at this time. For **Ebba**, aunt to Aelflaed and sister of Oswy, who was now King of Northumbria, her devotion to God was greater than her obedience to her brother. When she was ordered to marry the King of the Scots, she refused and instead entered the convent at Lindisfarne, later founding a double monastery at Coldingham near Berwick, where she died in 683.

Osyth, believed to have been the daughter of a Mercian lord, Frithwald, did not escape so easily. She grew up at a Benedictine convent and was then forced to marry Sighere, the king of the East Saxons. She founded a monastery at Chich in Essex, now St Osyth, which she was finally able to enter for a while, before she was possibly killed by Danish raiders about 675.

When Edwin had come to the throne of Northumbria, he had done so with the aid of the King of the East Angles. A later King of East Anglia, Anna, whose family and nation were Christian, had several daughters, of which one, **Etheldreda** (or Audrey) was born around 630.

Anglo-Saxon princesses

Etheldreda was a very beautiful young girl, whose devotion to God was such that she vowed she would not marry. Unlike Ebba, she remained obedient to the man who had authority over her, her father. This meant that she had to break her vow of celibacy, but her first husband died after three years. She was made to enter a second marriage this time to Egfrid, the younger son of Oswy, but the marriage was never consummated. Eventually her husband allowed her to enter the convent at Coldingham which his aunt had founded.

From there, Etheldreda moved to the Isle of Ely where she founded a double monastery around 672, over which she remained abbess until her death in 679. The present Ely Cathedral stands on its site. She lived in a most humble manner, eating only one meal a day, and wearing uncomfortable clothes. When she died, she was buried in a plain wooden coffin, but she was later reburied in a stone coffin, at which time her body was said to be unmarked and a wound in her neck which had been present at her death was healed.

Ely became an important pilgrimage centre, due to the

reverence shown to this Anglo-Saxon princess, and many fairs were held in her honour. These were known as St Audrey's fairs, and gave rise to the word 'tawdry', meaning something cheap such as would be obtained at such a fair.

Her intercession was often called upon, no doubt during her lifetime as well as afterwards, and the story of her life is told in a series of sculptures in Ely Cathedral today.

Etheldreda had three sisters, **Ethelburga**, **Withburga** and **Sexburga**, and a half-sister, **Sethrida**, all of whom became saints of the Church. After twenty-four years of marriage, Sexburga entered the convent at Minster in Sheppey, which she had founded, but later moved to Ely where she died around 699. The other daughters of Anna also entered convents, Ethelburga and Sethrida at Faremoutier in France, and Withburga at Dereham in Norfolk.

Violence and the Celts

While their sisters on the eastern side of Britain had their own problems regarding marriage, some of the Celtic women had different problems from their menfolk. **Dympna** was believed to be the daughter of a Celtic king who lusted after her incestuously. She fled from him, but was pursued and killed together with her chaplain in about the year 650. Her relics were found at Gheel, near Antwerp, in the thirteenth century. **Winifred**, or Gwenfrewi, was the niece of Beuno, who both educated her and helped her become a nun. She lived on the borders of England and Wales, where Caradog made amorous advances towards her, which she rejected. He was so annoyed that he struck off her head, which fell to the ground but it was miraculously restored by her uncle, Beuno, and a spring of water then appeared where her head had touched the ground. This spring is now a well of healing at Holywell, in Flintshire, and is dedicated to Winifred. It is one of the better known holy wells in Wales. Henry VII's mother, Lady Margaret Beaufort, (see p. 117) surrounded it with a stone building, and pilgrimages still take place there.

Winifred became abbess of a double monastery at Gwytherin in the mountains above Llanwrst, where she died in 650. Her relics remained there for some centuries until they were removed to the Benedictine abbey at Shrewsbury in 1138.

The Word spreads

The growth of Christianity through the royal princesses and other women continued. **Ermenburga** was another princess from Kent and the granddaughter of Bertha. She married the king of Mercia and later founded the convent of Minster in Thanet where she eventually died around 650.

Mildburga, Ermenburga's elder daughter, continued this ministry as she moved north and established the Benedictine convent of Wenlock in Shropshire, where she became abbess until her death in 720. **Mildred**, perhaps the best known of Ermenburga's daughters, was educated at Chelles in France where she refused an offer of marriage. She entered the convent at Minster where her mother was abbess, and where she in her turn became abbess. She was renowned for her gentleness and kindness and lived until 725. **Mildgytha** followed her sister to Minster and eventually became abbess at a convent in Northumbria where she died in 676.

Edburga was also a princess of Kent who became a follower of Mildred at the convent of Minster in Thanet. She followed her as abbess there until her death in 751, and also corresponded with Boniface, whom she met on a pilgrimage to Rome, supplying him with books and vestments. She wrote the Epistle of Peter for him in letters of gold and he was grateful for all that she did for him in spreading the Word and giving him spiritual encouragement. Boniface was himself a source of encouragement to many of the religious of this period and it was not surprising that they in their turn gave him much support particularly in his missionary work in Germany.

Cuthburga was the sister of Ina, the King of the West Saxons, and was married to Aldfrid, King of Northumbria before founding a Benedictine convent in Wimborne with her sister Queenburga around the year 713. She died fourteen years later but the convent was to be a major influence in the conversion of Germany for among those who helped Boniface were some nuns from her community including his niece, **Walburga**, and cousin, Leofe. Walburga, whose father, Richard, was a West Saxon king, had been born in Devon and grew up in Dorset. Known in Europe by different forms of her name, such as Walpurgis, Walburga's name actually was the

Anglo-Saxon form of the Greek name *Eucharis*, meaning gracious or pleasing. She came from a noble and saintly family, but her father died on his way back from a pilgrimage to the Holy Land.

Walburga travelled to join her uncle, Boniface, together with a number of other nuns from the abbey at Wimborne. Walburga had been at Wimborne for twenty-seven years, when the then Abbess, Tetta, asked the nuns to join Boniface in Germany. They went under the direction of Leofe or **Lioba**, who had been born in Wessex around 700 and educated in the convent in Thanet before she moved to Wimborne. She became the abbess of the community in Germany, and was renowned for her patience, intelligence and beautiful personality. 'Princes loved her, noblemen received her and Bishops gladly entertained her and conversed with her, for she was familiar with many writings and careful in giving advice.'[6] Even Charlemagne and his queen loved her dearly and Boniface gave her his cloak before he set out to convert the Frisians on which mission he died. Her name, Lioba, means 'beloved,' reflecting the great love others felt for her.

The nuns travelled the dangerous route across to Europe, and their voyage was later commemorated in a picture by Rubens in the church of St Walburga at Antwerp. They settled first at Bischofsheim, near Mainz, where Lioba founded a monastery renowned for its excellent training and this community became esteemed as a centre of prayer and counsel and also for helping the poor nearby. Walburga went on to a double monastery at Heidenheim, between Munich and Nuremburg, to be an abbess there whilst her brother was also abbot. When he died, she took sole charge, but in 760, she moved to become the abbess of a double monastery at Eichstad, where she remained until her death nineteen years later, one year before the beloved Lioba died.

To these women, because of their help to Boniface, can much of the conversion of the Germans be attributed. Walburga is often shown with a flask of oil, for she studied medicine and through her faith, skill and prayers, many were cured. At the place near the monastery of Eichstad where she was buried, oil with healing properties flowed from the ground and this became known as St Walburga's oil.

The lives of these two saints were written not long after

their deaths; they could be said to be the forerunners of all English missionaries, and the community at Wimborne was the first of many which sent out sisters to distant parts of the earth to teach and spread the Gospel of Love.

Despite the growth of Christianity at this time, the way of life was still very violent. **Werburgh**, who was born at Stone in Staffordshire, was an example of one princess whose life, like that of Winifred, touched on both the gentleness of the Christian saints and the warlike nature which pervaded much of Britain. Her mother, Erminguild, one of the daughters of Sexburga, married Wulfere, King of Mercia, which was then the last remaining pagan part of Britain, and converted both her husband and his kingdom. Werburgh's mother, her aunt, Ercongota, grandmother and great-aunts were all considered to number among the saints of the Church of this period. However, on her father's side, Werburgh was the grand-daughter of the heathen King Penda, who slew five kings, including two saints. Two of her brothers were killed in revenge by an evil knight who wanted to marry Werburgh, and who later made reparation by founding the Abbey of Peterborough and the Priory of Stone where her brothers were buried.

After her father died in 675, Werburgh's mother went to the convent at Minster, which her mother had founded, and Werburgh herself became a nun at Ely. She was an attractive young woman, with all the spiritual graces of being simple, unspoilt, very gentle, patient and devout. Her father was succeeded by his brother, Ethelred, who then handed over to Werburgh the headship of all the monasteries for women in his realm. By her own example and with gentleness, she guided the nuns in her care. She ate only one meal a day, and often spent the nights in prayer. She was in charge of the convents at Ely, Trentham and Hanbury in Staffordshire and Weedon in Northamptonshire. She wanted to be buried after her death at Hanbury, but the sisters at Trentham, where she died in 699, were reluctant to let her go. However, the nuns at Hanbury somehow had their way, and eventually Hanbury became a place of great pilgrimage.

It was only after another one hundred and fifty years that her relics were moved to Chester, for fear of the Danes. They were deposited in the church of St Peter and St Paul and an abbey was built which afterwards became a cathedral. This place also became a place of great pilgrimage and pilgrims wore the badge of St Werburgh to betoken their visit to the shrine. During the reign of Henry VIII the pilgrimages to Chester ceased with the abolition of the monasteries.

Werburgh is often shown with geese in pictures of her because of a legend about her coming to an agreement with a flock of wild geese, who were becoming a nuisance, that if they left her alone, her cook would leave them alone. She was even supposed to have brought back to life some geese which had previously been killed and placed in a pie. Other abbesses who became saints at this time included **Cyneburga**, aunt to Werburgh, who died around 680, her sister **Cyneswide** and relative, **Tibba** who were venerated at Peterborough abbey.

Into the dark world of Saxon Britain, these royal princesses had become beacons of light as they spread the Gospel throughout the length and breadth of the country, but over this period, women were also active on continental Europe.

Growth in Europe

At the beginning of the century, a young woman, **Theodolinda**, had married the King of the Lombards in Italy, and converted him to Christianity. There were many followers of the Aryan heresy at the court of her husband, but Theodolinda argued against them with a theological knowledge which surprised them coming from a woman. She died in 628 by which time she had convinced them of the rightness of her thoughts.

Two years earlier, **Gertrude** had been born at Landen, now in Belgium, to Itta and Pepin. When her father died, Gertrude was nearly fourteen and she helped her mother found a monastery at nearby Nivelles. She became the first abbess there when she was old enough, and did her duties well despite her young age. The influence of the Celtic Church had reached these parts also as it is recorded that Gertrude encouraged monks, particularly Irish ones, to work in the neighbourhood. When she was thirty, Gertrude gave up her office to devote herself to study and extreme penitential discipline, but she died when she was only thirty-three in 659.

A young girl, Gudula, was brought up at the convent of Nivelles which Gertrude had founded. She was the daughter of **Amalburga** who was married with three children, including **Gudula** and her sister, **Reineldis**. Gudula left the convent to join her parents at Ham, near Alost, where she spent her time in religious devotion and good works. She died in 712 and is a patron saint of Brussels. Before that Amalburga and her husband had joined separate religious communities, Amalburga going to the Benedictine community at Mauberge in Flanders until her death in 690. Reineldis also became a nun, but was murdered by raiders at Sainte in 680.

A little earlier, a young girl was captured by raiders in England and taken as a slave to France. It was in 641 that **Bathildis** was taken prisoner, but only eight years later she was married to King Clovis II. By 657, she had become a widow but was now Regent for her son Clothaire III. As Regent she fought the slave trade, founded the Abbey of Corbie and gave much money to other church establishments. After another eight years she was removed from her Regency and went to a convent she had founded at Chelles, near Paris, where she lived in humble surroundings and was often very ill, until she died in 680. It was at this convent at Chelles that Mildred was educated and no doubt the older Bathildis listened often to the young Mildred as she spoke about the country from which the older nun had been taken as a young girl captive.

Further east, but still in northern France, a baby was born blind to the wife of an Alsatian nobleman. **Odilia**, Ottilia or Adilia, was born in Obernheim and it is said that Adalric, her father, may have turned her away from home because of her blindness. Brought up in a convent near Besançon, Odilia was believed to have been miraculously cured when she was twelve. She was then allowed to return to her father's castle at Hohenburg, now Odilienberg, in the Vosges, where she founded a monastery. Odilia became abbess and remained there until she died around 720. This monastery became popular in the Middle Ages as a place of pilgrimage for those with eye diseases.

Whereas Odilia was known to be a minister of healing for eye troubles, a young English princess, **Frideswyde**, was responsible for men becoming blind. Born the daughter of Didan, king of a region in the upper Thames area, Frideswyde had a church built for her by her father in which to worship.

She developed this church into a Benedictine nunnery where she eventually became abbess. However, the King of Leicester, Algar, was attracted to this beautiful princess and asked for her hand in marriage. Though she refused him, he would not accept an unfavourable reply, and sent ambassadors to carry her away. The ambassadors were struck down with blindness, and so he set out to fetch her himself. Frideswyde, meanwhile, hid among the pigs which were roaming the woods at nearby Bampton, but Algar continued to pursue her, until eventually he too suddenly became blind.

It was three years later before Frideswyde returned to Oxford. After she returned, Oxford became a prosperous town which no one dared attack and many believed this was because of her presence. Thanks to the influence of Frideswyde, Oxford became a town of great importance long before it became a seat of learning. Frideswyde died in 739 and eventually became the patron saint of Oxford.

The iconoclast

Meanwhile difficulties were arising for Christians in the east and south of Europe. The use of icons was being attacked in the Eastern Orthodox churches and it was a woman, **Irene**, who was born in 752 and Empress of the Eastern Roman Empire from 797–802 in her own right, (the first woman to be so) who restored orthodoxy and the veneration of icons in 780.

Living at around the same time as Irene, **Anna**, the daughter of John, a deacon, was born in Byzantium and married soon after her parents died. Her uncle, an ascetic monk with the gift of prophecy, had had his tongue cut out by the iconoclast Emperor, Leon Isauuros, but his speech was restored miraculously and he prophesied that Anna would do much in the service of the Church. When Constantine VI became Emperor, with Irene to guide, knowing of his suffering from the hands of the previous emperors, Anna's uncle was invited to the court for consultation and to give a blessing. As he left court to return to his hermitage, he met Anna who was by then pregnant with her second child. He predicted the death of her husband and family, which were to be part of her sharing in the sorrows of this world as a Christian.

When this did happen, Anna gave away her possessions and travelled to various churches, praying before the icons for guidance. She met a monk from Mount Olympus who ordained her as nun, and then she dressed up as a man and sought refuge in a monastery on Mount Olympus. Thinking she was a eunuch, the prior accepted her and taking the name **Euphemanios**, she led a life of deep humility and devotion.

However her servant from home began to search for her, and found the monk who had ordained her. The two then continued looking until they came to the monastery where they learnt there was a eunuch living. Certain that this was Anna, they asked to see 'him'. Anna realized she could no longer remain at the monastery and went with her servant and the monk to another where she applied herself to a life of asceticism, and also was blessed in working miracles.

These miracles attracted many people, some of whom joined the community, which grew so that they had to move to a place called the Monastery of the Avramites. There Anna's fame continued to grow, but the devil caused one of the monks to spread insults and slanders against her. When someone criticised him, saying that Anna was possibly the young woman who had given away her possessions some years ago, he then tried to attack Anna and tear her clothes as she was walking in order to discover if she was really a woman. Immediately he became blind and paralysed. He was made to leave the monastery and returned to his home, where some time previously he had committed a murder and there he was hanged.

To avoid scandal, Anna left the monastery and went with two monks to a place called Steno. There they stayed for some time until she moved to another place called Sigma where she spent the rest of her life healing the sick and working other miracles.

The Empress Irene's death brought to an end the dynasty of the Isaurians and from then until the Macedonian dynasty established itself in 867 was a time of great transition. Although a council at Nicaea, held in 787, decreed that there was nothing theologically wrong in depicting either Christ or the saints in icons, there was a further period of iconoclasm, (attacks on the use of icons because of fear of idolatory), from 815–842, which was again brought to an end by a woman, the Empress Theodora. This later restoration of the veneration of icons was known as the Triumph of Orthodoxy, and is remembered each year on the first Sunday of Lent.

One young woman who suffered as a result of the iconoclasm was **Kassianne**. Born in Byzantium during the reign of Irene, Kassiane came from a noble family, and was well educated in both spiritual and secular studies. St Theodore the Studite (759–826) praised her for her learning and her piety. When the stepmother of Crown Prince Theophilus decided it was time for him to choose a wife suitable to be his Empress, she gathered all the beautiful daughters from the aristocracy and Theophilus was asked to chose from among them by giving a golden apple to the lady of his choice. Approaching Kassiane, he asked her whether it was not true that all evil things derived from a woman, meaning the sin from Eve. Kassiane answered modestly that also all good things derived from a woman, meaning the Holy Virgin. Theophilus found this answer offputting, demonstrating a feminine cleverness that he was not prepared to accept in his wife. He chose Theodora instead and she it was who restored the veneration of Icons at the end of her husband's reign.

Kassianne left the court and moved to Constantinople where she founded a convent, calling it *Icassion* after herself. There she became abbess, spending much time writing and composing hymns. Twenty-three of her hymns have been included in the liturgical books of the Eastern Orthodox Church, and her *Troparion* – 'Lord, she who has fallen in many sins', is familiar to generations of Greek Orthodox Christians. In 1897, the German scholar, Karl Krumbacher wrote of her 'originality and cleverness, combining the tender sensitivity with deep piety and strong descriptiveness'.[7] Her work has also been described as being characterised by deep theological knowledge, her poetry as offering a divine fragrance and smell of incense written in graceful language. In her hymns lies the light of the Spirit.

'Lord, she who fell into many sins has recognized your Godhead and has joined the myrrh-bearing women; weeping she brings myrrh for you before your entombment. "Alas," she cries, "what night is upon me, what a dark and moonless madness of unrestraint, a lust for sin. Accept my welling tears, you who procure the water of the sea through the clouds;

incline to the grievings of my heart, you who made the sky bow down by the unutterable abasement (of your incarnation). Many times will I kiss your undefiled feet, and then dry them with the hair of my head; those feet whose footfalls Eve heard at dusk in Paradise and hid in terror. Who will trace out the multitude of my transgressions, or the abysses (unpredictability) of your judgements, Saviour of souls? Do not overlook me, your servant, in your boundless compassion".'[8]

Kassiane lived during a difficult period for the Eastern Orthodox Church and was whipped for venerating icons but was also known to have visited monks in prison and in exile, giving them comfort and support. As has so often happened in the history of the Church and its people, it is at the time of greatest difficulties or persecution that there comes much growth and deep spirituality, expressed, in Kassiane's case, in both writing and music.

The threat of Islam and violence

By this time, the great scourge of Christianity, Islam, was beginning to spread throughout northern Africa and across into Spain. Whilst the Christian message was spreading through the work of men and women in northern Europe, further south, Christians were dying for their faith.

Eurosia was one such woman who was born in Bayonne in France according to legend. One of the muslims, a Moor, wanted to marry her but when she refused because she was a Christian, she was hunted down and slain by Saracens at Jaca in the Pyrenees.

In 835, **Pomposa**, a nun at Peñamelaria in Spain, was known to have been beheaded at Cordova by the Moors, and no doubt there were many other Christian women who suffered in this way for at that time Spain was ruled by a Muslim African ruler, Abd ar-Rahman, who persecuted the Christians.

Other women who were to die at the hands of this ruler include the sisters **Nunilo** and **Alodia**. Daughters of a Christian mother and Muslim father, they were brought up in Adahuesca, Spain, as Christians but beheaded for their faith in 851.

A young girl, **Flora**, was born during this period to a

Muslim father in Cordova. She became a Christian but then was denounced to the authorities by her Muslim brother. Flora was punished by being whipped and handed back to her brother for him to control but then she managed to escape. After a little while, both she and her friend, **Mary**, also a Christian, surrendered themselves to a magistrate who threatened to sell them into prostitution if they did not relinquish their faith. Eulogius wrote his *Exhortation to Martyrdom* to them, saying 'Do not fear, no harm can touch your souls whatever infamy is inflicted on your bodies'. They continued to remain faithful to Jesus Christ, their Lord and Master, and as a result were both beheaded in the same year as Nunilo and Alodia.

However all was not lost on the Iberian peninsular, for there are others who are known to have given their lives in the service of their Lord in a different way, women such as **Trigidia** who was the daughter of the Count of Castile. She became abbess of a Benedictine convent at Ona, near Burgos, built by her father and she died naturally in 925.

Further north, life was not necessarily safe even for those living within religious communities. **Wiborada** who was born in Aargau in Switzerland founded a hospital with her brother based on their home. When he became a monk at St Gall, she became the bookbinder in the monastery library. Eventually she became a recluse and many were attracted by the depth of her spirituality. When the Hungarian barbarians invaded in 926, she was able to prophesy their coming to the monks so that they escaped, but by doing so, she died in the onslaught. She gave her life to save her brothers in the monastery, following the example of her Lord.

However the period was stormy and attacks came not only from the south and east. Violence was once again sweeping through Britain by this time, and again Christians were dying for their faith. Although churches were still being built, they were being built in sheltered places away from the sea coast for many were being sacked and burnt by the Danes attacking from the north and from the sea. Among those who died at this time was another **Ebba** who was the abbess of the convent at Coldingham which her namesake had founded two hundred years earlier. She and her community were killed in 870 when the Danes set fire to their convent.

One name known throughout English-speaking Christian countries is that of good King Wenceslaus, but very few are aware of the woman from whom he learnt his kindness and who gave him a Christian upbringing. **Ludmilla** was born in 860, the daughter of a Slavic prince, and married Borivoy, the Duke of Bohemia and founder of the Premyslid dynasty. After her marriage, she followed her husband in becoming a Christian. They built a church near Prague and tried unsuccessfully to force Christianity on their subjects. No doubt some of their zeal at their new found faith was responsible for this over-enthusiasm.

When her husband died, their sons succeeded him, and Ludmilla was responsible for the upbringing of her grandson, Wenceslaus. However, her Christian influence over him angered some of the more pagan members of the court, and when the father of Wenceslaus died and his mother became Regent, Wenceslaus was taken away from his grandmother who was later murdered in 921.

Although the extreme persecutions of the Christians were now over, life continued to remain difficult for the women of this period, as not only Christians but people of other faiths and none began to travel more widely. Many of the Christians took their faith with them to new lands, and the influence of the royal princesses at this time was very important. 'English churchmen should never forget the wonderful work done by women in the early days of the conversion of England.'[9]

But there were other women such as Radegund, Clothilde and Bathildis who also fought against the tyranny or difficulties arising from disputes among their menfolk and even in the hills and countryside of the Celts, particularly in Ireland and Wales, it was often the women who were the gentle saints, while their menfolk continued to fight and curse.

Often the only way for women to escape this personal violence and also to use those gifts of intellect which God had given them was to enter the monastic life, especially when, as in Ireland, this was seen as the better way for a devout Christian to spend her life. So through prayer, through marriage and through bearing the wrongs of their menfolk, Christian women took the Church through the dark ages into the gentler early medieval times when literature and the arts began to be used more in the service of God.

It was during this latter period until the fourteenth century that many of the stories in this chapter, previously passed on by word of mouth, were written down. Although often legendary and influenced by the romanticism of the early middle ages, there is no reason to doubt that behind the legends was more than a grain of truth, a belief confirmed in some cases through more contemporary writings such as Bede's *A History of the English Church and People.*

CHAPTER FIVE

Visions of Love

'And afterwards, I will pour out my Spirit on all people. Your sons and daughters will prophesy, your old men (folk) will dream dreams, your young men (folk) will see visions. Even on my servants, both men and women, I will pour out my Spirit in those days.' (Joel 2.28, 29)

★ ★

T HUS BEGAN a more peaceful interlude, after the birth pangs and early increase, a time of continuing growth, of establishing the faith on a more secure footing in some countries and reaching out to new territories in other places, perhaps a pre-adolescent phase in the Church's history, when squabbles existed, but the stormy period of the Reformation was yet to come.

This was the time of the Crusades, the age of Chivalry, when men went to war and their womenfolk coped with the difficulties of living back home. For the men there was no problem as to what they should be doing; those who did not fight for their Church in the crusades were busy defending their lands, developing social and economic change, or encouraging the growth of the monasteries.

'Many medieval thinkers never bothered to consider woman's place at all, since her necessary subjection to man was considered too natural to question and obviously part of the divine order of things.'[1] But once again for the woman of the Middle Ages there were practically only two alternatives – to enter into the bonds either of Holy Matrimony or of Holy Church.

Their spiritual influence varied according to which role they took, but it continued strongly throughout this age, and while their menfolk were fighting the crusade against the muslim invader, the women were fighting a deeper and more spiritual battle.

Amongst the earliest of women writers at this time was one **Roswitha** or Hroswitha who was born around 935 possibly in Lower Saxony. Roswitha may have been connected to the royal house of Germany, and she entered the Benedictine convent of Gandersheim in the Harz mountains at an early age. She described the foundation of this convent, an important one of its time, in a well written story, one of many manuscripts relating the historical events around her which she wrote either as stories or dramas. Her writings were kept in a convent until rediscovered at the end of the fifteenth century when their worth was recognized and they were published with Albrecht Dürer providing the title page and frontispiece for each play.

Roswitha describes how her only desire in writing was in using 'the small talent given her by Heaven, to create under the hammer of devotion a faint sound to the praise of God'.[2] She tells how much she owed to two abbesses under whose rule she lived for their suggestions, information and encouragement in her literary work. These abbesses were highborn and influential women, one being Abbess Gerberg, niece of Otto the Great. At this time many convents were centres of learning, where women were allowed to study, with opportunities to exchange ideas and read classical and spiritual writers and often preferable to the confined atmosphere of a castle, where women could only sew or gossip. Often there were two groups of women living there, those who took religious vows, and those who retained their property and servants, and might even leave to marry. The latter group would be known as canonesses. In her writings, Roswitha brings out moral truth, as she sees it, and will use examples of miracles or conversion to bring about the right dénouement. Her plays were probably performed by her sisters in the convent, perhaps before an important visitor. Such plays as *Abraham*, *Callimachus* and *Paphunutius* may have been adaptations of earlier legends. Various dates are given as to her death, but it was towards the end of the tenth century or possibly at the very beginning of the eleventh.

The royal mothers of Europe

Despite their often beneficial influence, mothers had their problems then, as they still do, particularly with difficult sons or sometimes daughters-in-law. **Matilda** who was born around 895 was no exception. Matilda was the daughter of Count Dietrich of Westphalia and Reinhild of Denmark and married Henry I the Fowler, King of the Romans in 913, six years before he became Emperor. Of her sons, one, Otto, became Emperor and another became St Bruno, Archbishop of Cologne. She gave away much wealth to help the poor, but after her husband died in 936, two of her sons Otto and Henry complained about her generosity to the poor as well as to the Church. She continued her charitable giving, bearing their complaints with great patience and also founded three convents and a monastery before her death in 968. Known also as Maud, she was remembered for her kindness and generosity.

Another mother who had problems with her son was **Olga** of Russia, who failed to convert him, but like Ludmilla in the last chapter had a great influence over her grandson.

Born around 879, Olga came probably from the town of Pskov, where it was believed that she was a ferry woman. Igor, prince of Kiev, was crossing the river one day and he began to talk with Olga. He was so impressed with her wisdom that when in 903 he felt it was time for him to marry, he sent for her. He was cruelly murdered in 913 leaving his widow with a three year old son, Svyatoslav. She began to rule the land for her son and became widely known for her wisdom. Olga travelled widely and brought administrative and economic stability to her land. She was loved greatly by the Russian people for her humanitarian outlook.

In 955, she made the difficult journey to Constantinople where she was received by the Emperor. Impressed by the hymns she heard sung by the Orthodox choirs at a dinner held in her honour, she asked to know more about the religion from which this music came. The patriarch himself taught her and she was baptized into the Church. After the baptism service, the Patriarch blessed her, saying 'Blessed are you among Russian women that you have loved the light and rejected darkness; you will be blessed by the children of Russia until the end of time'. At her baptism, Olga received the name Helena.

She returned to Russia with several priests and built the church of St Sofia in Kiev. Through her influence the message of the Gospel began to spread throughout Russia and many came to know the light of Christ. Her son, Syatoslav, steadfastly rejected the Christian faith mocking those who wished to be baptized, much to his mother's shame. She was deeply upset by his lack of faith but prayed constantly that God's will be done. 'If God wishes to show mercy to my people and to the land of Russia, He will make their hearts turn to God, as he did mine.' Despite her son's rejection of Christianity, her grandson Prince Vladimir was baptized and through him the whole of Russia became a Christian country in 988, nineteen years after his grandmother died.

Olga built many churches throughout Russia, including one dedicated to the Holy Trinity on the banks of the River Velikaya, after she had seen a vision of the 'Light of the Thrice Radiant God' there. 'She was the first among the Russians to enter the Kingdom of God and children of Russia will always praise her for even after her death she continues to pray for Russia.'[3]

The influence of a woman in the conversion of Russia was repeated in another European country at this time. The first thousand years of the Church had almost ended when the name of Princess **Dobrawa** appeared in the Latin annals written in Czech, Polish and German. Dabrowska or Dobrawa was the daughter of the Czech prince, Boleslaw I, and the first named Christian woman in Polish history. In 965, she married the pagan Polish sovereign, Mieszko I of the Piast dynasty. She tried to win him over to Christianity by all possible means. After their wedding, because it was Lent, she intended to make a sacrifice by mortifying her flesh and abstaining from eating meat. Her husband urged her to change her mind and Dobrawa agreed in order to attract him to other spiritual matters. In such ways she was able to bring her husband closer to God, and Dobrawa's personal influence was a great factor in his conversion.

The baptism of Mieszko and other nobles of the period in 966 is an historical fact. Their marriage had been political, but Gall Anomia in his *Chronicle* writes, 'After his marriage to Dobrawa, Mieszko I renounced his seven previous wives.' Dobrawa's son became the first crowned Polish king, Boleslaw Chrobry, called Wielki (1025) and he was the first of a line of kings who ruled until 1370. Her daughter, Swietoslawa

(Gunhild or Astrid) was the wife of Eryk, the Swedish King, and later the Danish King, Ewen. Dobrawa was also the mother of Saint Olaf and the Danish King Knut (Canute) who conquered England.

Through the conversion of their nation by Dobrawa and Mieszko, Christianity had spread from Rome through Czechoslovakia to Poland and the plans which the German princes and archbishops had made for a mission to convert the Slavic nations were abandoned. By 1054, after the schism between East and West, the Church in Poland became the boundary of the Western Church.

A contemporary of Dobrawa, Bishop Thietmar from Meresburg, who was an honest man but slightly hostile towards Poland, describes her in the following way: 'Her Slavic name, Dobrawa, means "good" . . . and she lives up to her name.' The conversion of Poland had far-reaching consequences, for as a result three quarters of the Polish vocabulary comes from the Czech language. Poland also became part of the western civilization at this time, and began to benefit from Greek and Roman art and literature, developing a great knowledge and experience in law, administration and politics. So it was that by her conversion of her husband, Dobrawa had a tremendous influence on the affairs of Poland even beyond her death in 977.

Around the same time as Dobrawa was coverting Poland, a young woman had been crowned Empress of the Holy Roman Empire as wife of Otto. **Adelaide** or Alice was born in 931 and became the wife, first of Lothaire, King of Italy, and then the second wife of Otto, the son of Matilda. She was widowed when she was only nineteen and then imprisoned before finally marrying Otto and, in 962, being crowned Empress. Otto died eleven years later and for the next twenty years, Adelaide's life was full of troubles because of her daughter-in-law and afterwards her granddaughter-in-law. For a while she even left the court. After 995, she had a more peacable life, building monasteries and convents and was described by many of those who knew her as a kind and generous woman. Odilo, an abbot from Cluny, wrote that she was a marvel of beauty and goodness. She died in 999 at the convent she had founded at Seltz in Alsace.

Another woman who married one destined to become

Emperor was **Cunegund**, who was the daughter of Siegfried and Hedwig of Luxembourg and became the wife of Henry II, the duke of Bavaria, a saintly man who became King of the Romans in 1002 and Holy Roman Emperor in 1014. While he founded the see of Bamberg, she founded the Benedictine convent at Kaufungen in Hesse. They had both been great supporters of the Benedictines, and after her husband's death in 1024, Cunegund entered the convent that she had founded and remained there until her death in 1033.

Royal influence continues in Britain

The influence of women in Britain was continuing, with women like **Edburga** who was the daughter of Edward the Elder and granddaughter of King Alfred. Edburga became abbess of the monastery at Winchester which her grandmother had founded and was especially venerated at Pershore where her remains were buried after her death in 960 and where pilgrimages were made in her memory.

Edburga's nephew, Edgar, became king the year before she died, and two years later, his daughter, **Edith**, was born to a woman called Wufrida at Kemsing in Kent. Wufrida took her baby to Wilton Abbey, where Edith grew up until she became a nun there at the age of fifteen. Her mother became abbess and Edith remained in the abbey, even though her father, the King, offered her the abbacy of other monasteries. She refused these, and possibly also the throne after her half-brother was murdered, on the grounds that she preferred 'to serve her sisters in the most humble capacities, like Martha herself.'[4] This she did until she died at the young age of twenty-three.

On a lesser scale there were those like **Wulfrun** who eventually died around 994. Wulfrun was a wealthy Mercian lady who founded a monastery on the site of what is now St Peter's Church in Wolverhampton. She became the patron saint of Wolverhampton.

Another wealthy woman who was to have much influence in the church, especially in recent times was the Lady **Richeldis de Faverches**, who in 1061 had a vision of The Blessed Virgin Mary at Walsingham in Norfolk, in which she was asked to build a chapel beside a well of pure spring water, which was to be a replica of the house at Nazareth where

Mary and Joseph had cared for Jesus as a child. The house became a centre of pilgrimage in the Middle Ages, but was destroyed in the Reformation. In 1938 it was restored, and is now one of the main centres of pilgrimage in Britain.

Towards the middle of the eleventh century a young English girl had been born in Hungary while her father was living there in exile with his German wife, having moved there after the Danish King Canute had conquered England. The girl, **Margaret**, returned to England in 1057, when she was twelve, with her parents, sister and brother to live in the court of her uncle, the saintly King Edward the Confessor. Although her father died soon after, Margaret enjoyed the time of prayer and worship conducted by the Benedictine monks at the court.

After the Norman conquest, Margaret moved north with her brother, Edgar, and the rest of the family. The King of Scotland, Malcolm, made them welcome and found Margaret to be a young woman of great goodness, kindness and spirituality. Although she had thought of entering a convent, Margaret married Malcolm instead.

Strong-willed and deeply religious, Margaret sought to bring a civilising influence over her rough, warrior husband and his wild country. She even tried to end the slavery that resulted from the constant feuds and raids of the Scottish people.

Margaret not only built churches but encouraged people to use them. She founded monasteries and restored the abbey at Iona. She brought books and learning into the court – her illuminated Book of Gospels is now in the Bodleian Library in Oxford. She tried to teach the king to read but was unsuccessful so instead she read to him herself from her holy books. Afterwards he would piously kiss the books and he later arranged that they should be splendidly rebound in her honour. Margaret won respect and love from all who came into contact with her, making herself available to listen, talk or give counsel to anyone who needed her. She was generous to the poor, and became personally involved in providing for them and for orphans. 'Each day the Queen entertained nine little orphans and twenty-four poor persons; and in Lent and Advent the King and Queen invited three hundred poor people to dine, and served them from the dishes of the royal table. It was a common sight to see this great and beautiful lady on her knees washing the bruised and stained feet of the poor, or sitting beside the couch of the sick, and nursing them.'⁵

Malcolm continued with his fighting, but many of his prisoners were cared for by Margaret. Her spiritual life developed, and with it the spiritual life of the court and of Scotland. Within Edinburgh Castle is an oratory dedicated to Margaret, where she often used to pray and meditate before the altar. During this period, she had six sons, of whom three were to become kings of Scotland, and two daughters, of whom one, **Matilda**, was to marry Henry I, King of England. The present royal family is descended from Margaret through Matilda. In 1072 she and her husband founded the Benedictine abbey at Dunfermline.

Malcolm was eventually surprised and killed in a battle at Alnwick in Northumberland in 1093 at a time when Margaret was ill. She died just four days later and was buried in Dunfermline Abbey. Margaret was canonized by the Church in 1250 and made a patron saint of Scotland in 1673.

Her chaplain, Turgot, wrote about Margaret, 'Let others admire the tokens of miracles which they see in others, I, for my part, admire much more the works of mercy which I saw in Margaret. Miracles are common in the evil and the good, but works of true piety and charity belong to the good alone. The former sometimes indicate holiness, but the latter are holiness itself.'⁶

Matilda spent some time in a nunnery at Wilton under the care of her aunt Christina when she was young. Although encouraged to wear the veil, 'to escape the lust of the Normans', she never became a nun but instead, as the last of the Saxon princesses through her mother's line, married the king of England, Henry I. There was some dispute over whether she had been professed as a nun, but Anselm supported her denials and they remained good friends throughout their lives. She rejoiced at his return to Britain after a quarrel with her husband was settled and ensured his well-being wherever he stayed by careful but lavishly furnishing any lodgings in which he was to stay.

Like her mother, Matilda was very devout and her spirituality also had its practical side. She founded the hospital of St

Giles in London and spent much of her time in caring for the sick, even washing the feet of lepers and kissing them, and her generosity in other ways could be overwhelming as in the case of the magnificent candelabra covered with jewels which she presented to the humble Cistercian order at Cluny in France.

While Margaret and Matilda had continued the royal tradition of spreading the faith in Britain, over in Europe royal women continued to voice their beliefs. One woman who made use of her great influence in the cause of Christianity was **Ida** who belonged to one of the most powerful families in France and was born in 1040. Herself descended from Charlemagne, she had married Eustace II, Duke of Boulogne who was related to both the English and French royal families and had been involved in the battle at Hastings in 1066. Though proud of her nobility, Ida was also a very pious woman and founded many monastic establishments, helping others and distributing her wealth widely to numerous charities.

She encouraged her sons to join the Crusades, and Godfrey the middle son became conqueror of Jerusalem in the first Crusade. Her youngest son had been destined for the Church, but he too joined in the defence of Christianity, which was how the crusades were seen, eventually becoming 'King of Jerusalem'. Later, Ida became an oblate of St Vaast Benedictine monastery in France where she died in 1113.

Further north, in Sweden, another woman, **Helen**, devoted herself to caring for the poor after the death of her husband. Helen was born in Skövde in Västergötland and made a pilgrimage to the Holy Land, but when she returned she was falsely accused of murdering her husband and was killed by relatives around 1160.

Women like Helen and Wulfrun need to be mentioned, because they represent the vast majority of ordinary women who rarely receive mention in any book written during their own times, because they were not important enough for their stories to have been written down. But millions of such women have existed in every age, some wealthy, like Wulfrun, and probably Helen, but mostly the poor and pious who keep the Church alive with their devotions as so many women do to this day.

Hildegarde and other religious

Many may not even have been able to write their name, but one who could not only write her name but was skilled in many different ways was **Hildegarde** of Bingen, born in 1098 in Böckelheim, Germany. She was brought up by **Jutta**, who lived as a hermit but founded a Benedictine community near Diessenburg, which she directed as prioress for twenty years before her death in 1136.

Hildegarde herself was a women of many parts: poet, playwright, musician, artist, scientist, prophet, reformer, visionary, mystic, and spiritual guide. She became a nun at Diessenburg when she was fifteen and prioress after the death of Jutta.

Hildegarde had received visions from an early age and she was instructed by her confessor to write these down. About 1147, she moved with her community to Rupertsberg, near Bingen where she composed hymns and other music for the use of her nuns. She wrote a great deal and while some people approved of her writings, others rejected her particularly as she would speak to all and sundry regardless of their rank. She travelled widely, addressing groups of clergy and founding another house at Eibingen.

In her concern for the environment, Hildegarde speaks strongly to our own age. She felt women and men were estranged from creation, and constantly brought images of juice and the greening of the world into her writings. She would describe the Holy Spirit as pouring the juice of contrition into broken hearts, and describes the sense of rhythm, the harmony that was needed to tie us back into the earth. She uses homely images of God, one who hugs us so that we become encircled by the arms of the mystery of God.

Her best known work, *Scivias*, is apocalyptyic, expressing in symbolism and allegory warnings of the wrath to come. The following extract, however, from *The Divine Works of a Simple Man* shows how closely she sees God's relationship with all creation:

'I am the high and fiery power, Who kindled all living sparks and I breathed out no human things unless I judge them as they are. I placed that encircling wing with My wings above it rightly, that is surrounding them with wisdom. But I burn in the fiery life of the substance of the divinity above the beauty of the fields, and I shine in the waters, and I burn in the sun, and the moon and the stars, and with an aerial invisible wind, by a certain life which sustains all things, I quicken all things vitally.'[7]

Hildegarde saw humanity losing its contact with creation, and aimed to bring people back into working alongside nature within the framework which God, our creator has given to all. Much of her poetry and songs also relates to nature as well to the saints. In an offering to Mary as a branch of the tree of Jesse she combines the two. 'Hail, O greenest branch, sprung forth in the airy breezes of the prayers of the saints. So the time has come that your sprays have flourished; hail, hail to you, because the heat of the sun has exuded from you like the aroma of balm.'

Another visionary of this period was **Elizabeth of Schönau** who was born in 1126 and was a friend of Hildegarde. She entered a double monastery when she was twelve at Schönau, near Bonn, was professed nine years later and became abbess when she was thirty-one. In her writing *The Book of the Ways of God* she spoke out against the spiritual laxity that existed at that time. Elizabeth died when she was only thirty-eight, unlike her friend, Hildegarde, who lived until she was eighty-one. Evelyn Underhill was later to write about these two Benedictine sisters that they 'were the first of that long line of women mystics, visionaries, prophetesses and political reformers – combining spiritual transcendance with great ability, of whom Catherine of Siena is probably the greatest example.'

Another abbess who was involved in writing at this time, particularly on things of science and poetry was **Herrad** of Hohenbourg. Herrad was born in Landsberg, Alsace in 1130 into a noble family. She entered the convent at Hohenbourg and became abbess there around 1167. For the remaining twenty-eight years of her life, Herrad appears to have had unlimited energy and founded not only a priory nearby to supply priests for saying Mass, but also an Augustinian church and convent, farm, hospital and hospice.

Herrad wrote *Hortus Deliciarum*, a well illustrated anthology of science, which she collected to inform and delight her nuns, and to help them develop their service to God. It is a religious encyclopedia containing nearly twelve hundred different texts from many different authors, particularly Peter Lombard and

Honorius Augustodunensis, and is one of the major works of the twelfth century. Besides her expert editing, Herrad herself is believed to have written some of the poetry and helped with some of the illustrations. The work is an example of the intellectual and artistic ability present amongst the women in twelfth century convents, ability which often failed to be recognized outside the convent walls, even in Herrad's case.

While Hildegard and Herrad were using their many talents in the service of God in the north, a young girl, **Rosalia**, was hiding herself away from the world further south. Born in 1130 in Palermo of noble parentage, Rosalia became an attendant at the court of the queen, Margaret of Navarre. She was an attractive young girl, and spoilt by the riches of court life. When she was about fourteen, the Virgin Mary appeared to her in a vision, warning her that her beauty was a threat to her soul. Rosalia slipped quietly away from her home, taking very little with her except a few books and a crucifix. Two angels guided her along a path towards a cave hidden among trees on the mountainside, and there she stayed for several months.

Warned by the angels that her parents were searching for her, she moved on to a grotto to which she had been led, and remained there for another sixteen years until her death in 1160, devoting herself to a life of penance. She supposedly ate nothing but the Eucharist which appeared miraculously.

Her hiding place was not discovered until 1625, when her body was discovered in a sheath of rock crystal. She had cut an inscription in the rock explaining that her disappearance was due to her love of her Lord, Jesus Christ. There is little doubt that had she remained in her family, she would have been married probably against her will to a rich noble. The people of Palermo accepted her as their patron saint in 1625, after her prayers were believed to have brought a serious plague to an end. She was canonized the following year.

Two years before Rosalia died near Palermo, a baby girl was born at Huy in Holland. **Jutta** married while she was still young and had become a widow by the time she was eighteen. She spent the next ten years looking after lepers, and in 1182 she became a solitary until her death in 1228. Although her own family were negligent in their spiritual life, her constant prayers for them eventually succeeded in turning them back to the Christian faith.

Another person who cared for lepers was **Marie** of Oignes. Marie was born at Nivelles in Brabant in 1176 of wealthy parents and was married when she was fourteen to a young man whom she persuaded not only to share in her work for the lepers, but also to live with her as brother and sister. They used their money to help the sick, living in poverty themselves, and eventually, in 1207, Marie went to live in a cell attached to the Augustinian priory at Oignes. Her life there was one of asceticism and holiness until her death thirty-one years later, teaching others and offering her devotion to God through the Eucharist which attracted others to her way of life.

Cardinal de Vitry was greatly influenced by her and wrote about her life and through him, Marie's form of life, which became the start of the Beguine movement, was accepted by the hierarchy.

The Beguines were not exactly nuns as they neither lived in convents, took vows, nor renounced their property and they could return to the world or marry. They began in the twelfth century in the urban parts of the diocese of Liège, spreading around northern France and southern Germany. Holy women would often attach their cells to an hospital or abbey, but did not become full members of a community. Often they were the daughters of families not sufficiently wealthy or well born to enter a convent. Later, many of them adopted the rule of the Third Order Franciscans.

The Beguine movement grew at the time of the Crusades, when there were many more women around than men. There were about two thousand Beguines in Cologne alone, and they worked among the poor in the Rhineland area. Rome did not like these patterns of religious behaviour, since they did not fit into established categories. 'So the bishops and the Inquisition kept a close watch, and frequently acted to break up groups of . . . beguines who looked like toppling over into heterodoxy.'[8]

Often they would be accused of heresy, and if this was not possible, then the accusation was of laziness or illicit begging. They would frequently be involved in teaching or nursing and sometimes in cloth-making, which annoyed the Guilds.

Although Jutta and Marie were prepared to look after those who were sick, especially those whose sickness was very visible, many women were isolated because of their leprosy or other sores. **Seraphina** was born in San Geminiano in Italy and became paralysed as a young girl. When her parents died, she had little help despite her condition which constantly worsened. Sores developed which were so bad that only one of her friends could bear to treat them. But throughout her sufferings until her death in 1253 she remained patient and gentle, a true witness to her faith.

The Augustinian order was growing not only with the priory at Oignes but elsewhere including the manor at Lacock in Britain. **Ela**, who was born in 1187, was heiress to the earldom of Salisbury and married to the illegitimate half-brother of King Richard when she was only nine. She had eight surviving children by the time her husband died thirty years later. During this time she had been greatly influenced by Edmund Rich who was later to become Archbishop of Canterbury and was well known for his saintly ways, his knowledge and preaching.

After her husband's death, Ela began to set about the founding of a nunnery at her manor of Lacock, to follow the Augustinian rule. The first nuns were veiled in 1232, and Ela entered the abbey herself in 1237 or 38, becoming abbess in 1239. There were about twenty nuns in the abbey, which was founded to give 'shelter to the countess and any of her descendants inclined to religious life and to pray for the souls of the countess, her husband and the whole family connection'.[9]

Ela was eventually buried in the choir of the abbey at the age of seventy-four. Not only did two of her granddaughters become nuns there but many of her family were also involved with the foundation. Ela was perhaps typical of the heiress who was married for political purposes, but took the opportunity later of developing her piety in a way which not only enabled her to offer her life to God, but also kept both herself and her family well off both spiritually and materially.

Life was not always easy for the noblewomen though, especially if their fathers or husbands were not in favour with the monarch. **Annora** and **Loretta** were the daughters of the marcher Lord William de Braose. Loretta was married to the Earl of Leicester about 1196 and was widowed eight years later. Annora was the wife of Hugh de Mortimer and both sisters suffered when King John, who had succeeded his brother Richard by then, turned against their father. In 1214, through the influence of their brother, the Bishop of Hereford, Annora was released from prison where she had been held, and Loretta received back her property.

After a while, Loretta began to make preparations to become a recluse and was enclosed in a cell just outside Canterbury in 1221 until her death in 1266. She was supported by both Stephen and Simon Langton, the archbishop and archdeacon of Canterbury at that time. Probably this situation afforded Loretta the security she desired as well as the opportunity for devotion. She exercised a great deal of influence from her cell, particularly in encouraging the Franciscans to come to England and gave them continual help after their arrival. Thomas of Eccleston, an early historian, wrote 'how she cherished them in all things as a mother her sons, sagaciously winning for them the favour of magnates and prelates by whom she was held in highest regard.'[10]

Meanwhile, Annora became enclosed at Iffley in about 1231 and was known only from the grants of royal money for the recluse at Iffley where she died ten years later.

The problems between monarchs and their nobility were not confined to England especially when either the kings or the nobles were often away on their crusades. **Blanche** of Castile who became Regent for her son also had her problems, this time with the barons in France.

Born in 1188, Blanche married Louis VIII and gave birth to eight living children before her husband died. Her son, St Louis IX, was only twelve when he succeeded to the throne and Blanche acted as regent for her son both when he was young and again when he went away on Crusades.

She was known to be both devout and ascetic and was also an able administrator in coping with the strong barons during her son's minority. She was often very headstrong though in the way she ruled and clashed both with the University of Paris and the Chapter of Notre Dame. Blanche, who died in 1252, was not such a saintly character, especially in her dealings with the barons and other authorities, but she was devout and the demands she made on others were never any greater than those she made on herself. It is probable that those who objected to her rule resented any woman holding power, particularly one as able as Blanche, an objection which has been held by many throughout history.

Juliana also had problems with those in authority. She was born in 1192 near Liège in Flanders, and after being orphaned when she was five, she was looked after by the Augustinian nuns at Mount Cornillon. She joined the community, spending her time in devotion to the Eucharist and studying the Church Fathers and eventually becoming prioress. Juliana proposed that the Church should celebrate the feast of Corpus Christi initially to two other women who lived nearby, and then to some priests who appeared at first to approve of the idea. However because some senior clerics did not approve, she was suddenly condemned as being a visionary and an embezzler, and was expelled from the monastery.

Bishop Robert had her restored and he proceeded to try to introduce the feast, but when he died she was again driven out and went to the abbey of Salzinnes in Namur and later to Fosses where she died in 1258. When Urban IV became pope three years later he affirmed the feast having supported Juliana earlier and the office was written afterwards by Thomas Aquinas.

Women and the Franciscan orders

The Benedictine, Cistercian and Augustinian religious communities amongst others were flourishing in many parts of Europe at this time, but in 1210 a young man called Francis had his rule approved by the Pope. **Giacoma** di Settesoli was born in 1192 and was already a very wealthy widow with two small sons when she came to know Francis of Assisi. She was so impressed with him that after Francis decided to start a third order for people such as herself who had commitments in the world, Giacoma became a Franciscan tertiary. She dedicated her life to the upbringing of her sons, the worship of God and the service of the poor. Francis was attracted by her dedication and humour and called her Brother Giacoma, an acknowledgement of the energy she expended in the Franciscan work.

Descended from the noble Roman family of Frangipanis, Giacoma's ability in baking the almond cakes named after her family meant that Francis was often offered these cakes when he visited her in Rome. Some say it showed a tiny weakness in his otherwise strict regime. Francis appeared to treat Giacoma as an honorary man to overcome his general disapproval of close female company.

When he knew he was dying, he sent a letter to Brother Giacoma, asking her to bring cloths in which to wrap his body, a cushion for his head, candles and some of the almond cakes she used to make for him in Rome. However Giacoma had already received a premonition about his death and was on her way to him, bearing with her these very things and she was with him when he died. She was buried near him in the basilica when she herself died in 1273.

The daughter of a noble family, **Clare** was two years younger than Giacoma and had turned down two offers of marriage while she was still young. When she was eighteen, after hearing Francis preach several times, she ran away from home to follow him, and Francis put her in the care of the Benedictine nuns at Bastia. When her sister joined her, their family arrived to try to take them back forcibly, but Francis moved them to San Damiano near Assisi where they started a community which became the Community of the Poor Clares. She and her community led an austere life, living entirely on alms, even through an illness which lasted twenty-eight years until her death in 1253.

Clare and Francis were very close spiritually but met together only occasionally. Their love was a love which reflected the love each had for their Lord. On one occasion, when they were eating together with some of the brothers at la Portiuncula, the whole area became covered as if by flames and people rushed from miles around to put the flames out. When they arrived they found Clare and Francis with the brothers in a state of ecstasy sitting at table, and it was this divine ecstasy which was at the heart of their relationship.

Clare told her nuns to 'Pray and watch at all times! Carry out steadfastly the work you have begun and fulfil the ministry you have undertaken in true humility and holy poverty. Fear not, daughter! God, who is faithful in all his words and holy in all his deeds, will pour his blessings upon you and your daughters. He will be your help and best comforter for he is our Redeemer and our eternal reward.'[11] The following is a blessing of Clare: 'The Lord be with you always and be you with Him always and in every place'.

One of the first well-known members of the Franciscan order was **Elizabeth** of Hungary. Born a princess of Hungary in 1207, she married the Landgraf of Thuringia when she was fourteen. After her marriage, Elizabeth often visited the humble peasant cottages nearby despite her husband's disapproval. Legend tells how once when she was taking a full basket of food and wine, her husband asked her angrily what she was carrying. She told him she had some roses which she had been picking, but he did not believe her and tore the covering away. Under the white cloth, transformed from the bread and wine by a miracle, lay several beautiful roses.

When her husband died after six years of marriage, whilst on the Crusades, she abandoned her rank and became a Franciscan of the third order, devoting herself to the care of the sick and poor at Marburg. Conrad of Marburg became her confessor, but treated her very badly, though her spirit was never broken. She died when she was twenty-four, and was canonized only four years later.

Her cousin, **Agnes** of Bohemia, was born in 1205 a princess in the Premyslid dynasty in Czechoslovakia, granddaughter of Ludmilla (see p. 68) and sister to Wenceslaus.

Agnes joined the order which Clare had founded and became a symbol of devotion to Christ by resigning her privileges and serving the poor and sick. Agnes became a Poor Clare in Prague, at the convent which she and her brother Wenceslaus had built and to which Clare herself had sent five nuns. Agnes became abbess there after a hundred other girls had joined her. She died in 1282. As so often happened, the saintliness of the better known Wenceslaus was encouraged by his grandmother, cousin and sister.

Three other members of the family were the sisters **Cunegunda**, **Jolenta**, and **Margaret**, who were the nieces of Elizabeth and daughters of King Bela IV of Hungary. Cunegunda, who was born in 1224, married King Boleslaus V of Poland when she was sixteen. When he died in 1279, she joined the Poor Clares at the convent which she had founded at Sandeck where she lived until her death in 1292. She gave generously to those in need and helped to build many hospitals and churches and also ransomed many Christians who had been captured by the Turks. She was also known as Kinga.

Jolenta was born in 1235 and when she was five she went to Poland to join her sister, the Queen. She married at the age of twenty-one, founded several religious houses and, after she was widowed, joined her sister at the Poor Clares at Sandeck before becoming superior at Gnesen in Poland until her death in 1298.

Margaret of Hungary was born in 1242 and entered a Dominican convent which her father had founded near Budapest when she was twelve. Apart from asking to remain within the convent when a marriage was suggested with the king of Bohemia, Margaret did not demand any special treatment as a royal princess. She went out of her way to seek the most menial tasks and would do the demanding work of helping the worst of the poor and the sick. She spent long hours in her work and prayer, fasting frequently and eventually died in 1270 worn out with the tasks she had set herself. A maid servant spoke of her kindness and goodness, describing her as 'much more humble than we serving maids'.[12]

Yet another **Jutta** who lived around this time was born in Thuringia where Elizabeth lived and married a nobleman when she was fifteen. After he died while away on a pilgrimage and her children had grown up, she gave away her fortune and entered the religious life. She did not remain in a convent but lived by begging alms, most of which she gave away to sick travellers. She eventually settled in Kulmsee in Prussia as a hermit where she spent the last four years of her life in prayer and blessed with divine gifts before she died in 1260. Eventually Jutta was to become one of the patron saints of Prussia.

Once again the women of a royal household had played a large part in encouraging the growth of Christianity in their countries. As they move through an arranged marriage to a new country or new part of a country, they take their deep spirituality with them and strengthen the faith of yet another land.

Women of education

One noblewoman who also travelled widely was **Devorguilla** de Balliol. Devorguilla was the wife of John de Balliol, one of the great robber barons of the north, who died in 1269. She was descended from the royal house of Scotland and heiress to the Lordship of Galloway, ruling a large part of south west Scotland. She and her husband also had large estates stretching throughout eastern England and they moved frequently around them all.

After the Bishop of Kirkham had been attacked by de Balliol's men, he imposed a penance on Devorguilla's husband that he should support four students at Oxford. This was the beginning of the foundation of Balliol College, but it was only after her husband's death that Devorguilla made the future more secure for the College. She loved her husband, and saw in Balliol the means of expressing that love in perpetuity, by calling the foundation after him.

After her husband died, Devorguilla carried his heart around in a casket wherever she went, as a token of her love for him and a reminder of their union in Christ for eternity. She arranged for a Cistercian monastery to be built on her land in Dumfriesshire, so that this heart could be laid to rest there after she died. So it was that in 1273 Sweetheart Abbey was founded.

After that she concentrated the rest of her life until she died in 1290 supporting these two foundations, ensuring that the students should attend church and say masses and that the richer students should help those who were poorer.

Mechtild, too, was of noble family and well educated. Born around 1210, she first had her visions at the age of twelve. When she was between twenty and twenty-five years old she joined the Beguine community in Magdeburg, but later she became a Dominican.

She was a mystic with a deep love for God, and was drawn to the idea of Christian perfection, striving by mortification of her body to reach that inner detachment she desired to enable her to become united with God. Much of her writing in the *Flowing Light of the Godhead* dwells on the love of God, the love of God for us and his creation, and our yearning love for God. The book is composed in seven parts, of which six may have been written while she was still a Beguine.

At the time she wrote, faith in the Church was waning, and much of her writing is prophetic as well as mystical. She denounced abuses of the faith in churches and particularly in convents and considered many clergy to be grieviously lacking in spirituality, often giving them counsel or advice regarding this. Writing to a canon, Mechtild compares our constant need to give thanks to God, who is so much greater than us, with 'that it soars so high, the eagle owes no thanks to the owl'. She warns the clergy 'O thou Crown of Holy Christen-

dom, how greatly has thou lost lustre! Thy jewels are fallen
out, since thou dost outrage and bring dishonour on the holy
Christian vows. Thy gold has become tarnished in the morass
of unchastity, for thou art become degenerate and art lacking
in true love ... Alas, O thou crown of the holy Priesthood,
how diminished thou art, and verily thou now possessest
naught but priestly power, with the which thou fightest against
God and His elect. For thus saith the Lord: "My shepherds of
Jerusalem have become murderers and wolves, for that they
slay before My very eyes the white lambs, and the sheep are
all sickly for that they may not eat of the wholesome pasture
that grows on the high mountains, the which is godly love and
holy doctrine".'

Like others who try to reform where they see wrong, she
was persecuted for many of her writings and found the persecution hard to take. On being told that her writings deserved to
be burnt, she prayed to God, and heard him tell her not to
mistrust her powers, since they were from him, and no one
can burn the truth. Eventually, in 1270, she took refuge in the
Cistercian Convent at Helfta in Thuringia where she continued her work and writings. Mechtild had a great love for the
Church, but above all was her passionate love for God which
shines through her writings.

> '*The day of my spiritual awakening*
> *was the day I saw and knew I saw*
> *all things in God and God in all things.*
>
> *A fish cannot drown in the ocean ... all things are safe in their*
> *element ... God is our element.*
>
> *I who am divine am truly in you.*
> *I can never be sundered from you;*
> *However far we be parted never can we be separated.*
> *I am in you and you are in Me,*
> *We two are fused into one, poured into a single mould,*
> *Thus, unwearied, we shall remain forever.*'

Mechtild makes Understanding to converse with Conscience,
accusing Conscience of being both proud and humble. 'Conscience explains that she is proud because she is in touch with
God and humble because she has done so few good works.'
True prayer 'makes a sour heart sweet, a sad heart merry, a

poor heart rich, a dull heart wise, a timid heart bold, a weak heart strong, a blind heart seeing, a cold heart burning'.

When describing her return to grace after confession, she writes 'grace came again to wretched me, and I creep back like a beaten dog into the kitchen'. Describing how love flows from the Godhead to humankind, she writes: 'It goes without effort, as does a bird in the air when it does not move its wings.' Some of her writings recall the beauty of the *Song of Songs*:

'I come to my Beloved like dew upon the flowers.'

Perhaps her writings are summed up in the following:

> *O thou God, out-pouring in thy gift!*
> *O thou God, o'erflowing in thy love!*
> *O thou God, all burning in thy desire!*
> *O thou God, melting in union with thy body!*
> *O thou God, reposing on my breast!*
> *Without thee, never could I live.*

Mechtild spent the last twenty-seven years of her life at Helfta, where **Gertrude of Hackeborn** was then abbess. Gertrude and her sister, Mechtilde, were daughters of a powerful family and as a result their first convent at Rodarsdorf was well endowed. Gertrude, who was born in 1232, became abbess there at the age of nineteen, later moving to Helfta where she again became abbess, making it a centre for mysticism, counsel and study before her death in 1292.

Mechtilde of Hackeborn entered the convent at Rodarsdorf in 1248 at the age of seven by her own desire. She also moved to Helfta where she was mistress of novices and became a great friend and guide to **Gertrude of Helfta** who was fifteen years her junior. Gertrude had also entered the convent when she was very young, in her case when she was five, and she probably remained there all her life. Both women had mystical experiences, Gertrude's beginning in 1281 when she had a vision of Christ. She wrote about these experiences in her books *The Book of Special Grace* and the *Revelations of Mechtilde and Gertrude*. Mechtilde of Hackeborn died a year after her namesake and Gertrude of Helfta, (Gertrude the Great), four years later. Gertrude of Helfta is the patron saint of the West Indies.

A young girl called **Hélène** was born in Anjou in 1235,

about the same time as Mechtilde joined the Beguines. She left France as a child to become the wife of Uros, King of Serbia, one of the great Nemanyic dynasty, and nephew of Sava who founded the independent Serbian Church. Although by birth a Roman Catholic, Hélène became Orthodox when she married but kept links with the Roman Catholic Church, building several foundations for them, and being loved as much by them as by her Orthodox subjects. After her husband's death, her son allowed her to continue to govern part of the coastlands. There she founded a school for orphaned girls to learn domestic skills, which was unique for its time, and there are still traces of French influence in both the cooking and embroidery designs of the region.

Hélène also built a large and beautiful monastery to be her burial place, and was buried there one very cold and snowy day in February, 1314, mourned by her many subjects who had so greatly loved her. This monastery was to become a centre of the cultural and religious life of the Serbs, during the Turkish occupation which lasted for five centuries. At the end of the seventeenth century, it was completely demolished by the Turks, but after the Second World War, it was rebuilt. The community of nuns who now live there feel that this monastery is a symbol of the reawakening of the Serbian Church at a time when the 'people are turning with thirst and hope to hear the Gospel of life'.[13]

The Word is spread by many women throughout Europe

All over Europe, women were continuing to make their contribution in the service of God. From differing walks of life, in differing ways they offered themselves at different times of their lives to help the spread of Christianity by word or prayer or example. Such women as Margaret of Cortona, Angela of Foligno, both from Italy, Marguerite Parète of Valenciennes and Mahaut of Artois from France, Notburga from the Tyrol, Elizabeth or Isabel of Portugal and Elizabeth de Burgh from England.

Margaret was born into a farming family in Laviano, Italy in 1217 but ran away from home to live for nine years as mistress to a wealthy man. After he was killed, she became

penitent and through a period of depression (self-mortifica-
tion), and working in hospitals she became a recluse. She then
joined the Franciscans as a tertiary in Cortona and founded a
hospital where she encouraged a group of women, the Pov-
erelle, to work there. After eight hard years, Margaret was
accused of immoral behaviour with the friars, and although
she was found innocent, the smear remained. She died when
she was fifty, at which stage she had once again gained
respectability for her healing powers and work in bringing
others to know God's love.

Angela was born in 1248 into a prosperous Umbrian
family, married young and had several children. Although
different in some ways from that of Margaret, Angela also
lived a worldly and sometimes immoral life until the time of
her conversion when she was about thirty. This conversion
initiated a long period of self-discovery and deepening awareness of the nature of God. It was a time of temptation and
penitence, which she describes in her writings and is one of
the 'classic statements of the inward flowering of mystical
awareness'.[14] When her husband and her children died, she
became free to devote herself to God. She also became a
Franciscan tertiary, joining with several others in a life of
complete poverty and prayer. By the time she was thirty-six,
she was already known as a spiritual teacher.

Angela describes her many battles against the sinful part of
her nature, particularly her strong will, self-indulgence and
pride, the source of much suffering for her. Yet she also
recognized within herself a potential for a rich interior poverty
and deep humility to be reached through the light of God's
infinite goodness and greatness.

Sometime after 1290, she founded a sisterhood in her native
town of Foligno, where the women took religious vows, but
lived and served in the community, giving themselves to the
sick and needy.

Angela's Franciscan calling emerges in her writings, where
she concentrates not only on the Passion of Christ, but on his
concern for the poor. She had a great insight into the spiritual
significance of poverty. Hers was the Christ who walked
among the poorest of the poor, and died abandoned and
naked on the cross. This spirituality becomes linked to an
intense joy in the service and following of Our Lord.

'Christ . . . made himself poor and needy, laying aside his own power. He, the omnipotent, for whom nothing was impossible, desired to appear and to live in the world as a man, weak, infirm, and impotent, in order that beside the human miseries, the helpless childhood and other burdens which he took upon himself for our sake, he who was without blame or sin might appear as but a feeble man. He truly endured much weariness in his journeyings, visitations and disgrace . . . The mighty Lord and King of kings was despised and rejected, but we are always seeking to be exalted and preferred, living in freedom, bearing no yoke.'[15] Angela died in 1309.

Marguerite Parète who was born around 1265 was also a writer. A Beguine who lived in Valenciennes, Marguerite's offering to the Church was both theological and spiritual. Her battle was not with her own sinful nature but with the Church theologians who would not accept anything which was outside the normal thinking of the Church. It was the time of the Inquisition and Marguerite was one of its martyrs. Amongst other works that she wrote was a book called *Mirror of a Simple Soul*, showing a way to God which brought liberation. She tells how when the soul is liberated that it comes closest to God, and conversely, when the soul is closest to God it becomes liberated, a theology expressed by Augustine as 'Love God and do what you will'.

Her book, written when she was in her forties, was rejected by the theologians and she was sent to the Inquisitor, Wilhelm de Paris. When she was put on trial, she refused to answer and Marguerite was burnt at the stake in 1310. Her book was passed down through the monasteries as written by an unknown woman, until it was rediscovered in 1943.

In 1311, the Council of Vienna decided to excommunicate the Beguines. The Inquisition began its work in earnest in the 1230s, but was more efficient in the south of Europe. During the fourteenth century, despite the official Church opposition to many religious communities particularly new ones, small groups of lay men and women came together in poverty and obedience, sharing a devotional life following Christ as their rule and his life and doctrine as their breviary of life. Among those who encouraged such communities in the Low Countries was Gerard Groote who 'turned his house [at Deventer] into a refuge for pious women'.[16] Among those who later belonged to a similar community for men in Deventer was Thomas à Kempis.

Meanwhile, a young peasant woman from the mountains of the Tyrol became a kitchen maid in the household of Count Henry in Rattenberg. Born in 1264, **Notburga** was dismissed by her mistress after she had worked there for a little while for giving some of the scraps which were meant for the pigs of the household to the poor people who lived nearby. After her dismissal she found a job with a farmer at Eben, and continued to give food away, often depriving herself in order to do so.

Following the death of her previous mistress, Notburga returned to work for Count Henry, until she died probably in 1313. Many stories were written about her, and she became the patron saint of servants. It is good to hear such stories, because so often it was the rich and powerful who had their histories written down, but this story tells of a simple women who knew that the commandment of Christ was to love one's neighbour however costly that love might be.

Another women at this time, from a completely different background and yet with the same desire to follow this commandment of Our Lord, was **Mahaut** of Artois. In contrast to Notburga who was poor and without influence, Mahaut was related to some of the most influential people of the period. A countess, Mahaut was also a great niece of St Louis IX, cousin to one king and mother-in-law to another. She was married in 1285, but her husband was killed in 1303, so she had to bring up her three children and look after her territories in Burgundy and Artois. She was accused by some at court of using sorcery to poison the king, but after an inquiry was held she was acquitted.

Mahaut frequently gave money to help the poor, with concern that they should receive it before the winter got too cold. Her servants were looked after well even when they became too old and sick to work. She preferred to use women apothecaries and also had women musicians and singers. She founded several hospitals, ensuring that those attending were always well cared for, and died in 1328.

The influence of these women, particularly if they came from royal families spread widely. **Elizabeth** or Isabel of Portugal was called after her great aunt, Elizabeth of Hungary. Born in 1271, Elizabeth was the daughter of Peter III of

Aragon and married Denis of Portugal when she was twelve. Like Mahaut and many other women before her, she too cared for the poor around her and was helped by her husband in her work by setting up a hospital, a 'rescue home' for women and an orphanage. Several times she interceded between her husband and their son, Alfonso, who led an armed revolt against his father, organising treatment for the wounded of both armies. She suffered a great deal from her husband's neglect, jealousy and infidelities, but through her patience and loving kindness she changed his ways.

After he died, Elizabeth wanted to enter the order of the Poor Clares, but lived instead in a house close to the convent at Coimbra which she had founded. She also became a Franciscan tertiary and devoted her life to helping the poor people of the neighbourhood in the service of God. In 1336, her son, now King Alfonso IV, went to war again and in trying to act as peacemaker, Elizabeth wore herself out. She was successful in bringing peace, but died shortly after. Throughout her life Elizabeth was very devout in her attendance at Mass and in her prayers. It was this devotion to God which sustained her when all else seemed dark.

The founding of colleges

While some of the nobility, and others, were devoting their lives to helping the poor on the continent, two wealthy women in England were following the example of opening education to some of the poor which Devorguilla had set earlier in the thirteenth century. Born just five years after Devorguilla had died, **Elizabeth de Burgh** was the granddaughter of Edward I and daughter of Gilbert de Clare, Earl of Gloucester.

By the age of twenty-seven, she had already been widowed three times. Her third husband was executed after a quarrel with Elizabeth's brother-in-law about the Clare inheritance and Elizabeth and her son were imprisoned in the abbey of Barking. Eventually, she was released and managed to retrieve some of her lands in Wales, Ireland, East Anglia and Dorset, but lived mostly at Clare Castle in Suffolk, from where she received the title, Lady of Clare.

She lived a life of luxury, but also gave much away on education and alms for the poor. She gave generously to the

Augustinian Order, who made an abbey at Clare their mother house, and also to the Minoresses, the Franciscan nuns. In 1336, she gave money to found Clare College at Cambridge, which at that time was a small and struggling hall. She died in 1295 and is remembered on the seal of Clare College where she stands surrounded by the scholars whom she helped both during her life and in her will.

Marie de St Pol was a close friend of Elizabeth, and their lives were not dissimilar. Marie also founded and endowed a Cambridge college, Pembroke, (in 1347) and gave generously not only to the college but to religious houses, hospitals and many other good causes.

Mystics and visionaries

This was a gentler period generally, when spirituality was often developing through writings and mysticism, yet the visionaries and mystics were often people who suffered much, either because their writings or their spiritual devotions to God brought them closer to his passion also.

Bridget of Sweden was one such person who in later life became a visionary, while attempting to continue to live within society. Born around 1303 she married a nobleman while she was still fourteen. They had eight children of whom one, Catherine, is also venerated as a saint. In about 1335, she became lady-in-waiting to Blanche, wife to King Magnus, and she tried to influence their lives and those of others at court. Much affected as a child of ten by a sermon on the Passion, the following night she had seen Our Lord in a vision in which he had told her how much he suffered because of men's indifference to him. Following this, her whole life became centered on bringing people back to leading Christian lives.

Though mocked at court for this, she eventually received permission to go on a pilgrimage to Compostella with her husband. Her husband fell ill on the way home and did not recover until she promised he would enter a monastery. After he died in 1344, Bridget continued to upbraid the court for its sinful ways, as well as founding an Order of the Holy Saviour, the Bridgettines, principally for women. She told about her visions in her book called *Revelations*.

She travelled to Rome in 1349, where she lived in great personal poverty, looking after the poor and sick and offering advice to the Pope and others on the ecclesiastical and political problems of the day. Bridget's daughter, Catherine, joined her mother there but her son, Charles, caused her many problems with his profligate life.

Bridget died in Rome in 1373, soon after making a pilgrimage to the Holy Land. She is described as being humble, gentle and charitable, but also appears have been an intense person. She was keen to purify her soul, and made frequent confessions, constantly weeping for her sins. 'God gave her such a horror of sin that one careless word of her own instantly brought a bitter taste to her mouth, while the bad language of others was a stench in her nostrils.'[17]

She was canonized in 1391 despite opposition from Fr Jean Gerson, who distrusted any visionaries especially if they were women. He tended to blame both Bridget and Catherine of Siena (see p. 102) for the schism in the Church after encouraging the Pope to return from Avignon.

Bridget's writings influenced many people and Margery Kempe (see p. 101) is known to have heard them and visited Bridget's chamber in Rome on a pilgrimage there. Although a mystic, Bridget had lived a normal life but wrote of her longing for reform of the Church and higher society.

Perhaps now one of the best known English mystics, but one whose name was long forgotten after the Reformation is **Julian** of Norwich who was born around 1342. By the time she was born, the comparative security of the age of chivalry had become confused, the storm clouds of the Reformation were brewing on the horizon with the rise of Lollardry and its challenge to the traditions of the Church. It was the time of Crecy and the Black Death, a world which was full of greater violence and of change, a world not dissimilar in these ways to our own, giving rise to much insecurity and fear.

Julian, who probably took her name from the church to which she was attached, was one of many anchorites in this period, recluses who were regarded as part of the welfare services 'worth maintaining for the spiritual good derived from their prayers and penances'.[18] She was one of a number of English mystical writers at this time, and was probably the first woman to write a book in English, even though she thought of herself as unlettered. That there may have been doubts that a woman such as herself should write are answered in her own words 'Because I am a woman, ought I therefore to believe that I should not tell you of the goodness of God, although I saw at that time that it is His will that it be known.'

An anchorage cell may have consisted of several rooms, and it is believed that Julian may have had at least two servants, but an anchorite was not allowed to leave her cell, and lived a life of prayer and self-denial. An anchorite would also teach and act as a spiritual director.

On the 8th May 1373, possibly before she became a recluse, Julian received sixteen visions while she was very ill. She wrote her first version of these very soon after, but it was nearly twenty years later, after much meditation that she wrote the much longer *Revelations of Divine Love*.

Before her visions, she had been praying for three favours from God, in order to know him more fully. These were to understand his passion, to suffer physically while still a young woman of thirty, and to have as God's gifts three wounds, the wound of true contrition, the wound of genuine compassion and the wound of sincere longing for God. Regarding the first favour, she had asked to understand his passion in such a way that she could share some of the pain and suffering of those who loved him and were present at his crucifixion, and even some of Our Lord's own sufferings. In her Revelations she writes 'I saw the body which was bleeding copiously, apparently as the result of the flogging. The fair skin was broken and there were deep weals in the tender flesh of that dear smitten body. So copious was the hot flow that neither skin nor wound could be seen: it was all blood. The most precious blood of our Lord Jesus Christ is in truth both costly and copious. Look and see. The costly and copious flood of his most precious blood streamed down into hell and burst the chains and freed all there who belonged to the Court of Heaven. The costly and copious flood of his most precious blood overflows the whole of earth, and is available to wash all creatures (if they are willing) from their sin, past, present or future.'[19] Later she writes, 'Christ showed me something of his passion near the time of his dying. I saw his dear face, dry, bloodless, and pallid with death. It became pale, deathly and lifeless. . . . That blessed flesh and frame was drained of all blood and moisture. Because of the pull of the nails and the weight of that blessed body it was a long time suffering. For I could see that the great, hard hurtful nails in those dear and tender hands and feet caused the wounds to gape wide and the body to sag forward under its own weight, and because of the time it hung there. His head was scarred and torn and the crown was sticking to it, congealed with blood; his dear hair and his withered flesh was entangled with the thorns and they with it.'[20]

There are many passages which reflect the Divine Love as revealed to Julian, of which the best known include the vision of the hazelnut in which insignificant object, Julian sees the reflection of the whole of creation which lasts and ever shall because God made it, he loves it and he looks after it.

Julian sees Jesus as a complete human, both male and female and, as Mother Jesus, bearing us into new life. In her writing which reflects earlier saints such as Anselm, she dwells on the motherhood of Jesus, seeing the pain of his death as the pain of labour. We become united with him, his very flesh and blood, and through Mother Christ we grow and develop, nourished by his Body and Blood. 'God', she writes, 'is as really our Mother as he is our Father. Our own mother's bearing of us was a bearing to pain and death, but . . . Jesus . . . bears us to joy and eternal life! Blessings on him! Thus he carries us within himself in love. And he is in labour until the time has fully come for him to suffer the sharpest pangs and the most appalling pain possible – and in the end he dies. The human mother will suckle her child with her own milk, but our beloved Mother, Jesus, feeds us with himself, and with the most tender courtesy, does it by means of the Blessed Sacrament, the precious food of all true life. The human mother may put her child tenderly to her breast, but our tender Mother Jesus simply leads us into his blessed breast through his open side, and there gives us a glimpse of the Godhead and heavenly joy – the inner certainty of eternal bliss.'[21] Julian also declares God's promise that 'All shall be well and all shall be well and all manner of things shall be well', and tells how she 'learned that love was our Lord's meaning. And I saw for certain that before ever he made us, God loved us; and his love has never slackened, nor ever shall.'[22]

Julian lived on for many years, probably until after 1413. Until the Reformation, her writings were popular, but it was only earlier this century that her writings became more widely known again. She was commemorated as a saint in the Church of England in 1980.

One women who is known to have visited Julian of Norwich is **Margery Kempe**, born around 1373, who became the wife of a burgess of Lynn and the daughter of its mayor. She had fourteen children and writes in her autobiography, discovered in the 1930s, how she had a mental breakdown after the birth of her first child, during which she had a vision of Christ talking with her, clad in a mantle of purple silk. Despite, or perhaps because of, her many failures to follow the ways of Christ, she became convinced that she had a special vocation to pray and weep for sinners and to go on pilgrimages for the good of their souls.

Margery lived apart from her husband after a while and was obviously quite an eccentric even for a mystic, often breaking into loud sobs in the middle of a sermon, which must have been somewhat disconcerting for the preacher. However she was also instrumental in calming stormy weather at sea on her pilgrimages and on one occasion when a large fire had broken out at Lynne, she prostrated herself before the altar with shrieks and groans at which a heavy snow shower immediately quenched the flames, even though the sky had been clear only moments before. Margery could see the holiness in the poorest of women suckling a child. While in Rome, Margery had dreamt that she had become a bride of Christ, with the saints Bridget of Sweden and Catherine of Siena as her bridesmaids, and henceforth she was to dress in white. This habit, together with her strange behaviour, meant that she was accused at times of being a Lollard, but the charge was dismissed by the Archbishop of York. He later accused her of preaching which was, according to the clerics who advised him, against Paul's teachings in the Epistles.

When her husband became senile and incontinent, she returned home to look after him. After his death, Margery went on a pilgrimage and when she returned, she persuaded a priest to put her thoughts and life experiences down in a book. It was this book which was forgotten after a while only to be discovered in 1934 in Yorkshire.

Margery delighted in her mystical visions with a simple naïvity and appears to have been a very human person, self-conscious but very devout. In her book, Margery changes from a simple faith, 'Every time I hear a robin sing, I am filled with thankfulness and praise,' to describe some of the wildest fantasies that she experienced. Through her life she also shares with other women the common difficulties often associated with childbirth or with caring for the elderly and demonstrates how, even in such circumstances, they can still continue to offer their lives in the service of God, though perhaps not in the same way as herself. She writes 'On the day of purification, which is Candlemas, all the people were in church with their candles and in contemplation I saw our Lady with Joseph offering her son to Simeon, the priest in the temple. I heard songs so beautiful that I was transported with love for our Lord and could not hold my candle to offer to the priest. . . . Every time I see women being purified after child-birth it is as though I see our Lady.'[23]

Prayer and politics

While Julian was meditating on her visions in the East Anglian city of Norwich, another young woman in Siena in Italy was attempting to heal the religio-political disputes in the Church. **Catherine** Benincasa was born in 1347 the twenty-fifth child of a Sienese dyer. She made a vow of celibacy at a young age and entered a Dominican order as a tertiary at the age of sixteen, remaining in her own home. She lived as a recluse there for three years, speaking only to her confessor and spending her time in prayer.

Then in 1366 she began to lead a more active life amongst the poor and the sick, including those suffering from the plague. She attracted a group of people around her, priests and laity, young and old, rich and poor, including an Augustinian friar from England, Brother William. The number of young men attracted to her began to cause scandal, but she was cleared of any charge and instead became widely known for her intellect, her visions and her holiness.

Catherine also started to involve herself in some of the religio-political disputes of the day. The papal court was at that time in Avignon, in France, and Catherine went as emissary from Florence to bring Gregory XI back to Rome as part of an effort to bring peace to the rebellious Italian states. On the one hand attempting to heal the divisions within the Church, Catherine was also concerned at the corruption that existed there. 'She looked deep into the roots of problems, noting the pride and corruption of the human heart, then invoked the model of Christ, into whose image all persons must be reformed.'[24] She did indeed bring about much healing, but her success in bringing Pope Gregory back to Rome was marred by his death shortly afterwards in 1378. His successor, Urban VI, proved unpopular, and the College of Cardinals declared his election invalid. They elected Clement VII, an election which caused the great schism with rival popes. Catherine remained faithful to Urban, constantly pleading his cause with political and religious leaders. The strain told on her health which was never very strong and she died in 1380. She had received the stigmata five years earlier, whilst praying in the church of Santa Christina. In 1970 she was made one of only two woman doctors of the Church, the other being Teresa of Avila (see p. 120).

Catherine never learned to write. Her letters and her book *The Dialogue* were all dictated to a scribe. 'I have given you my Son as a bridge, that you may not drown in, but pass over, the flood – the stormy sea of this dark life. See then how indebted my creature is to me, and how foolhardy it is to persist in drowning rather than accept my remedy.... Consider the bridge that is my Son, and see how its great span reaches from heaven to earth; see, that is, how it links the grandeur of the Godhead with the clay of your humanity.... No heaping up of earth alone could ever have sufficed to make a bridge great enough to span the torrent and open the way to eternal life.'[25]

Catherine was effective in reforming the world and the Church hierarchy because of the saintliness of her life. From the depths of her contemplations, with a life rooted in her love for God, she was able to bring a social consciousness which challenged the religious and secular institutions of her time.[26] Through her life it can be seen how women can be effective in the work of the Church when their life is centred on prayer and a deep love for God.

Prayer was the essence of life too for **Dorothy** of Montau in

Prussia. Born in the same year as Catherine, when Dorothy was seventeen she married a wealthy swordsmith from Danzig. Although her husband was bad tempered, her patience and prayers had their effect on him in the same way as they often help and are needed in such circumstances. After he died in 1390, she lived as a recluse at Marienwerder, where she supposedly had many visions, until she died in 1395. She is greatly honoured in that locality, and became, together with Jutta, (see p. 88), a patron saint of Prussia.

While Dorothy was coping with her difficult husband in Prussia, a baby was born in 1371, to the king and queen of Poland and Hungary. **Jadwiga** was the youngest daughter of Casimir III and his wife, Casimir being the last of the Piast dynasty and the most powerful amongst the Christian rulers of the world. Casimir encouraged the foundation of religious communities which built and staffed hospitals, schools and developed farming. The nuns of these communities developed education for girls 'who proved themselves to be more interested in learning than did the laymen'.[27]

Although the right of succession of the thrones of Poland and Hungary passed through the male line, at this time there were no male heirs, so it was left to the daughters of Casimir to become the heirs. However, because she was the youngest of the three daughters, Jadwiga could not receive a throne as her two sisters would. Therefore as Archduchess of Austria, with an enormous dowry she had, at the age of four, already become a useful pawn in the hands of the politicians as a means of enlarging the country through marriage to the six year old Wilhelm of the Hapsburg dynasty. Jadwiga was sent to live in Vienna and Wilhelm joined the court in Buda in Hungary so that they could learn more about each other's countries.

However after the death of her sister, Katarzyna, in 1378, Jadwiga became heir to the throne of Poland, and became even more important to Polish politicians. After her father died in 1382, her sister became Queen of Hungary. Jadwiga moved from Vienna to Krakow, where she was crowned when she was ten years old, although women were not really allowed to become monarchs in Poland. At her coronation, therefore, she was dressed in clothes not normally worn by women including the Alb, Tunic, Dalmatic and Cope, which were indicators of her responsibility as a priestly administrator. After making her vows in accordance with the rites of the Kingdom, Jadwiga was anointed by the Archbishop, who made the sign of the cross and placed the crown on her head, her hair flowing freely as befitted a virgin. The Archbishop then proclaimed in Latin, 'Know this, that the crown elevates you to be a member of our ministry.' Like Bridget before her, through circumstance, Jadwiga had become a member of a ministry normally denied to women, a ministry which was to be greatly blessed.

According to the sacred formula of the laws of Poland, Jadwiga was crowned not to be Queen but to be King of Poland. As a result, she signed official documents as King of Poland. Although she had some independence, as far as her marriage was concerned she was not consulted, for she remained the centre of Polish political activity which still yearned to expand eastwards.

Negotiations began to offer the Grandduke of Lithuania, Jagiello, the promise of Jadwiga and the crown of Poland. In order to facilitate this, the previously arranged marriage to Wilhelm had to be prevented. Although there are no historical records to show it, it is known that Jadwiga was very unhappy about the newly-proposed marriage, and tried to escape from Krakow, even attempting to force the door of the palace. In the end, Jadwiga gave way to the pressure from those around, because of the deep faith she held which demanded her obedience, and when she was twelve years old she married Jagiello, a man twenty years older than her, in the Cathedral.

At his side, Jadwiga not only cemented the Polish/Lithuanian union, which lasted for several centuries, but also brought the faith of Christianity to Lithuania in 1387, a very important event as it was the final part of Europe to be converted to Christianity, and the beginning of the Age of Christendom. In this way Jadwiga was following in the footsteps of so many of her sisters in being an apostle of Christ taking the Gospel to new lands.

Despite her reluctance, her short marriage was successful, although her only child, Elizabeth, died within three weeks. Jadwiga herself died a few days later when she was just twenty-five years old. She had led an intensely religious life and was widely known for her good works and her charity.

When she died in 1399, she left all her silver, jewellery and treasures to the University in Krakow which had been founded in 1364. She also financed various faculties in Prague University (for Lithuanian students) and was active in peace negotiations with the commander of the Crusader order of Sayno, guaranteeing peace in that area for as long as she lived.

She was greatly loved by the people of Poland and an attempt was made to canonize her. After her death, her beneficial influence was no longer present and war again broke out, beginning a new and more violent chapter in Polish politics.

A woman of literature

One of the most important women writers of this period, a woman who is little known in Britain, was **Christine de Pisan**. Christine was born in 1363 in Venice, the daughter of Thomas de Pisan, who was known for his knowledge of medicine and astrology. When she was five, she moved with her mother to Paris to join her father who had become court astrologer to the King, Charles V. Christine grew up at court, where she revelled in spending much time in the sumptuous library in the old Louvre castle, reading and meditating on the many books contained there.

When she was fifteen, Christine married Etienne de Castel, the King's notary and secretary whom she loved dearly but two years later, after the King died, both her husband and her father lost their posts. By the time she was twenty-five both men had died leaving her with three small children. She began to write poetry for her own enjoyment but also to earn some money to support herself and her family. She studied Aristotle, and through her poetry and writings gradually began to become well-known, so that she was invited to other courts.

Her interest lay particularly with the cause of women and her love for her adopted country, which was in the throes of the Hundred Years War at the time. She recognized the importance of women's influence on the world and appealed to the Queen Isabella to use her influence to help put an end to the disputing between the rivals for the regency during the King's illnesses. Christine also helped to make such authors as

Dante more widely known, taking titles of her poems from his writings. Dante had lived a century before, and in his writings had placed woman in heaven beside the Deity. At this time, women continued generally to be either deified or held to be evil incarnate as in the times of the Church Fathers.

Christine studied men and women as God made them and as she found them. In attacking Ovid's *Art of Love* and *The Romance of the Rose*, she stirred up opposition against herself, but was supported by many who then formed fellowships in the defence of women. Christine wrote about these in her poetry and also argued that the shortcomings of the few should not condemn the many. When it was pointed out to her that other books were full of the condemnation of women, she replied that those books were not written by women.

Christine went on to write *La Cité des Dames*, an account of an imaginary city where women of all times and countries who have distinguished themselves may shelter. Philosophers and poets have always defamed women, she writes, and appeals to God, asking why such a thing should be seeing that He Himself made them, giving them inclinations which seemed good to Him and that He does not err. 'God created the soul, and made it as good in woman as in man, and that it is not the sex, but the perfection of virtue, that is material.' Replying to the suggestion that women are not fit to plead in Court because they are not sufficiently intelligent to apply the Law even if they learn it, Christine shows how in history women have always shown great judgement and intelligence in the management of affairs, a statement which would appear to be very true.

Regarding marriage, she indicates that it is not always the blessed state that it is meant to be for a woman, when it not infrequently happens that a husband returns from enjoying himself only to beat his wife. Christine also saw no reason why girls should not be educated as well as boys, for their learning ability is just as great. How often have those statements been repeated over the centuries. The recognition of her own wide knowledge is shown in the way the English King Henry VII commanded Caxton to translate and print a book she had written on the history of military strategy, entitled *Le Livre des faites d'armes et de chevalrie*. It was still quoted as an authority in the reign of Henry VIII. In a further book, Christine counsels

well-born women not to attach too much importance to the
material things of this world, to be charitable, to ensure their
children are educated and to inform themselves so that they
may replace their husbands as leaders of the household when
the husbands are obliged to be away. She also counsels servants about not taking bribes, for God is everywhere and will
notice, while she reminds the poor that they will have recom-
pense in Heaven.

Christine was worn out with disappointment after the defeat
of her country at Agincourt, and retired to the convent of
Poissy which she knew so well. She remained there for fourteen
years, silent to the outside world, before writing a final hymn
of praise (see below) for the deeds of Joan of Arc. She died at
the age of sixty-six, at the very moment of the consecration of
the Dauphin, Charles VII. From her writings, the following
verse of the hymn of praise for Joan of Arc speaks strongly of
her views on men and women:

> *'Mark me this portent! strange beyond all telling!*
> *How this despoiléd Kingdom stricken lay,*
> *And no man raised his hand to guard his dwelling,*
> *Until a Woman came to show the way.*
> *Until a Woman (since no man dare try)*
> *Rallied the land and bade the traitors fly.*
> *Honour to Womankind! It needs must be*
> *That God loves Woman, since He fashioned Thee!'*

Perhaps it is with such a potent piece of writing that this
particular chapter in the history of Christian women needs to
end. From the turn of the millenium until the times of Christine de Pisan the story of both Europe and Christianity had
moved on. Throughout this period women had been at the
forefront in the development of spirituality and in holding the
fort back at home for their menfolk during the crusades.

Both in their writings and in the visions and mystical
experiences, women could be seen to be using the spiritual
gifts which they had been given by God. While these were
sometimes rejected as not being appropriate gifts for women,
as a whole they were acknowledged by the Church even
though, during the changes in the Reformation yet to
come, many of these offerings were often to be lost for several
centuries.

The spread of Christianity to new countries within Europe, which women such as Eurgain and Bertha had initiated, had now come to fulfilment with the conversion of the final piece in the European jigsaw of Lithuania by Jadwig. The martyrs of this period were fewer in known numbers but wider education and spiritual searching meant that difficulties were beginning to arise within the Church, difficulties which would erupt with the Reformation. However apart from the trials of the Inquisition, this period had been a quieter one for the womenfolk, even if their men had spent it, as so often happens, engaged in feuding and fighting for king or religion.

CHAPTER SIX

A Planting of the Lord

'The Spirit of the Sovereign Lord is upon me, because the Lord has anointed me to preach good news to the poor. He has sent me to bind up the broken-hearted, to proclaim the year of the Lord's favour and the day of vengeance of our God, to comfort all who mourn, and provide for those who grieve in Zion – to bestow on them a crown of beauty instead of ashes, the oil of gladness instead of mourning, and a garment of praise instead of a spirit of despair. They will be called oaks of righteousness, a planting of the Lord for the display of his splendour.' (Isaiah 61.1–3)

★ ★

As THE Western Church grew into adulthood, so it grew away from some of the original purity and unity of belief. While there still remained many very devout Christians in all parts of the Church, the adolescent squabbling of the early medieval period was developing into outright family fighting. Misunderstandings and misinterpretations meant that the Church based on Rome was beginning to splinter and with the splintering came some wounding. Throughout Christian history there have always been martyrs, but the deaths which occurred at this period were more often between differing sections of the Church than from secular oppression as the rumblings of discontent burst into the battlefield of the Reformation.

The Reformation was partly a protest about the secular power which had been exploited by the hierarchy within the Church, but this protest did not extend itself towards the abuse of the power which men held over women. The role of Mary the virgin which had seen the feminine side of God partitioned off into worship of the mother of Jesus, was dismissed as idolatry by the Protestants, but the feminine in God was not to return as might have been expected. Far from it, women were to lose their place in the eyes of the churchmen and equality as one of the marks of Christianity was a thing of the distant past. Luther's view was that women were inferior to men, but women's voices were being raised in protest at being treated only as domestic appendages.

Calvin gave women more opportunities, but generally women were not used in the public ministry of even the Reformed churches.

'Marie Dentière, the daughter of a shopkeeper, preached publicly and wrote a defence of women; Argula von Grumbach publicly protested on behalf of a university teacher who had been wronged; Katherine Zell, the wife of a Reformed minister in Strasbourg, defended clerical marriage.'[1] 'Thus the Reformation achieved less than one might expect towards the liberation of women. It cherished the ideal of motherhood as opposed to virginity, but simultaneously reinforced the view that women are created for domestic roles. It supported the education of girls, and affirmed the right of all Christians to study the Bible and approach God directly in prayer, but discriminated against women in public worship, perpetuating the idea that ordination and church government belong to men. Although some small Protestant groups affirmed the right of women to preach and serve in the diaconate, the mainstream Protestant Churches continued, in this respect at least, in the tradition of the medieval Church.'[2]

However it was through the women of the Reformation period, who read the Bible and taught what they found there to their households that the Reformation spread throughout Europe. The women as well as their menfolk died for their newly found Protestant beliefs at this time, as Roman Catholic women too were to die for holding to their beliefs. The Church was now searching for new opportunities and beginning again to spread in more ways than understanding. From the freer availability of the Bible in their native tongues, there came a planting of the Word of God not only in the hearts and minds of the educated, but also following that planting the word of God reached out to new places and new sections of the community. With the discovery of the New World, women were amongst those who saw the new lands as virgin territory for the spreading of the Gospel which they held so dear. For those who found their gifts not very acceptable to the hierarchy in Europe, America was far enough away to offer them the freedom to use those gifts in the service of God.

Opposition and pain

When women have been successful in their work, this has often appeared threatening to some men, especially if that success deprives those men of what they see as the femininity of women in any way. One who suffered from such success was **Angelina Angioballi**. Angelina was born in 1377 at Montegiove, near Orvieto in Italy, married at fifteen and widowed by the time she was seventeen. She became a Franciscan tertiary and gathered around her lay tertiaries who preached the desirability of virginity. Because of the numbers who joined her she was denounced as a sorceress and Manichean heretic but the charges against her were dismissed. She and her companions then went to Assisi, and in 1397 she founded an enclosed convent of the third order regular of St Francis at Foligno where she died when she was fifty-eight years old.

In Holland at the same time lived one **Lydwina** who was patient in suffering in a different way. Lydwina was born in 1380, one of nine children of a labourer and his wife in Scheidam in Holland and was injured while she was skating when she was sixteen. She became an invalid, suffering more and more as the years went by but bearing the pain patiently as reparation for the sins of others. Eight years after her accident she began to receive supernatural gifts. Eventually she became blind and also extremely thin, living only on the Eucharist until her death in 1437.

One who received opposition from women rather than men was born not so very far away at Corbie, Picardy, in northern France. Nicollette Boillet was a year younger than Lydwina and was born the daughter of a carpenter. From her childhood she was known as a deeply religious person with her own little oratory in the corner of the yard. She became attached to the Beguines and then a Franciscan tertiary and went to live alone in a little hermitage beside a church, where many people came to her for advice.

In 1406, **Colette** (as she became known) had a dream in which Francis appeared to her asking her to bring the Poor Clares back to their original strict rule of life. She was struck blind and dumb for three days and was uncertain what to do but her spiritual director, Henri de Baume, encouraged her to go to meet Peter de Luna, the papal claimant who lived in Nice. He was impressed with her and not only professed her into the Poor Clares order, but also gave her authority over many of the houses so that she might reform them.

She met a great deal of opposition and hostility from the nuns as she travelled barefoot across Europe, but persisted in her efforts until she achieved success. Her influence spread throughout France and into Flanders and Spain and altogether she founded seventeen convents under the reformed and stricter rule, besides reforming several others. Colette was well known for her great faith and holiness and her determination to do what was right despite the opposition. She died in Ghent in 1447, but her communities of the Poor Clares of the Colettine are still found throughout the world today.

One who would have been very aware of the influence of both Clare and Francis was **Rita** of Cascia who was born in 1381 in Roccaporena, near Spoleto in Italy, the scene of one of the visions of Francis. She had hoped to become an Augustinian nun, but had been forced to marry a very hard and dissolute man. In their eighteen years of marriage she was very unhappy and when her husband died in a fight, her two sons wanted to avenge his death. She tried to dissuade them but they insisted and themselves died as a result. This left Rita free to follow her first desire and in 1413 she entered the Augustinian convent in Cascia.

She spent her time in caring for others and praying for those who failed in their devotions. She was often very ill but lived an austere life in the convent until her death in 1457. In many parts of the world she is considered to be 'the saint of desperate cases'.

Another Italian woman who cared greatly for those in need was known as **Frances** of Rome. Frances Busso was born in 1384 into a wealthy Roman family, and married Lorenzo de' Ponziani when she was only thirteen. From an early age, Frances was concerned with the sufferings of others, often visiting the poor and the sick. During the plague which struck at one time, she took it upon herself to nurse the worst of those afflicted. She led a very simple life, caring not only for her husband and children but also the many around who needed her help.

When their home was sacked by an anti-papal army in

1408, her husband was wounded and a year later he had to escape while Frances turned their home into a hospital to care for those injured in the war. Two of her children died of the plague and one of her sons joined his father, who by now was himself very sick. In 1414, he returned to Rome but was so ill that Frances had to spend much of her time nursing him back to health.

She established a community of women, the Oblates of Tor de' Specchi, to continue her works in association with a Benedictine monastery nearby. In 1436, after her husband had died, she entered this community herself for the remaining four years of her life and became superior there albeit with great reluctance. She was a mystic and a visionary and had much influence within the Church. 'Her last years were marked by extreme austerities, and many supernatural gifts were added to her earlier power of healing.'[3]

While Rita and Frances were following their vocations in other parts of Italy, a young girl, **Antonia**, was growing up in Florence. Born in 1400, she became a widow while she was still young. After first joining the Franciscan tertiaries, Antonia then entered a convent at Foligno, of which she became superior, before moving to take charge of the convent at Aquila. She wanted to follow a stricter rule and was moved to a house, probably one of those which Colette had reformed where Clare's rule was obeyed more strictly and there she remained until her death in 1472.

She suffered a great deal through illness and family quarrels, often brought about by her troublesome son. There are many in this history and elsewhere who have looked with a sad and yearning love on the misdemeanours of those sons whom they have cared for from the cradle and Antonia must be amongst those who can be counted as patron saints for such women.

A Woman at war

How often must women have wondered when, after giving their all in the service of God and their menfolk, they are abandoned, perhaps forgotten or even treated harshly by those they would help. There can perhaps be no name better known in this context than Joan of Arc. Her worth has already been mentioned in the previous chapter, and though her story is well known, no apology is needed for its retelling here.

Joan was born **Jeanne** La Pucelle in the village of Domremy in Normandy in 1412. She was burned to death less than twenty years later, accused of witchcraft and heresy in Rouen. At the time she was born, the English and French were at war. The English had joined forces with the Burgundians to attack the forces of the Dauphin, Charles. Joan was very devout and prayed often for the safety of her country. When she was about thirteen, while she was praying, she heard voices urging her to save France from the enemy. The certainty with which she spoke about these voices enabled her eventually to obtain an audience with the Dauphin. After undergoing a searching examination by some leading churchmen, she was given a suit of armour and allowed to join the commander of the French army.

At that time much of the French army was being besieged at Orleans, and the plans of the Commander were being thwarted by a strong wind which prevented rafts taking French soldiers across the Loire from sailing. Joan prayed for a change of wind and God answered her prayer. Immediately the soldiers were able to cross, with Joan among the leaders. The defeat of the English there led on to other victories and Joan persuaded the Dauphin to be crowned King at Rheims. All France wondered at the bravery and skill which Joan showed, but even more they wondered at her strong but simple faith in God, from whom her success had come.

The battles were not over, however, and while helping to relieve Compiegne, she was captured by the Burgundians who sold her to the English. She was imprisoned by them for nine months during which time she was brutally treated, but she remained constant in her devotions and prayer. She was then brought before a court presided over by the Bishop of Beauvais and was accused of witchcraft and heresy. She was urged to confess that her 'voices' were the work of the Devil rather than God, but refused steadfastly to deny that they were from God.

For fifteen long sessions she answered her accusers with her faith and fearless good humour. Only once did she falter, when she realized what her faith in her voices was leading to, a death which would be hideously painful. When asked how she could invoke heaven and yet be in opposition to the church militant, she replied that she would defer to the church militant provided that it did not command her anything to do that was impossible.

It is interesting to note that what was meant by the church militant was the hierarchy, the clergy and theologians, who alone, according to themselves, were qualified to express the divine will. When asked whether or not her voices commanded her to submit to the church militant or its judgement, she replied that they commanded her to obey Our Lord first, not the Church. She could not act contrary to God's command. She was handed over to the authorities to be burned to death in the market place of Rouen and there she died, holding in her hands a simple cross, a symbol of her faith in the crucified Lord.

In 1456, only twenty-five years later, Pope Callistus III appointed a commission which declared that Joan's condemnation had been obtained by fraud and deceit and that she was a true Christian. However it was not for another four and a half centuries, in 1920 that Joan was canonized by her church, for her virtue and obedience to the voice of God.

'With Joan, the mediaeval tradition of the prophetic woman confronts the claim of clergy and doctors to monopolize the public word pronounced in the name of God. Joan forcefully reminds her judges that ecclesiastical power is in the service of holiness, and not the contrary'[4]

Women of peace

Eight years after the Pope's commission into Joan's trial, another Joan was born, the daughter of Louis XI and Charlotte of Savoy. **Joan of France** was both hunchbacked and had disfigured skin and so her father, who disliked her intensely, married her off to Louis, Duke of Orleans when she was only twelve. Her husband also disliked her greatly and the marriage was never consummated. As a result, when he became King in 1498 and wanted to marry someone else, he obtained an annulment of his marriage to Joan. She did not object, accepting the situation with the great patience which she showed in all her adversities.

She proceeded to found a contemplative order, the Annonciades of Bourges, and then also established a confraternity to pray and work for reconciliation until her death in 1505.

Another Joan who lived slightly earlier was **Joan of Portugal**. Also of royal parentage, Joan was born in 1452 in Lisbon, the daughter of King Alfonso and Elizabeth of Coimbra. She lived in a frugal manner until she was twenty when she entered the Dominican convent at Aveiro. While her father and brother were away fighting the Moors, she acted as regent and she remained in line to the throne until 1485, when the succession was established and she became free to take her final vows. She died only five years later at Aveiro.

While the men continued to fight their battles, the women continued to attempt to use their influence for peace. The Lady **Margaret Beaufort**, was born in 1443 the daughter of John Beaufort, the first Duke of Somerset, and her first husband was Edmund Tudor, Earl of Richmond, brother to Henry VI. Her husband died after a short marriage, but their son was to become Henry VII after Richard III was killed at the battle of Bosworth in 1485. Margaret was instrumental in bringing the Wars of the Roses, between the houses of York and Lancaster to an end. Her second husband, Henry Stafford, died in 1482 and she then married Thomas, Lord Stanley, who later became the Earl of Derby.

Margaret gave encouragement to many young men including two who were to become Bishops and the pioneer printers, Caxton and Wynkyn de Worde whose edition of Walter Hilton's *Scale of Perfection* was dedicated to 'the right, noble Margaret, as ye see, The King's Mother of excellent bounty . . . This mighty Princess hath commanded me T' imprint this book her grace for to deserve.'[5] Margaret translated a book called *The Mirror of Gold for the Sinful Soul* herself. Her interest in learning encouraged her to establish both Christ's College, where she had an oratory built and St John's College at Cambridge following in the footsteps of Devorguilla de Balliol, Elizabeth de Burgh and Marie St Pol a couple of centuries earlier. She was also responsible for endowing the Lady Margaret Professorship of Divinity at Oxford, and under her patronage, Erasmus prepared his revised edition of the New Testament. Her generosity towards the students of Oxford was eventually rewarded in 1879, when Lady Margaret Hall was founded with Elizabeth Wordsworth, niece of William and daughter of Bishop Christopher, as the first principal. Not only did Margaret give generously to the universities and others, she was, as mentioned earlier, responsible for erecting a building at the well of St Winifred at Holywell. Her faith was such that eventually she took monastic vows and lived in a community until her death in 1509.

Italian women of the fifteenth century

At the same time as Margaret was practising her faith in Britain, another young woman was deepening hers in Genoa. **Catherine Fieschi** was born in 1447 into a noble Italian family, and from an early age was drawn to the religious life. She was refused admittance to the convent where her sister was living, because she was too young. She was, however, forced to marry at the age of sixteen, in order to unite two factions in the city where she lived. Her husband was both unfaithful and profligate, and Catherine remained unhappy until eventually she was abandoned by her husband in 1473.

It was then that she had a conversion experience and began to live a life of extreme penance and mortification. When her husband returned to her four years later, his life also had been changed and he joined her in living with the poor and caring for the sick in a hospital at Pammatone. For twenty years they lived in this way, guided by the Holy Spirit in all they did. After her husband's death in 1497 Catherine had many mystical experiences and in 1499 she left her work at the hospital attracting a group of disciples around her whom she led with deep spiritual insight until her death eleven years later.

Catherine 'combined an interior life of ecstatic and incessant contemplation with an exterior life of unflagging activity'.[6] She received communion every day, a practice which was unheard of by most people of her day. Catherine spoke of her conviction that a total surrender of will and rejection of earthly concerns were necessary to achieve union with God. About this union she wrote 'God seems to have nothing else to do than unite himself to us'. Purification of the soul required a high degree of inner and outer mortification, where self becomes nothing. Catherine's words are 'ecstatic, aching with love, singing in the thrall of rapture, speaking of a joy and desire that transcends all else.'[7]

After experiencing such a period of ecstasy, when she felt on fire and pierced to the heart by the love which God had shown her, her prayer was 'O Love, is it possible that you have called me with so much love and have revealed to me in one moment what no tongue can describe?'[8] She felt the keenest sorrow for her sins for to her they had been committed against God's great goodness.

'I saw that Love's eye was so open and pure. His sight so keen and His vision so far-reaching, that I was astounded at all the imperfections he found and showed me so clearly that I was obliged to acknowledge them . . . When the creature finds himself cleansed and purified and transformed in God, then he sees what is true and clean.'[9]

Angela Merici was born in Lombardy three years after Catherine had experienced her conversion. She was orphaned at an early age and eventually became a Franciscan tertiary, giving catechism lessons to the village children. She was invited to Brescia to do similar work at which she was very gifted, but although she did well in this work, it did not appear to her to be her true vocation.

She went on a pilgrimage to the Holy Land, during which journey she lost her sight. On returning to the very same point on her journey home, her sight was miraculously restored. She also inspired the crew and other passengers with her calm courage when the ship nearly foundered during the voyage. She was asked to stay in Rome by the Pope, Clement VII, but preferred to return to Brescia to await God's will for her.

In 1535, Angela together with a number of her companions formed a group to bind themselves in God's service, the Company of St Ursula. At first they were just a society of young women, living in their own homes and offering their lives to help the poor and the ignorant. There was no community life, no vows, no religious habit. They began to teach in the children's own homes. The group developed into the first teaching order of women and the order of Ursulines, as it was known, began to spread. Angela herself died in 1540, not many years after her Company had begun its work but the community continued to grow. Now the Ursuline Convents are well known for their education of girls throughout the Christian world.

Like Catherine, **Lucia Brocadelli** was also deeply religious from a young age, yet she was forced to marry despite having made a vow of virginity as a girl. Born in 1476 in Narni, Italy, Lucia married a count when she was fifteen. He respected her vow of virginity and three years later she became a Dominican tertiary, retiring to a place called Viterbo. She became prioress of a convent in 1499 but was not a good administrator and when she was forced to resign only six years after her appointment, she suffered much indignity and bad treatment at the hands of the others at the convent, bearing it with great patience and humility, remaining there until her death in 1544.

Teresa of Avila

Another woman attracted to the Church from a very young age was Teresa de Cepeda y Ahumada, more commonly known as **Teresa of Avila**.

Teresa was born in Avila in Castile, Spain in 1515 of Jewish descent on her father's side. It is said that at the age of seven, she decided to seek martyrdom with her baby brother, by walking to the country of the Moors, where they thought they would then be beheaded and so be with God for ever and ever. They did not get very far before they were discovered. When she was twelve, her mother died and at the age of twenty-one Teresa entered the Carmelite Convent of the Incarnation at Avila.

At first she was not well, and when she gradually got worse it was felt it would be better if she left the convent for a while, but she was able to return in 1540 when her health began to improve. Fifteen years later Teresa began to see visions and hear voices and these mystical experiences continued for many months. At first Teresa did not fully understand these happenings, and it was only after several years of spiritual desolation, with little help from her spiritual advisers, that Peter of Alcántra persuaded her they came from God.

For five years from 1557 she was involved in a reformation movement which was a response through prayer to the difficulties of the Church. Then in 1562 she wrote her *Life of St*

Teresa, a book about her life to that time. However her dearest concern was the instruction of the thirteen nuns at her Reformed Carmelite Convent of St Joseph founded that same year despite much opposition, for whom she wrote her second book *The Way of Perfection* a year later.

Over the next twenty years, Teresa founded seventeen different convents under her newer stricter rule. Often they were poor, with strict enclosure, and a discipline which included silence as well as great austerity. This reformation was taking place some century and a half after that which Colette had introduced into the Poor Clares and was a reaction to the laxity which had crept into the Carmelite movement. Teresa's influence in the reformation of the women's side of the Carmelite movement spread also to the men's communities, particularly through John of the Cross who was much influenced by her.

Teresa began writing *The Book of Foundations* in 1573, but opposition remained to the Reformed or Discalced Carmelites and from 1575 onwards there were many disputes within the Carmelite order. Not only was John of the Cross imprisoned at this time, but fifty of the nuns at Avila were also excommunicated. However, Teresa concentrated on her main work and *The Interior Castle* was written in 1577. Three years later the Discalced Reformed Carmelites were recognized as a separate order. Teresa died in 1582 at Alba de Tormes where she was buried.

Several characteristics of Teresa speak to us in today's world. The first is her biblical training, for her constant reading of the Bible is evident in all her writings. She wrote a commentary on the *Song of Songs* and it is possible that her deep knowledge of the Bible may stem from her Jewish background. Despite this biblical background, the Inquisition forbade publication of her books.

Secondly, from a very young age her whole life had been centered on Christ. She wrote about prayer in her books and had a constant need to pray. In 1554, she received a vision of Jesus and His passion which influenced the rest of her life.

The third characteristic of Teresa which speaks to us is that of her humanity. This was based on her knowledge of Christ in his human experience together with her own vivid feelings and the experience of being a woman with all its dignity and capacity to love. She was both intelligent and intuitive, founded her Reformed Order of Carmelites for both men and women and challenged the established male authorities. Her qualities included tenderness, friendliness, optimism and cheerfulness.

Teresa never thought that God had bestowed favours on her because she was better than others. She considered herself only a very humble instrument chosen by Him to manifest His Glory to others. Through her personal determination she overcame both her physical as well as her spiritual weaknesses, for Teresa was never very well. She was sensitive to the need for equality and admitted both fallen women and young unmarried mothers into her communities.

The first woman Doctor of the Church, the literary value of her writings have given her universal stature, and her deep sense of solidarity gives her life a missionary dimension. Teresa shared her wealth, both spiritual and material, and welcomed all comers. In her struggles with the hierarchy, she remained persevering yet discreet, treating everyone as her equal. She was not averse to criticising God himself when after feeling particularly annoyed with the way it appeared that he was yet again frustrating her, she told him it was no wonder he had so few friends after the way he treated them. Despite her initial reluctance to take office or responsibility, once she had done so she prided herself on her reputation as a sound organizer and a good business woman.

Teresa discerned the Holy Spirit in the whole of life and this included ecumenical dialogue, an idea which was certainly less common in Spain because of the Inquisition, but was developing elsewhere.[10] Two of her prayers are still widely known today:

> *'Let nothing disturb thee,*
> *Nothing affright thee.*
> *All things are passing,*
> *God never changeth.*
> *Patient endurance attaineth to all things;*
> *Who God possesseth in nothing is wanting:*
> *Alone God sufficeth.'*

The second of these prayers demonstrates her thoughts about the service of God:

> *'Christ has no body now on earth but yours,*
> *no hands but yours, no feet but yours.*
> *Yours are the eyes through which must look out*
> *Christ's compassion on the world.*
> *Yours are the feet with which He is to go about doing good.*
> *Yours are the hands with which He is to bless others now.'*

Teresa also wrote that 'it is important to understand that God doesn't lead all by one path, and perhaps the one who thinks she is walking along a very lowly path is in fact higher in the eyes of the Lord.'[11]

Only seven years after Teresa began her life in Spain, **Ragoula Benizelou** was born into a distinguished Greek family in Athens. Her father ensured that his only child was well educated although this was not normal for a young girl at this time. Married at the age of fourteen, about the same time as Teresa was entering her convent, Ragoula had become a widow only three years later, after which she refused the offer of another marriage choosing instead to become a nun.

The martyrdom of women continues

Greece was part of the Ottoman Empire and Ragoula founded a monastery which helped not only Christian but also Muslim women who were lonely or facing difficulties in their lives. Two hundred women from Athens joined the community to devote their lives to God as nuns, and many more sought shelter there. The women were taught to read and write but also learnt skills which would help them to earn a living afterwards. The monastery also contained a hospital for those who were sick and a hostel for travellers with nowhere else to go.

The success of the monastery attracted the attention of the Turks who did not approve of Mother Philothei as she was then known. They made trouble for her and the monastery, placing her in prison and restricting the activities of the monastery in order to cause financial hardship. Philothei did not give up, but after a while the Turks became so angry that they broke into the monastery and attacked Philothei, beating her to death. Beloved by the people of Athens for all her good works, she was canonized only ten years after her death.

Martyrdom continued to afflict women elsewhere, but not

always at the hands of heathens. A member of the household of Queen Katharine Parr, the wife of Henry VIII, **Anne Ascough** was endeavouring to reform the religious thoughts of the court in England.

Anne was born a year after Ragoula and was well educated with a gift for logical argument, a gift which led eventually to her martyrdom. After she married, her husband turned her out of his house because of her new ideas. She continued at court but was accused of introducing heretical books into the Queen's household while the men were away busily involved in issues of war. Her arguments were very protestant ones which were not to the liking of the newly formed Church of England, and as she was deemed to be leading others astray, she was first tortured on the rack, Chancellor Wriothesley himself taking a turn at tightening it. The Queen, though, continued to encourage daily Bible readings during which Anne's protestant views so outraged some that she was eventually burned to death and her body was cast out as the body of a malefactor, one of the first martyrs of the Reformation.

Katherine continued to encourage study of the Scriptures, although she incurred the King's wrath by discussing such matters with him. '"A good hearing it is when women become such clerks. And much to my comfort in my old age to be taught by my wife!," quoth he.'[12] Probably he was unaware how good an influence many previous royal wives had been in the history of the English Church.

There were many in court circles and elsewhere at that time who became entangled with the continual changing views of the monarchs between Protestantism and Roman Catholicism. Some died as martyrs, among them such women as **Alice Driver** and **Joan Waste**. Both women were poor, but were willing to stand up for what they believed to be God's truth. Foxe in his *History of Martyrs* describes how Joan 'went to Church daily to hear the Bible read in English and saved up money to buy a New Testament ... she would pay a prisoner from the debtors' prison or another poor person to read a chapter to her daily. She thus became convinced that the Roman observance of the Mass was not according to Christ's meaning in the Gospels and was led away to her burning holding her brother by her hand.'[13]

Others were not so firm in their beliefs or felt it was prudent not to declare them so openly and merely followed the monarch of the day, changing from one viewpoint to the other in the manner of the vicar of Bray. Many managed to retain their loyalty to their own aspect of the faith, giving way to royal or ecclesiastical pressure only when it was necessary and judicious so to do.

The Elizabethans

Among those living at this time were the **four daughters of Sir Anthony Cooke**. Katherine was a great scholar in both Greek and Latin, and Elizabeth, who married first Sir Thomas Hoby and then Lord John Russell, was a great friend of Katherine Parr and probably Anne Ascough, although she also enjoyed the pomp of Roman ceremony and disliked extreme protestantism. In Elizabeth's reign, Elizabeth Hoby tried to restore a national church which included both Roman Catholic and Protestant features, and also translated a tract on the *Way of Reconciliation touching the True Nature and Substance of the Body and Blood of Christ in the Sacrament* in 1605.

Her sister, Ann, the mother of Francis Bacon, was also a great scholar and one who had taught the young Prince Edward when she herself was still young. She was strongly puritanical and a counsellor of many great men and was also known for her translation of the *Apologia pro Ecclesia Anglicana*, a work approved by the then Archbishop.

The fourth daughter was Millicent, Lady Cecil, to become Lady Burghley. Though Protestants, the Cecils conformed under Mary by receiving Holy Communion at Wimbledon parish church, he for reasons of state, she with a patient waiting until the right faith would arise again. She gave generously to the education of the poor as well as maintaining scholars at St John's College in Cambridge. She also provided Bibles in Hebrew and other languages besides other books and supported many widows and orphans in such a quiet way that often her husband was unaware of what she had done.

Queen Elizabeth herself was born in 1533, the daughter of Henry VIII and Anne Boleyn. She lived in these throes of the Reformation period, after her father had turned away from the Church of Rome in favour of the Protestants although he still kept to Catholic order and doctrine. Elizabeth's half-brother, Edward, who succeeded to the throne was more Protestant and during his reign it was the turn of the Roman Catholics to suffer for adhering to the old faith. Their sister, Mary, changed the country round yet again, with Protestants being martyred this time, so that Britain did not know whether it was Protestant or Catholic when Elizabeth came to the throne at the age of twenty-five.

Elizabeth was determined, therefore, to take the middle road, so that the Church would be both Catholic and Protestant, and both sides would feel that they could now belong to the Church of England. She did not insist on the use of ornaments in churches, but retained crucifixes, lights and vestments in her own chapel. At her coronation, she accepted an English Bible, and kissed it, but was crowned by one of Mary's bishops with all Roman ceremonial.

Elizabeth did not approve of clergymen marrying, but many of them did, and there was a wider degree of tolerance allowed then than for some time past. The Liturgy was authorized to be read in English, and Edward's prayer book was used with only slight alterations. Elizabeth joined the administration sentences of two prayer books together in the Communion service, thus combining the acceptance of the real presence with the idea of the memorial, so that the presence was thought of as more spiritual than corporeal. Elizabeth described the Communion in her own words as 'Christ was the Word, who spake it; He took the bread and break it; and what His word doth make it, that I believe and take it.' By combining different thoughts in this way Elizabeth shows her desire to bring all her subjects into the fold of an inclusive Church of England.

Elizabeth also changed her own title from being 'Supreme Head of the Church', to being 'Supreme Governor in all things ecclesiastical and temporal'. She did endeavour to accept many who did not conform strictly in accord with the guidelines of the Church, and turned a blind eye to many Catholics and extreme Protestants who remained outside the Church. But she also helped the Calvinist cause in Scotland against the Roman Catholics, and tried to help the Huguenots in France. Although excommunicated by the Pope, this did not worry her especially as during her reign many Popes were to come and go while she continued to remain on her throne until her death in 1603.

Despite her liberal attitude to many, Elizabeth could be quite firm with any she thought were attempting to undermine the Church of England which was so dear to her heart.

One who suffered in this way was **Margaret Clitheroe** who was born two years before Elizabeth came to the throne. Margaret was the daughter of a wax chandler in York, and was baptised in St Mary le Grand where her father was churchwarden. He had been responsible for bringing back the old Catholic services when Mary Tudor came to the throne, but when Mary died, he accepted the Elizabethan religious settlements as did many of the York inhabitants. Margaret was brought up in this Church of England and learnt her duties in running a household, but could neither read nor write.

She was married at the age of fifteen to a prosperous butcher, who was sworn in as a special constable in 1572 to hunt down Roman Catholic suspects. In that same year, Margaret herself became a Roman Catholic. The young couple lived in the Shambles in York, and their family grew. Margaret was strict in her dealings with others but remained likeable and competent in business with a lively wit.

In 1576, the Roman Catholic priests who had been trained abroad returned to England, and many were to receive shelter in the Clitheroe's house. Several times between 1577 and 1584, Margaret was sent to prison accused of sheltering the priests who were seen to be a threat to the established Church. There she learnt to read and write and study devotional books. Not only did Margaret shelter the priests, but Masses were also said in her house. By 1582, after a fierce persecution, many priests were captured and executed and Margaret herself became a suspect person, being sent to prison for eighteen months.

In 1585, it became a felony punishable by death to harbour a priest and on 12 March 1586, Margaret was arrested and put on trial. Margaret refused to plead because by so doing she would save her own children having to give evidence, and three days later she was sentenced to death by 'pressing'. Margaret was devoted to her family to the end, and sent her shoes and stockings to her twelve year old daughter to signify that she should follow in her footsteps in serving God. Her last words were 'Jesus, Jesus, have mercy on me.' She was a woman who had the courage to die for what she believed was right as so many others had done before or have done since.

Roman Catholic communities meet opposition from the Church

Difficulties for Roman Catholic women during this period did not always arise from the established Church but continued to arise from within the Church of Rome itself. **Mary Ward** was born at Mulwith, near Ripon in Yorkshire fourteen months before Margaret Clitheroe was pressed to death. Many of her family had been imprisoned for their Roman Catholic faith and she had lived in several different households when young. At the age of fifteen, while Mary was staying with her cousins near Selby in Yorkshire, she felt a vocation to enter the religious life. Her parents, however, made her wait until she was twenty-one, when she travelled to St Omer in Flanders to join the Poor Clares.

She did not settle with them, but gathered a number of like-minded Roman Catholic women around her, and returned to St Omer in 1609 with them to form her own community. She waited to find a suitable rule, and it was after a serious illness two years later and much prayer that she decided to follow the example Ignatius had set with the Society of Jesus some seventy years earlier. The community was to be free of enclosure and able to move freely, an idea which was considered acceptable for men, but never, according to the storm of protest, for women.

Mary was obstinate, objecting to the inferior status which women were given. 'There is no such great difference between men and women, yet women, may they not do great matters also? ... And I hope in God it will be seen that women in time to come will do much.' She founded her community despite the opposition.

In 1631 Pope Urban VIII supressed her Institute by Papal Bull and Mary was imprisoned in Munich. When she was released, she tried to plead her cause in vain. Despite this, she returned to York in 1637 and set up her community there. The members of the community followed a rule of life and lived in one house, wearing ordinary clothes and ministering to the people of York but moving to Hutton Rudby in the countryside nearby during the Civil War. Mary died eight years after her return to York and the founding of her community which became known as the Institute of the Blessed Virgin Mary.

Eventually the community was officially recognized by the Pope in 1877 and it still works in many and varied ways. It has been involved in the education of girls and now has a pastoral and ecumenical centre. One of its members, Sister Lavinia Byrne, was appointed to the post of co-ordinator for women at the newly formed Council of Churches for Britain and Ireland in 1990, a worthy successor to Mary in promoting the acceptance of the worth of women and their work in the churches.

Mary was not the only woman having difficulties with the Roman Catholic authorities. **Anne de Xainctonge** was born in Dijon 1567 and when she was a young woman she tried to set up an uncloistered order to help the educational needs of women. Despite strong opposition, and with the help of the Jesuits and Claudine de Boisset, she managed to found a convent in Dôle (then in Spain) in 1606. The order was that of St Ursula of the Blessed Virgin Mary and it spread widely through France and Switzerland. Anne died in her convent in Dôle in 1621 and all of the documents relating to her order were destroyed during the French Revolution.

Another order which was founded at this time was the Order of The Visitation started by **Jeanne Frances** de Chantal. Born in 1572, the daughter of M. Frémyot, then president of the Burgundian Parliament, Jeanne married Baron Christophe de Chantal at the age of twenty, had several children and was widowed eight years later. Four years later, Jeanne met Francis de Sales who became her spiritual director and their friendship grew, encouraged by a long correspondence. She devoted her time to caring for her children and the poor until, in 1610, Francis persuaded Jeanne to found her order. The order was primarily for the old and the sick who would have been unfit for other stricter orders. Despite initial opposition, the order grew and by 1636 there were sixty-five convents, which had increased to eighty by the end of her life.

She felt greatly the loss of her mentor, Francis de Sales, when he died in 1622 and her son who was killed five years later. Jeanne lived on until 1641 and not only was her life deeply religious but she was also an excellent administrator and had great strength of character. Vincent de Paul who knew her well, spoke of her as 'one of the holiest people I have ever met on this earth'. This holiness comes out in some of her writings. 'When you have committed some fault, go to God humbly, saying to him, "I have sinned, my God, and I am sorry." Then, with loving confidence, add "Father, pour the oil of your bountiful mercy on my wounds, for you are my only hope; heal me." . . . Sometimes put yourself very simply before God, certain of his presence everywhere, and without any effort, whisper very softly to his sacred heart whatever your own heart prompts you to say.'[14]

While talking to her sisters one day, Jeanne questioned them about why most Christians do not become martyrs. She then went on to describe what she calls the martyrdom of love which can be a thousand times more demanding than a bodily martyrdom. She told the nuns that it was to this martyrdom that the Daughters of the Visitation were called. In it, the 'Divine Love causes his sword to pass into the most secret and intimate parts of our souls and separates us from ourselves . . .' To one (herself) to whom this had happened, it 'mattered far more . . . than if tyrants had separated her body from her soul with the cutting stroke of their swords.'[15]

A Light to the Russians

Whilst martyrdom or community life was the way of life for some women, **Juliania Ossorgina** remained obedient to her family's desire that she should marry. Her husband was a wealthy and important official and they had thirteen children. Busy and efficient with her household duties, Juliania spent much time in prayer each night. Gentle with others, she was severe with herself, and during the great Russian famine of 1601–3 she gave away all her food and used herbs and roots to keep the people healthy.

Though illiterate, she had a deep knowledge and love of God, and served him through those she met by sacrifice and her overflowing charity. 'This profound devotion to the Saviour made her a shining light in the dark years of struggle and confusion in which she lived and died. Christians like Juliania

Ossorgina were the salt of Russia. The country could face any trial or danger as long as it could rely upon their labours and prayers.'[16] She was canonised soon after her death early in 1604.

The Church spreads its wings in the Americas

Concern for the social and educational needs of women was felt not only by Christian women in Europe. In 1492 Columbus had discovered America and five years later Vasco da Gama sailed to India. Christianity was beginning to spread to the New World and eventually right round the world. In South America the Dominicans and Franciscans were busy converting the peoples and encouraging settlers. In the East Christianity was growing through the influence of the Jesuits.

By 1586, there were many Spanish settlers in Peru. A young couple living in Lima had a baby daughter that year, Isabel de Flores y de Oliva, better known as **Rose**. Her parents were poor and as Rose grew up she helped the family by doing needlework and growing flowers. She had no desire to marry, but became a Dominican tertiary at the age of twenty, living in the garden of her home in a hut.

The penances she imposed on herself and her long periods in prayer brought criticism and eventually an ecclestiacal enquiry was set up to look at her mystical experiences. She was as patient with those who came to ask questions as she always was and continued to share in the sufferings of others by caring for the sick and poor Indians and slaves. Rose began the whole idea of social service in Peru, but died while she was still young in 1617. By 1671 she had become the first person to be canonized in the Americas and soon Rose became accepted in the Roman Catholic Church as the patron saint of the New World.

While Rose was the daughter of Spanish settlers, there was one young native born American who lived at that time and whose life both before and after her conversion was also one of caring.

Pocahontas was born in 1595 in Virginia as it was known to the settlers from Britain. In 1584 Raleigh had attempted to colonise this part of the New World, but the settlers had disappeared, probably having been killed by the native inhabitants.

In 1606, with King James on the throne of Britain, a second attempt was made to colonise America and these new settlers met with Pocahontas' father, a Red Indian Emperor. The Indians were not pleased to see the newcomers as there had been a prophecy that a nation would arise to take over their land, a nation which would in time subject and conquer them.

The settlers tried to make peace with the Indian people but they were very suspicious and were reluctant to trade. One man who attempted to act as envoy was captured and about to be put to death when the Emperor's most dearly loved daughter, the princess Pocahontas, took his head in her arms and saved him from execution. This action meant that for a while there was peace between her people and the settlers and the Emperor became content that the settlers should remain trading with the Indians.

Illness began to affect the settlers and when they were unable to provide enough food for themselves, Pocahontas brought provisions to them. Despite this there was still a certain amount of fear on the part of the Indians and the peace between the two peoples was fragile. This eventually erupted in a plan by the Indians to surprise the British. Pocahontas warned the settlers about this and told them to leave quickly. Instead of leaving the British crushed the Indians, who immediately sought peace again.

This uncertain situation continued until the Emperor decided it was time that these newcomers should return home or at least confine themselves to the nearby town. Instead the British planned to capture the princess to exchange her for some prisoners the Indians had taken. Her cousin betrayed her into the hands of the British, and she was then asked to bring about peace before she would be allowed to return to her father. Pocahontas was taken to Jamestown nearby where she was left in the care of a priest and there she learnt about Christianity. She was very keen to learn and quick to pick up the new religion. She soon renounced idolatry and was baptized. One of the men who lived there, John Rolfe, wanted to marry her and her father agreed. So Pocahontas did bring about a peace between the settlers and the British.

After their marriage, Pocohontas lived in Jamestown and had a son, Thomas. A great blessing came upon Virginia at that time, which was known as the Peace of Pocahontas.

In 1616, the family sailed to Britain, a cold, wet voyage to Plymouth first and then on to London. Despite her husband being a commoner, Pocahontas was received by the Queen and treated as the daughter of a prince. She was taken to plays and balls and generally received well by the ladies of the court. Later that year the young family moved away from Ludgate to Brentford because the air in London was making Pocahontas ill. She found it difficult to accept the misery, depravity and poverty which existed in London and could not understand the strange king who, unlike her own father who caressed and encouraged his people, actually appeared to dislike his people and hold them in contempt. The following March, it was decided that they should return to Virginia, but the young princess died while waiting to sail at Gravesend. Her son was also too ill to return so her husband returned without them much to the grief of the Indians.

Five years later the Indians rose up against the British, killing 347 men, women and children in one settlement and in response the British military destroyed them, sparing only the young to work for them and for conversion to the Christian faith. Thus the prophecy made to the Indian people was fulfilled.

Pocohontas' story is not only interesting as the story of one conversion among the Indians but it also questions the witness of Christianity when a pagan princess can show more caring and love than many of the so-called Christians around her.

Japanese martyrs

While the conversion of the Americas was not without its difficulties, in Japan the Christians were beginning to experience a persecution to rival that of the early centuries in Rome. After the Franciscan and Jesuit missionaries had brought Christianity to Japan, their success infuriated the 'Shogun' Hideyoshi who began to persecute the Christians, both missionaries and native. In 1614, Christian worship was banned in Japan. In October, 1619, following the desire to exterminate the Christians by the brutal Tokugawa, Richard Cocks witnessed fifty-five people of both sexes being burnt alive, including babes in their mothers arms with their mothers crying out to Jesus to receive their souls.

One such incident is described by Boxer as a spectacle with tens of thousands of witnesses. 'When the faggots were kindled, the martyrs said "Sayonara" (farewell) to the onlookers who then began to intone the Magnificat followed by the psalms *Laudate pueri Dominum* and *Laudate Dominum omnes gentes*, while the Japanese judges sat on one side.' Boxer also describes some of the other horrific ways in which the martyrs died. 'The victim was tightly bound around the body as high as the breast (one hand being left free to signal should they decide to recant) and then hung downwards from a gallows into a pit which usually contained excreta and other filth, the top of the pit being level with his knees. In order to give the blood some vent, the forehead was lightly slashed with a knife. Some of the stronger martyrs lived for more than a week in this position, but the majority did not survive more than a day or two ... One young woman endured this for fourteen days before she expired.'[17] That she could have saved her life if only she would deny her Lord shows the strength of her faith.

Among those who were martyred were **Beatrice** da Costa and her daughter **Maria**. The magistrate tried to make them and the five priests tried with them apostasize and ridicule the holy faith by threatening to immerse them in boiling water. They were bound hand and foot and taken to a hut in the mountain at Unzen where there was a lake of boiling water. From there the prisoners were taken one by one to the edge of the lake and urged to abandon the teachings of Christ. When they refused, the guards tore the clothing off the prisoners and ladled the boiling water over their naked bodies. The young Maria fell to the ground in her agony, which made the guards think that she had given way, but when they took her away, she pleaded to be allowed to join the others again.

The magistrate did not want to kill the prisoners yet, but to let them suffer first, and Beatrice and the priests had to undergo this torture of the boiling water six times. In addition, Beatrice was given the extra punishment of being made to stand for hours on a small rock, exposed to the insults of the crowd. Eventually the magistrate saw that he was not winning and brought the prisoners back to Nagasaki, where Beatrice was placed in a house of ill fame. Some time later the women and priests were martyred, probably in 1629.

The horrors of the Japanese persecutions would be difficult

to surpass. The women such as Beatrice and Maria only had
to give way and deny their faith in God, but their trust in his
love was sufficient for them. These women continued the
witness of Christ by martyrdom which has been the role of
many Christian women and men throughout the centuries.

The Civil War

While these terrible persecutions were continuing in Japan for
a short time life was quieter in the Church in Britain following
on from the difficult period of the Reformation. Towards the
beginning of this period, a wealthy couple from Somerset
decided to endow a college at Oxford.

After the death of her husband in 1609, **Dorothy Wadham**
continued with their scheme to found a college at Oxford in
the style of the Somerset architecture which they loved. Many
of the first scholars came from the West Country, especially
during the first century of its existence, because of the connection of the Wadham family with Somerset. Dorothy died nine
years after her husband, having ensured that the foundation
was by then fully established.

Unfortunately Britain in the seventeenth century was to go
through a violent phase with the Civil War between the more
Catholic 'Cavaliers' and the Protestant 'Roundheads'. Families became split over religion and loyalty and many people
were to die as a result. Later on that century, perhaps as a
result of the Civil War, many trusts were set up to help poor
people in the parishes.

Elizabeth Newcomen was typical of some of the wealthier
ladies of her age and when she died in 1664 she left money in
trust for the poor, to provide twenty aged women with clothing
and to educate poor children. For many this was the only
public way they felt able to demonstrate their Christian faith.

During the Civil War there were many noblewomen whose
faith was greatly tested on both sides. Even within families
there were divided loyalties and **Mary Rich**, Countess of
Warwick who was born in 1625 was one such woman. Though
a Puritan, Mary was also close to the royal family and there
must have been times when her deep faith alone sustained her
amidst the terrors of those days. She spent much time in
meditating and writing about her thoughts in a book. Her

love for nature was reflected in these meditations so that many have titles such as 'Upon a flower that opened itself towards the sun', or 'Upon seeing a hog lie under an acorn tree and eat the acorns, but never look up from the ground to the tree from which they fell'. Within her meditations she often experienced a mystical closeness to Jesus receiving either great joy or great suffering as she considered his passion and death.

Her husband was a man of violent temper, who frequently swore and blasphemed, but despite the pain this caused her, she nursed him in his sickness and he gradually became more gentle. She died when she was fifty-three.

Other women like **Lettice Mary Tredway** who was born in 1595 in Northamptonshire moved abroad. She joined the Canonesses Regular of the Lateran at Beaulieu when she was twenty-one. In 1634, she founded a convent for English canonesses in Paris and became its first abbess. She remained abbess there until two years before she died in 1677. She also helped found a seminary to train priests for the English mission.

The mission fields of North America

Missionary work had been expanding far beyond Europe and for some like **Marie** of the Incarnation the call to go to new mission fields was strong. Born in 1599, Marie Guyart entered the Ursuline convent in Tours after the death of her husband, realizing that her calling was to take the Gospel to the Indians of North America. She eventually arrived in Quebec on 1 September, 1639 after three months of difficult travel by boat. Many times on the journey they thought they would be shipwrecked by the storms but once Marie had safely arrived she set to work to bring salvation to the souls of the Indians.

Despite the murder of other missionaries by those very people they had come to convert, Marie continued with her work. This martyrdom of other missionaries led Marie to meditate on the significance of such a death. 'The last, physical death takes place after an essentially spiritual and personal development: it comes as the crown of the life of the religious and to fulfil his desire for total communion with the passion of Christ. Thus violent death is no longer the most important feature of Christian martyrdom. It is a gift which God alone can decide to grant.'[18]

Marie of the Incarnation was not only a witness to the Jesuit missionaries, but she had 'an extraordinary personality. She was a woman of action who was also a thinker, a pragmatist and a mystic'.[19]

In a letter to her son, written in 1647, she tells of the blessings which God pours on the new Church as well as the afflictions which he allows to happen to it including the many deaths of Christians, especially Father Jogues, SJ. In describing the way Fr Jogues met his death, she concludes 'How sweet it is to die for Jesus Christ! That is why his servants desire to suffer with so much ardour. Just as the saints are always ready to do good to their enemies, so we do not doubt that he, being in heaven, asked from God the salvation of the one who struck the death blow. For when this barbarian was taken some time later by the French, he was converted to the faith, and having received holy baptism, he was put to death with the feelings of a true Christian.'[20]

Marie became known as the Teresa of the New World and before she died in 1672 she was able to see great changes in the relationships between the native born inhabitants and the settlers. Throughout all the dangers of life in the New World, she felt the presence of God guiding her. 'The closer one lives to God, she said, the more clearly one sees one's way in temporal things.'[21]

As the known world began to grow, so missionary work became all important. **Marguerite Bourgeoys** was born in Troyes, France twenty-one years after Marie of the Incarnation and three years after Pocohontas had died. When she was twenty Marguerite tried to enter a convent but was refused. In 1652, she went to Montreal as a teacher, housekeeper and helper in the hospital. When a school was built six years later, Marguerite returned to France to encourage other women to come out to Montreal. Two years after that she made another trip home and gained the support of the king, Louis XIV for her work.

Returning to Canada, she founded a community, the Congregation of Notre Dame of Montreal, which was officially approved in 1676. However the church authorities remained reluctant and so the sisters were unable to make their first vows for another twenty-two years, only two years before Marguerite died. During her lifetime, Marguerite opened many schools, including a boarding school in 1673 and a school for the Iroquois three years later.

Ecumenism in Europe

Living at the same time in Hungary was another women of great faith. Hungary at that period in its history was a divided country, suffering under the rule of two foreign powers, the Hapsburgs and the Turks, and fighting for her liberty and independence. People were seeking freedom in their worship, and there was religious conflict.

Born in 1600, **Zsuzsanna Lórántffy** lived in an age of change and civil strife, when life was hard and far from peaceful and materialism and power struggles were rife. Zsuzsanna's own life was not easy for her parents died while she was still a child, but when she was only sixteen she fell in love and married György Rákóczi. They were very happy together, with Zsuzsanna caring not only for the household, but also helping her husband in his work, advising him about wider matters while they continued to live at the dearly loved home which she had inherited from her father at Sárospatak. When her husband was elected Prince of Transylvania in 1630, they shared their life between Gyulafehérvár, the centre of his Principality and Sárospatak.

After the death of her husband, she returned home to devote her life to the people. The castle buildings, the beautiful garden, filled with valuable plants and flowers, the hospital, where the old and sick were cared for were all signs of her untiring humanity.

The most important part of her life, however, was the secondary school in Sárospatak. More and more pupils, both boys and girls, came to study here, mainly from poor families, and new buildings were needed. Talented students were sent abroad for higher education so that they could return to teach in the school. Zsuzsanna even invited the famous teacher, Amos-Comenius, to teach at the school. Sárospatak became widely known as the 'Athens of the River Bodrog', but it remained a school for the poorer children.

Zsuzsanna's strength came from her deep faith. Her Bible was always open on her desk. She not only read it night and morning but whenever her husband needed to make decisions she sought God's will through studying her Bible. God's word was the light of her feet, which is why she offered everything in his service; money, time and effort. Her patience and tolerance were an example to others when all around people were fighting for their religious beliefs. She could not agree with either the more impatient fanatics or the strict orthodox wing of Calvinism. She gave a helping hand to the Greek Orthodox Rumanians in their cultural problems, and in the 'peace-making of Linz' her husband was the first to assert the right of the poor to practise whatever faith they chose.

A letter was discovered in which a friar from Rome expressed his gratitude for her donation, and when her Roman Catholic brother-in-law visited her, she arranged for a Roman Catholic priest to be available. She could well be said to be among the forerunners of ecumenism. Towards the end of her life, her much loved son died and Zsuzsanna had difficulties at the school amongst the teachers and pupils. In 1660 she wrote, 'When I lost my loving husband and son, I did not cry as much as I do now. You see, my God, that, like a mother with her children, I tried to bring up these pupils to serve God and their country. But what gratitude do I receive for taking care of them?' She died only a few days later.

In 1990, the churches in Hungary received their schools back from the State after nearly forty years, including its famous school at Sárospatak which Zsuzsanna and her husband founded. At that time, the women of the churches were again reminded of Zsuzsanna's devotion to God through her example of service to the poor, her strong faith, and her whole life offered in God's service.

Women of France

Born in Brittany, the same year as Marguerite Bourgeoys, **Catherine** de Francheville came from a devout Catholic family and lived at home until she was thirty-five years old. After the death of her fiancé, she became deeply involved in a life of prayer and visiting the poor.

In 1661, she felt the call of God in the words of a sermon and knew that she must give her life totally to God. Moving into a room close to the Cathedral in Vannes, where she had been living, she would spend the mornings in prayer and meditation and the rest of her time in simple and humble service to the poor. She was generous with the fortune she had been left, some of which was used to help in the construction of a Jesuit retreat house for men. She began to receive women into her own house for eight-day retreats following the Spiritual Exercises of St Ignatius, and these attracted women from all social classes.

However the Church authorities began to be suspicious of these gatherings and forbade retreats in private homes. The Ursulines helped to take on these retreats until the Jesuits were forbidden to lead them. Eventually, after much opposition, Catherine was allowed to arrange retreats for women again. A retreat house was built and the importance and value of this work was recognized as the number of retreats increased. Later a community was formed, 'The Community of the Daughters of the Blessed Virgin', which established other houses mainly in Brittany.

Catherine died in 1689, but her community flourished. However, during the French Revolution, the retreat houses were closed but gradually members got together to open new houses to develop the educational and spiritual values of individuals. The community became known as 'The Sisters of La Retraite' and still flourishes today.

Another French woman who received opposition to the work she felt called to do was **Margaret Mary Alacoque**. Margaret was born in 1647 at L'Hautecourt, France, the daughter of a lawyer who died when she was eight. She went to a Poor Clares school at Charolles, became ill with rheumatism which kept her in bed for five years and then entered the convent at Paray-le-Monial in 1671. There she became mistress of novices and assistant superior, but between 1673 and 1675 she experienced four visions which concerned devotion to the sacred heart of Jesus, symbolizing his love for all people, and she felt that God was directing her to encourage this devotion.

Although many opposed her, both within and without the community, eventually the Jesuit confessor to the convent gave her his support, and this overcame the opposition. Margaret died when she was only forty-three. Born a year later than Margaret, **Jeanne** Marie Bouvier de la Mothe had also hoped to become a nun, but when she was sixteen, her mother made her marry Jacques **Guyon** who was an invalid. Her husband, who was sixteen years older than Jeanne, died after they had been married only seven years and Jeanne became influenced by a rather eccentric priest with whom she spent several years travelling around France, preaching and teaching. Eventually they were both arrested on the grounds of heresy and immorality, but Jeanne was released through the influence of Madame de Maintenon.

Her teaching still caused controversy, particularly between the theologians, Fénelon and Bossuet. Although she wanted to defend herself, she again finished up in prison, until eventually she agreed to defer to the Church authorities. Her books, many of which were of a mystical nature, were very popular and brought contemplative prayer to the ordinary person.

'There are two kinds of people that keep silence; the one because they have nothing to say, the other because they have too much: it is so with the soul in this state; the silence is occasioned by the superabundance of matter, too great for utterance. The infant hanging at the mother's breast is a lively illustration of our subject: it begins to draw the milk by moving its little lips; but when the milk flows abundantly, it is content to swallow, and suspends its suction: by doing otherwise it would only hurt itself, spill the milk, and be obliged to quit the breast.

'We must act in like manner in the beginning of prayer, by exerting the lips of the affections; but as soon as the milk of divine grace flows freely, we have nothing to do but, in repose and stillness, sweetly to imbibe it; and when it ceases to flow, we must again stir up the affections as the infant moves its lips . . .

'But what becomes of this child, who gently and without motion drinks in the milk? It drops gently asleep on its mother's breast. So the soul that is tranquil and peaceful in prayer, sinks frequently into a mystic slumber, wherein all its powers are at rest . . .

'The interior is not a stronghold to be taken by storm and violence but a kingdom of peace, which is to be gained only by love.'[22]

Life at Court

In Britain, life was beginning to stabilise after the Civil War, but a young girl, **Margaret Blagge**, although born towards

the end of the war, had been sent to the court in France to
escape the troubles. She returned to join the court in England,
where although she took her part in what was required of her,
the attractive young Margaret was able to keep herself pure
and free from all the scandalous behaviour of many in court
circles, acting as witness to her faith despite the ridicule this
caused. She was courted by Sidney Godolphin for nine years,
and married for only three years before she died at the age of
twenty-five, just after her son had been born.

One who contributed much to bring about the stability of
her country was the Queen, **Mary II**, who became the wife of
William of Orange with whom she ruled Britain.

Mary was born in 1662, the daughter of King James II and
her life also followed the stormy period of the Reformation
and the Civil War. While she was still young, Mary would
have seen Margaret about the court and quite possibly was
attracted by her devotion and piety. Mary's father was Roman
Catholic but her husband, William of Orange was a strict
Calvinist, who disliked the candles and flowers in his wife's
private chapel. She was herself determined to be both Protestant and Catholic and it is owing to her that Anglicanism
remains as the national religion of England. In fact as the
Church of England is the mother of Anglicanism, it can be
said that the whole of the Anglican Communion owes its very
being to Mary.

Mary's understanding of her faith was not just a shallow
understanding, for she was known to study much of the
theological thinking of her time, including Hooker's *Ecclesiastical Polity*. Her obedience to her husband was a priority in her
life, but when it came to her faith an exception was made as
his Calvinism clashed with her deeply held views on the
Anglican Church. She had been prepared to debate as much
with her father about his Roman Catholic viewpoint as with
her husband about his Calvinist views. Regarding the reading
of the Scriptures, she argued with her father that Jesus himself
commanded the Jews to search the Scriptures and St Paul
ordered his epistles to be read to all. 'Even under Mosaic
Law,' she continued, 'it was never ordained that only the
scribes and doctors and lawyers should be present, but even
the women and children.' Mary finds 'a great difference
between the Anglican Church separating from the Roman

Communion and our Nonconformists abandoning us.'[23] She criticised the Romans for refusing to allow the cup to the laity, referring to the words, 'Drink ye *all* of this'. Because she saw their error on this point, she could not agree that the Church of Rome could call itself infallible.

Mary desired to abolish the idea of the King and Queen receiving Communion alone, as had been introduced, and she was pleased that many of the nobility also received at her first Christmas Communion in England when she returned there with her new husband from Holland. Unhappy living in Holland, when Mary returned to live in Britain in 1688 as joint ruler with her husband she was able to work for that peace within the Church which was so close to her heart. She died of smallpox when she was only thirty-two, and Greenwich hospital was built in her honour.

During her lifetime, Mary encouraged the formation of various societies for religious study and prayer, including the Society for the Propogation of Christian Knowledge and the Society for the Propogation of the Gospel in Foreign Parts and her influence can be seen to continue to this day in many ways.

Mary's sister, **Anne**, was three years younger than Mary and became Queen in 1702. She was also very devout and determined that the true faith of Britain should be in a national church which was both Catholic and Protestant. As Supreme Head of that church she appointed bishops and also surrendered the tithes extracted from the clergy which had been given originally to the Pope and then to the monarch. This money became known as Queen Anne's Bounty and was used to augment those livings which needed it most.

The growth of Nonconformity

The last woman to be mentioned in this chapter leads us well into the next, for her influence over her sons was to open up the new dissenting movement within Britain. Though Mary had done her best to stabilise the Church in Britain, this had brought about a complacency which was much to the detriment of the Church itself.

Susannah Wesley was born in London, only four years after Anne, the last but one of the twenty-six children of

Samuel Annesley, a nonconformist minister deposed of his living in 1662 for refusing to accept the revised Book of Common Prayer and the Act of Uniformity.

Susannah was an intelligent child who rejected nonconformity in favour of Anglicanism when she was thirteen, and married the Revd Samuel Wesley when she was twenty. A year later Samuel was given the living of South Ormsby but being a family that began to increase rapidly, the Wesleys were very poor. Six years later, they moved to Epworth, where the stipend was much better, but Susannah's husband was still constantly in difficulties, and on occasion was sent to prison for debt.

Susannah managed to keep going despite the difficulties, although at times she suffered greatly both in health and from the poverty, for Samuel was not the easiest of husbands, having stormy relationships with both his wife and his parishioners. Samuel was an ardent supporter of the King, William of Orange but Susannah, who was opposed to William, refused to say 'Amen' at the end of a prayer for him. Samuel felt that he could no longer share a bed with her and left, not to be seen again by his family or parishioners for nearly a year.

Despite this break, Susannah had nineteen children of whom only ten survived and these she educated herself from the age of five. She brought the children up strictly according to her own 'method' and spent half an hour each week with each one individually, mainly talking to them on spiritual matters. They learned to say the Lord's Prayer as soon as they could speak, and learned passages of scripture as soon as they were able.

At one time when her husband was away she felt the Curate was not being sufficiently inspiring in his sermons and so she gathered groups of villagers in her kitchen for Bible study. The group grew until there were more than two hundred meeting in the church hall each night. Her husband wrote to her forbidding this partly on the grounds of her sex, but she continued knowing that in this matter, as in all others, her first duty was to God. Her reply to his objection about a woman leading was that, in his absence, she looked upon every soul he left under her care as a talent committed to her under a trust by the great Lord of all the families of heaven and earth. However she was concerned about leading the prayers because she was a woman, and she agreed only when the people insisted that she should.

Susannah was not strong, but she had an indominatible spirit and a deep spirituality. She wrote often to her sons at university about spiritual matters such as the Real Presence of Christ and justification by faith. Her opinion of how the clergy should direct their lives was salutary. 'Consider well what separation from the world, what purity, what devotion, what exemplary virtue are required in those who are to guide others to glory!' She rejoiced when the practice of weekly Communion began to be revived, 'for there is nothing more proper or effectual for the strengthening and refreshing the mind than the frequent partaking of that blessed ordinance'.[24]

There is no doubt that she had a profound influence on her children, particularly John and Charles. She was concerned about their activities, but when she realized how great was their contribution to the work of God, she supported them fully. It was her use of a 'method' in bringing them up which inspired the name for the group her sons started. She was herself caught up in the new way of thinking, and became converted to it. Susannah greatly encouraged John to develop the work of Lay Preachers, no doubt after her own experience in that work. To her it was important that people recognized 'heaven as a state as well as a place – a state of holiness begun in this life but not perfected till we enter on life eternal. God is Being itself, the I AM, and therefore must necessarily be the Supreme Good! Were He always present to our mind, as we are present to Him, there would be no pain nor sense of misery.'[25] Susannah, who died in 1742, could well be called the 'Mother of Methodism'.

This chapter is one which covers a period of tremendous change within the churches' life in Europe. Not only was the Reformation questioning the old order of the Catholic Church based on Rome, but new boundaries were opening up with wider fields of mission. A great number of those who were trying to bring about change in every branch of the Church were women but there was much opposition to them and not only from the men. However in the Protestant churches the way was beginning to open for women to take a fuller share in the work of the Church and even within the Roman Catholic Church women felt called to found new communities, often with stricter rules or with the intent of helping to educate or care for those women who were considered unworthy to receive it.

The social Gospel was also beginning to be preached again. The women represented here did not shrink from doing what they thought God had called them to do, whether it meant travelling to the distant New World or just fighting the hierarchy of the Church for recognition of a new order, being burned at the stake, as with Joan of Arc, or suffering even worse torture still, as with the Japanese martyrs.

It was unfortunate that with the breaking away from some of the traditions of the Church of Rome, the Protestant Churches did not break with the patriarchal system which they inherited until much later, indeed some have not yet made that break. The thought was there, for in some of the nonconformist churches, particularly within the Quaker movement, women were being allowed to lead worship and preach. A little later it was a Quaker, George Fox, who asked 'May not the Spirit of Christ speak in the female as well as in the male?' For the time being however, the Spirit did speak but was often ignored.

CHAPTER SEVEN

Fruits of the Spirit

'You did not choose me, but I chose you to go and bear fruit – fruit that will last.' (John 15.16)

Beloved let us love one another; for love is of God, and everyone who loves is born of God and knows God. In this the love of God was shown, that God sent his only Son into the world, so that we might live through him. If we love one another, God abides in us and his love is perfected in us. (1 John 4.7,9,12)

★ ★

THE NEXT period in this chronicle of Christian women is a time when women were beginning to make their voices heard in a way which had not happened before to such an extent. With education being more freely available to women as well as men, opportunities were now arising for women to use their skills in ways that could not be gainsaid by men any more. After the Reformation and the Civil War, there was an evangelical revival which gave women an opportunity for preaching at open-air or more informal meetings.

During the eighteenth and nineteenth centuries, women also became involved in missionary and social work following the commandment of Jesus not only to love but to take the love of God into the world. The deep spirituality of many women also blossomed in such creative ways as writing and music, and this was the age of many great novels and beautiful hymns. While many women used the gifts they had in this way although remaining confined to their homes because of their domestic situation, illness or for other reasons, others found themselves able to go out and spread the Word in foreign parts or fight against social ills. Even so there still remained that devoted core of women who found that their service to God would be as a member of a religious community or in following the way of the cross in martyrdom.

Marthas and Marys

One woman who combined some of all these gifts in her life was **Kata Bethlen** who was born at the very beginning of the eighteenth century. Kata, (Katie in English), was a highly respected Countess from Transylvania, who, during the eighteenth century, when writing autobiographies was in fashion, joined the many historians, scientists and even rulers to write about her own life. Coming from a strong Protestant background, her deep faith from an early age gave her a moral strength and honest outlook.

Life had never been easy for Kata. Her father died when she was eight and her mother ten years later. When she was only nineteen, Kata's first husband died and her second, Joseph Teloki, when she was just thirty-five. From the first marriage there were two children, but unfortunately they were taken away by relatives of her first husband in order that they should not grow up as 'heretics' and were subsequently brought up as Roman Catholics. Three children from her second marriage all died within one year of each other followed shortly by their father. She spent the next twenty-seven years living on her own, calling herself 'an orphan', and is remembered by the name Arva Kata Bethlen, (the Orphan Katie Bethlen). During this time she became quite ill and her estates were damaged by various natural disasters.

Now on her own, Kata was surrounded by many kinsfolk full of hatred for her and envious of her great wealth, but she did not feel abandoned, knowing the presence of God and her Saviour within her. The more trials she had to undergo, the greater and stronger her faith became. For her, saying prayers was not merely an exercise, but a necessity of life – a real conversation with God. Because of this it is no wonder that Church historians describe her as an outstanding writer of prayers. Many of her prayers can be found in her autobiography and later she published them in a separate book. All the evils of the world and all her frustrations and troubles only served to put her in closer touch with God. New troubles made her more modest and humble but constantly filled with trust, and disappointments would only increase her sense of forgiveness.

Kata was a very good woman, whose life was spent in doing

good to people. This, at least, she felt no-one could take away from her. She used her money in giving to the clergy, schools and churches, and helping many writers, scientists and poor people. She also gave money for the publishing of books. She supported science because she was interested in it and had a very rich library which would have been the envy of many a scientist both in her own country and abroad. Her knowledge of medicine was renowned throughout the world.

Kata was also an excellent housewife, famous for her cooking and her embroidery. Even today there are many examples of her embroidery in existence which, together with many gold and silver vessels, had originally been offered as gifts. Besides this she was involved in gardening, weaving, farming, growing grapes, candle-making, planting and tending fruit trees, etc. She set an example to all in her domestic and in her spiritual life, and her faith in Christ gave her the strength to continue through it all until her death in 1759.

There are many other suffering hearts who could well join with Kata Bethlen in her prayer, 'Oh, blessed mercy! You have given me the power to endure my innumerable crucifixions. Oh, mighty Lord, I'm weak and powerless, give me strength, please. Let your mercy be with me and strengthen me day by day. Don't abandon me, and forgive my frailty. Consider the redemption obtained by your Holy Son and let me spend my days in the praise of your Name, for your Glory and for the benefit of the Mother Church.'[1]

Kata Bethlen was one who possessed the virtues of both Martha and Mary, but **Dorothea Christiana Erxleben** was most definitely a Martha who spent her life fighting against wrongs.

Dorothea was born in 1715, the daughter of a doctor with modern views who taught his children Latin and medicine. When she was twenty-five after many years of study, Dorothea petitioned the Prussian king to confer a medical degree on her at Halle. Never before had a woman graduated in medicine there, but her request was granted and Dorothea became the first woman to obtain her medical degree.

Two years later, she published a paper entitled *Basic investigations of the causes which debar the female sex from university study* and later that same year Dorothea married. She continued her studies, devoting herself to medicine, not for personal gain or

fame, but for humanitarian reasons. She wrote a treatise
called *The far too rapid and easy, but therefore uncertain healing of
illnesses*. After her marriage she brought up her four children
and also applied for a medical doctorate. She became the first
woman to sit the examination, and on 12 June 1754 she
obtained it, again at Halle, thus proving to the sceptics
around her that women are capable of following academic
pursuits. It was then that she began her campaign for the
rights of women.

Dorothea published a book about the subject of women
studying, which deals with prejudices and self-imposed obstacles preventing the female sex from studying. The main objec-
tions suggested against women's abilities in studying were first
'that the path of knowledge is not appropriate for the female
sex because women are not capable of doing well at it'. In her
book, Dorothea denied women were lacking in the intellect
necessary for study. 'Though few women study,' she writes
'this does not mean that they are intellectually inferior. Both
men and women are people whose duty it is to use their
spiritual and intellectual abilities.'

The second objection is 'that the external circumstances of
women are such as to prevent study'. She deplored the fact
that many women, through defective schooling, do not have
the qualifications for university study and were refused permission to attend public lectures. To say that women should be
brought up solely to house-keep, brought the response that no
parent would decide a profession for a son as soon as he was
born, but it is established what a girl will do at birth. Despite
this, housekeeping and marriage do not prevent university
study. 'Ignorance, errors, prejudice and doubts will all disap-
pear' she believed, 'as knowledge increases for women as well
as men.' Unfortunately this prophecy was not entirely correct.

Dorothea continues by questioning why women may not be
appointed to public positions, giving examples from philosophy where women were found just as capable provided they
had studied thoroughly and were prepared for positions of
public responsibility.

The innate disadvantages of the female sex were said to be
dread of the effort required to study, and laziness. Dorothea
wrote 'Such habitual ideas have a powerful hold over people,
for example when they state that women should leave aca-

demic study to those who are accustomed to it – namely men.' She suggested following reason rather than tradition, ideals rather than materialism and teaching this to children. She wrote 'It does not help a child to look after its material needs but neglect its mind, to leave it great wealth but prevent it learning. Self-knowledge is the beginning of wisdom and one only reaches this goal through learning.'

Dorothea called on women to overcome arrogance and jealousy and ended her report with the following: 'It is never too late to learn, and if you did not do so in your youth, it is still always better to start in old age than to neglect your education completely!'[2]

Dorothea practised medicine in her home town with much skill and success until she died there from a chest complaint in 1782.

One hundred years later Elizabeth Blackwell was to initiate medical studies in America and Britain. Dorothea's story has crept into this book even though it has no mention of her faith because it was supplied by the women of East Germany in 1990 as an example of a woman of faith.

Nazaria was born in Brasov in 1697, a woman as remarkable for her spirituality as Dorothea was for her academic studies. After her husband and two children died in an accident she became a nun at the Hermitages in Scintieia and Bontesti in Muntenia. Ten years later she moved to Moldavia where she spent the remainder of her extremely long life. During her time in Muntenia and Moldavia, Nazaria studied the stories of other men and women who had shared Paul's vision of living their lives in Christ.

Following the examples of Mother Teodora of Sihla and Mother Mavra of Durau in the ascetic life, Nazaria was advised by the Abbot Paisie to take the great schema, that is to take upon herself an even more ascetic life, to leave the monastic settlement where she presently was and to go to the Durau Skete. Here she was to have as her spiritual adviser and confessor a highly experienced father, Joseph the Hermit.

While at Durau, Mother Olimpiada Herescu, who had founded a convent at Varatic, invited Nazaria to come as Mother to the community there. Nazaria remained in charge until her death, twenty-six years later. During this time the convent flourished and by 1811 there were almost three hundred nuns there from many different backgrounds, daughters of landlords, merchants, peasants, clergy, high officials, etc. She instigated the building of a wooden church in 1785, and later built the present church in brick and stone. She also led the newly founded convent at Agapia which was turned from a monastery for men into a convent for nuns.

Due to her beautiful spiritual life and motherly approach at Varatic, Mother Nazaria was able to establish a firm foundation which has lasted to the present day. Her many gifts, including kindness, humility and wisdom, ensured her being loved by all the nuns who not only obeyed her but also thought of her as 'a true spiritual mother'. Under Nazaria's rule, through her tact and desire to follow the will of God, the Convent at Varatic grew and became prosperous.

Mother Nazaria was an outstanding personality, blessed with a long life. She gave her community an example of what the life of a nun should be like, how their time should be spent in prayer, in work, and in enabling the soul to grow through pious reading, spiritual singing, counselling and living under the guidance of those nuns who had attained a special spiritual experience. She urged the nuns 'Breathe Christ and believe in Him. Live as though you are dying each day and then you will not err.' Having lived her life in the 'fragrance of the virtues' and in prayer, humility and obedience, she was buried in the Church of the Dormition of Our Lady in 1814. Her bones were discovered during repairs to the church in 1973, and were reburied with great joy and thanksgiving by the nuns and Protosyngelos Caliopie Apetri in the church, where a candle still burns constantly as a reminder of such a holy person.

Because of the way in which she lived her life, Mother Nazaria was a person who attracted much interest among her contemporaries. In a *Vitae Patrium* of 1888, Mother Nazaria from the Pion (Durau) Mountain, as she is known, was placed among such saints of the Rumanian people as Teodora from Sihla and Mavra from Pion.

The nuns from her convent today tell how 'her life of holiness has influenced many disciples as well as those who followed her in embracing the angelic life of this holy establishment throughout its years. The Convent of Varatic has in Mother Nazaria a lasting example of the foundation of a life in purity and holiness.'[3]

One woman who was acknowledged as holy by some and denounced as a heretic by others was **Selina**, Countess of Huntingdon. Lady Selina Shirley was born in 1707, the second daughter of the Earl and Countess Ferrars. When she was twenty-one, she married the Earl of Huntingdon and they were a very happy and devout couple until his death in 1746. They mixed a great deal in high society and within the literary circles of the day.

The Earl's sister, Lady Margaret Hastings, was attracted by the preaching of one of the stirring band of preachers who were affecting the Church of England at that time. She in her turn brought her brother and his wife to listen to the preacher. It was then that Selina became ill and while she was ill she had a conversion experience which resulted in her asking God for pardon and mercy. 'With streaming eyes she cast herself on her Saviour: "Lord, I believe; help thou mine unbelief." Immediately the scales fell from her eyes; doubt and distress vanished; joy and peace filled her bosom. With appropriate faith, she exclaimed, "My Lord and my God!" From that moment her disease took a favourable turn; she was restored to health, and what was better to "newness of life." '[4]

About the time that Selina got married, there were several young students at Oxford who were destined for the priesthood and who were more serious about their faith than many of their contemporaries. Constant in prayer, in fasting and self-denial they found the shallow piety of others in the Church difficult to comprehend. Amongst these students were the Wesley brothers and George Whitefield. In 1739, Selina sent for the Wesleys to preach in her chapel, the first of many such occasions. Selina and her husband also tried to persuade their friends to listen, but it was often too much for the nobility of that age, who found it difficult to accept that they could be 'as sinful as the common wretches that crawl upon the earth'.[5]

Selina's own attitude to her faith was much more humble. She writes to Charles Wesley, 'What blessed effects does the love of God produce in the hearts of those who abide in him. How solid is the peace and how divine the joy that springs from an assurance that we are united to the Saviour by a living faith. Blessed be his name. I have an abiding sense of his presence with me, not withstanding the weakness and unworthiness I feel, and an intense desire that he may be glorified in the salvation of souls, especially those who lie nearest my heart. After the poor labours of the day are over, my heart still cries, "God be merciful to me a sinner!" I am deeply sensible that daily, hourly and momentarily I stand in need of the sprinkling of my Saviour's blood. Thanks be to God, the fountain is always open; O what an anchor is this to my soul!'[6]

Selina appointed George Whitefield as her chaplain in 1748 and opened her house for her friends to hear his preaching a year later. In 1760 she opened a chapel of worship in Brighton so that people might hear her friends, the Methodist preachers, the first of many she was to open for their preaching. Five years after that she opened another in Bath as a place of worship in which the 'awakened clergy' could preach. Many of the nobility were attracted to the deep faith and good preaching which they heard there.

Three years later difficulties arose at Oxford when six young men whom she had recommended to study at St Edmund Hall were expelled from the University 'for holding Methodist tenets and taking upon them to read, pray, and expound the Scriptures and singing hymns in private houses'.[7]

The enthusiasm of these preachers caused difficulties for many of the more traditional in the Anglican Church, and when complaint was made to the King by one such, he advised the Church to make bishops of these enthusiasts. 'But we cannot make the Countess of Huntingdon a bishop' protested the complainant, to which the Queen replied 'And more's the pity, for she is certainly worthy to be one.'

Selina's relationship with the Church would not have been improved by her criticism of Mrs Cornwallis, the wife of the then Archbishop of Canterbury, whose expensive social life left much to be desired.

In 1768, Selina founded a college for the training of ministers for the Anglican and other churches at Trefecca, the home of Howell Harris in Breconshire. Howell Harris was himself sick by then, but the college became very successful and is still in use today as a church centre. The number of Selina's own private chapels increased until she had sixty-four scattered about the country. In many of these, frequent communion took place at a time when four celebrations a year was normal. It was the prerogative of the nobility to found their own private chapels but the excessive number which Selina had set up was seen to be a threat to the more moderate members of the Anglican Church and one such chapel in particular, in Spa-fields in Clerkenwell in London, was used as an excuse to bring the matter before the Consistory Court.

Selina lost her case, for church planting to the scale which she was now doing was not within her rights as a peeress and so her chapels, much to her regret, became dissenting chapels with her name attached, the Countess of Huntingdon's Connection. Like her friends the Wesleys, Selina had failed to keep her reforming movement within the Anglican fold.

Selina died in 1792 and was buried in Ashby de la Zouch and her name lives on in the church which she founded.

While Selina was considered odd in Britain because of her reforming zeal, in Russia there lived another woman who was also considered decidedly peculiar. **Xenia** grew up in St Petersburg and when she was twenty-six, her husband died suddenly without having had any Christian preparation for death. This so shocked Xenia, that she determined to offer the most precious thing she had to God, her sanity, as a sacrifice to obtain forgiveness for her husband, Andrew. She therefore prayed that she might appear mad and on the day he was buried, she did indeed appear to those around to have lost her sanity, insisting on wearing her husband's clothes to the funeral.

Her relatives and friends thought that her mind had gone because of the shock of his sudden death but Xenia only responded by comforting them and saying Andrew Fedorovich had not died at all but become incarnate in her for she had died long ago. This only confirmed their belief that her mind had gone especially when she began wandering the streets of St Petersburg asking them not to call her by her own name any more but by that of her husband, Andrew Fedorovich.

Having inherited her husband's possessions, Xenia gave her house to a pious Christian woman, Paraskeva Antonov, and asked her to let the poor stay in it free of charge, saying 'I will give away all my possessions today and my money I will donate to the Church for prayers to be lifted for the repose of the soul of Xenia, a servant of God'. Paraskeva Antonov, concerned about what Xenia was doing, asked for advice from her relatives and doctors. An examination proved that Xenia was in good health and confirmed her right to dispose of her property as she thought fit.

Xenia continued to wander the streets wearing her husband's clothing throughout the winter and summer and was subject to much mockery and offence, but her prayers were unceasing and she made no complaint at her treatment.

At this time a church was being built by the Smolensky cemetery and the workmen noticed that each night someone was laying bricks high upon the new building. After carefully watching they discovered it was Xenia who was working tirelessly on the building. Others noticed that Xenia often said and did things which had a particular meaning so that when she asked a favour from someone it was a sign of a coming misfortune and when she gave someone a gift it foretold great joy. Merchants would find that if Xenia took something from their shops then their trade would suddenly become very successful.

Mothers with small children would often ask Xenia to give them a blessing or just to pat their heads and during her lifetime many would take their sorrows and misfortunes to her. After her death in 1803, many people continued to visit her grave in the Smolensky cemetery and it became a place of pilgrimage. Because of the miracles which happened to those who prayed for her intercession after her death and the veneration in which she was held Xenia was canonized, the holiness of her life being demonstrated by her deep love for her neighbour, her humility, patience, meekness and clarity of vision.

Pastures new in missionary work

While Marie Guyart and Margaret Bourgeoys took their mission to North America in the seventeenth century, by the beginning of the nineteenth century, missionaries were travelling much further afield, although the work was no less dangerous.

Mrs Johnston travelled to Kingston, Jamaica with her husband, a missionary with the Wesleyan Missionary Society, in 1807. This was nearly thirty years before the abolition of slavery and Mrs Johnston was aware that much of her work would be amongst these slaves. Acknowledging the wretchedness and poverty in which many of them lived, she rejoiced that her future work would be among them knowing that in God's sight the soul of one human being is worth as much as that of another. 'I yearn to carry the Glad Tidings to the slaves,' she wrote, 'and may God bless my labours.'

Previous efforts to convert the slaves had been hampered by the owners of the plantations. They felt that the singing of the slaves disturbed others at night and prevented them from working so hard. There were strict rules which forbade teaching and preaching and others which restricted times of services which had to take place before sunset. Despite this Mrs Johnston used to meet secretly with some of the female slaves after dark.

The Johnstons moved to Dominica after a while where their living conditions were much worse but at least they had freedom to preach and teach. However Mrs Johnston was not able to withstand the bad conditions and died of marsh fever only four years after her arrival in the West Indies. In her last letter to her husband she wrote these simple words, a testimony to her faith. 'Follow Christ himself. He is the perfect pattern of His Church and of His ministers. If you follow Him you shall never miss your way. I know He hath loved me; and He will now upon the margin of the eternal world give me the witness of it, for I can shout "Victory" over death and the grave.'[8]

Preaching and teaching

Women were not only involved in preaching the Gospel overseas. Among the itinerant preachers who were well known at that time was **Mary Bosanquet**, a Methodist lay preacher, who lived from 1739 until 1815 and to whom John Wesley wrote encouragingly of her extraordinary call which proved to be the exception to St Paul's rule about women speaking in churches.

The preaching of the Gospel was also important to **Hannah More**, especially for those who otherwise might not have heard it. Hannah was born in 1745, the daughter of a schoolmaster and she learnt to read at the age of three. Her father allowed her to learn Latin, but refused to let her learn mathematics as he believed, like many others, that women were physically incapable of absorbing much learning. However Hannah was the youngest of five happy and intelligent sisters who set up a ladies' school in Bristol where the family had moved when Hannah was ten and where she later began teaching herself. She was engaged three times, but never became married, her third engagement finishing when her bridegroom failed to turn up at the church.

Hannah was greatly loved by many for her story-telling, including the young Tom Macauley, later to become the historian, and Marianne Thornton who wrote how attractive the More household was, 'with its roses and haycocks and strawberries and syllabub and huge brown home-baked loaves, its warm welcome for visiting children, its two cats called "Non-resistance" and "Passive Obedience" whom we fed all day long. And all these cheerful delights interspersed with wonderful stories from the Old Testament of the adventures of the children of Israel, told by Hannah with such eloquence and force that I fancied she must have lived amongst them herself.'[9]

Hannah used to love story-telling and writing but was told that this was not the sort of thing for young ladies to do. She would do well to learn from her betters and make puddings! Even so she must have continued in her writing for she later had a play performed in London.

It was to London that Hannah went when she was twenty-eight and where she met Samuel Johnson, Sir Joshua and Lady Reynolds, David Garrick and later Isaac Newton amongst others. Hannah wrote a ballad which brought her fame and some plays but was also known for her sympathetic and religious sensitivities. Dr Johnson asked her to accompany him to St Clement Dane's to receive his last Communion before his death.

Like Selina, Hannah became disturbed by what she felt was the lukewarm attitude of the respectable people of London society towards their religion. She began to write *Sacred Dramas* which attracted much attention and often presented a moral challenge to those around. Her tract on whether, even in the days of wigs, it was right to employ a hairdresser on a Sunday led to Queen Charlotte cancelling hers on that day. Hannah was following in the footsteps of such people as William

Wilberforce, whom she met when she moved to Sussex, by stirring the conscience of the nation.

It was William himself who said to her one day, after a visit to the caves and cliffs at Cheddar had been spoiled by the frequent importuning of the beggars, 'Miss Hannah, something must be done for Cheddar.' They began a crusade for better conditions and both spiritual and secular education for the rural poor with William Wilberforce providing Hannah and her sister with money with which to start charity schools.

However even organising Sunday Schools was fraught with difficulties. Neither the local farmers, who were disturbed at the thought of their labourers receiving education, nor some of the clergy were happy at what was happening. The situation was likely to take the people out of their control and anyway 'the poor were intended by God to be servants and slaves'. That women should dare to interfere with the teaching of such people in the way they did was intolerable. Teachers were not easily available either and Hannah and her younger sister spent much of their time ensuring that the teachers were properly trained. In 1793 there was held an Annual School feast at Bath at which nearly a thousand children from nine Sunday schools picnicked 'on beef, bread pudding and cyder' according to the *Bath Chronicle* of the day.

Hannah sold many of her tracts cheaply to pedlars and gave away many Bibles, Prayer Books and Testaments each year so that the poorer people would be able to read them but her works continued to be read by people of influence as well. She also started welfare clubs for women to help with times of particular distress or sickness.

Hannah continued to write until she was advanced in years, including a series of easily read moral tales which were very popular, a forerunner of many to come. However the title of her last book was *The Spirit of Prayer*, a contemplative book which was altogether more reflective. Although an Anglican who believed strongly in the Church, she did not value either baptism or confirmation highly enough to express concern in this direction for her young charges, and at that time neither Confirmation nor receiving Communion were as frequent as today. That she was well loved by the young people to whom she sought to bring a little light, both spiritual and material, is demonstrated by the two hundred children who accompanied her coffin through the streets of Bristol when she died in 1833 and the crowds of people who stood by to watch. It is interesting to speculate whether she was influenced in her early days in Bristol by the preachers whom Selina of Huntingdon had arranged to visit there.

Hannah More had not begun the Sunday school movement, for Robert Raikes and **Sarah Trimmer** who were both friends of hers had started others earlier, Robert in Gloucester and Sarah in Brentford. Sarah had also written a large number of books concerned with the teaching and understanding of baptism, confirmation, catechism and one called *A Companion to the Book of Common Prayer*, which Hannah More described as a 'laborious, judicious and valuable performance'. Sarah was able to write in such a way that she could convert many a doubter back to not only a Christian but an Anglican way. Her love for God in the Sacrament is expressed in this extract from a meditation on the Holy Communion. 'Adorable Saviour, how can I sufficiently thank Thee for the comfort, the satisfaction, the delight I have experienced in receiving the Sacrament of Thy Body and Blood? Blessed Lord, keep me thine for evermore. Thou knowest that I love Thee.'

Words and music

While Hannah and Sarah were writing books and tracts and engaged in building up the Sunday school movement, other women were becoming inspired to write hymns. The eighteenth and nineteenth centuries saw an explosion of hymn singing, following on the large number of hymns written by such people as the Wesley brothers and the evangelical revival. For virtually the first time women were welcome to offer their gifts to the Church in this way, and many did, composing some of the most beautiful hymns still sung some two hundred years later.

Henriette Auber who was born in 1773 was among the first of these women hymn writers. Henriette or Harriet was living in Hoddesdon in Hertfordshire when she wrote her best known hymn 'Our Blest Redeemer, ere he breathed'. She had been meditating on the sermon that she had heard that morning and wrote some of the verses that came to mind with a diamond ring on the window pane. This pane of glass disappeared some time after Harriet died in 1862. She also wrote a metrical version of the Psalter.

Not all hymn writers of this period were English speaking even within the British Isles. The evangelical revival had penetrated most parts of the Britain, and Wales was full of religious fervour at this time. No doubt some of it inspired the young **Ann Griffiths**.

Ann was born in 1776 on a hill farm called Dolwar Fach, at Llanfihangel yng Ngwynfa, in Montgomery in the heart of Wales and lived most of her life there. She was a lively child when she was younger, but after her mother died when she was eighteen, she was restricted by having to help run the home.

After hearing Benjamin Jones of Pwlheli preach one day, she joined the Methodist Society at Pont Robert and there met John Hughes the teacher and preacher whom she came to know well and who was her spiritual mentor. In 1804, she married a farmer from Meifod, and died after the birth of their first child in 1805.

During her short life, she composed many hymns and letters in her native language of Welsh, which, because it is little spoken outside her own country, meant that the beauty of her words was not greatly appreciated until her work was rediscovered and translated by A. M. Allchin in recent years.

He considers Ann to be a mystic and theologian of uncommon power; one who sees deeply into the things of God, who speaks of great but silent events in the world within us, declaring what she sees in memorable words. She speaks of the mystery of Christ and how we can know and enter here and now into the depths of God's love, His grace becomes as a consuming fire or a cleansing, healing stream, the furnace and the fountain being so close together.[10]

Like some of the earlier mystics, Ann never wrote much of her work down, but recited it to her companion, Ruth Hughes, who remembered it. After her marriage her husband wrote down as many poems as he could and gave them to Thomas Charles of Bala who arranged for them to be published. The following piece of her work has the title in Welsh and was translated by John James:

RHYFEDD, RHYFEDD, GAN ANGYLION
Awesome, awesome it was for the angels,
Awesome for men of faith, to see
Life's author and unfettered ruler
Who sustains all things that be,
Firmly wrapped within the manger,
Without a head-rest in his stall,
Yet by resplendent hosts of glory
Extolled above as Lord of all.

Another young Welsh woman whose life was to have far reaching consequences also lived about this time. **Mary Jones** was born in 1784, and lived in Llanfihangel y Pennant in North Wales. She longed to own a Bible of her own, so she saved up for five years by washing and mending for others and then walked the twenty-eight miles from Llanfihangel to Bala to buy one from Thomas Charles. Impressed and inspired by her devotion, Thomas returned to London where he started the British and Foreign Bible Society in 1804 to provide Bibles for people like Mary, especially in their own languages.

While Harriet Auber and Ann Griffiths were writing their inspirational hymns in Hertfordshire and Montgomery, in Hampshire and Bath lived a young woman whose descriptions of life as she knew it at that time were to become classical novels. **Jane Austen** was born in 1775 into a clergy family and was one of eight children. She inherited her serenity and her fine intellect from her father and her observation and humour from her mother. Her parents were very devout, and the whole family were fond of reading. Jane began writing at the age of ten and her first book was *Northanger Abbey* which was not initially successful perhaps because it was the first effort of a women writer.

Jane lived with her parents, spending her time when she was not writing helping in the house, teaching children, sewing and making music. She was very fond of her family particularly her sister, Cassandra, and believed that she would bring people to faith more by example than by direct preaching through her books. Throughout her comparatively short life, for she died when she was forty-two, Jane was a humble, lively and believing Christian.

The author of 'Nearer my God to Thee', **Sarah Adams**,

also lived around this time. Born in 1805, she was the same age as Jane when she died. Among Selina, Countess of Huntingdon's closest friends was a young preacher, Henry Venn. His granddaughter, **Charlotte Elliot**, was born in 1789 and herself became the friend of such people as Elizabeth Fry and Edward Irving. She was also much influenced by the Genevan evangelist, Cæsar Malan. She was never very well, even in her childhood, but she had a strong will and a deep faith which enabled her to work hard despite her poor health.

Charlotte is believed to have written her best known hymn 'Just as I am, without one plea' while staying with her brother in Brighton. The whole family were preparing for a bazaar to be held to raise money for a school for the daughters of clergy. The rest of the family had been busily occupied, during which time Charlotte had felt particularly useless, and she lay on the sofa. Armed with the knowledge that God loved her, despite her weakness and her doubts, she wrote what became one of our greatest hymns:

> *Just as I am, without one plea*
> *But that thy blood was shed for me,*
> *And that thou bidd'st me come to thee,*
> *O Lamb of God, I come!*
>
> *Just as I am, poor, wretched, blind*
> *Sight, riches, healing of the mind,*
> *Yea, all I need, in thee to find,*
> *O Lamb of God, I come!*

Charlotte wrote about her continual struggle to keep going in these words: 'My heavenly Father knows and He alone, what it is, day after day, hour after hour, to fight against bodily feelings of almost overpowering weakness and languor and exhaustion, to resolve, as He enables me to do, not to yield to the slothfulness, the depression, the irritability such a body causes me to long to indulge, but to rise every morning determined on taking this for my motto: "If any will come after Me, let them deny themself, take up their cross daily and follow Me." '[11] Charlotte lived until she was eighty-two, despite her weak health.

Improving prisons

Charlotte's friend, **Elizabeth Fry** was nine years her junior. Born into a large Quaker family at Earlham, near Norwich, Elizabeth Gurney was an attractive and lively girl who married Joseph Fry when she was twenty. Her husband's family were of a serious disposition and did not fully approve of their new daughter-in-law.

As a young woman she often visited the poor and decided after she was married to try to improve life for those in prison, founding the 'Association for the Improvement of the Female Prisoners in Newgate' in 1817. Amongst other changes she inaugurated, she arranged that prisoners should be separated by sexes and that female prisoners should have female supervision. The wild women of the prisons who were just as likely to assault visitors as to welcome them were transformed by Elizabeth's teaching. Maria Edgeworth, a contemporary, writes of a visit by Elizabeth to Newgate prison. 'The prisoners came in and in an orderly manner ranged themselves on the benches. All quite clean, faces, hair, cap and hands. On a very low bench in front little children were settled by their mothers. Mrs Fry opened the Bible and read in the most sweetly solemn sedate voice I ever heard, slowly and distinctly without anything in the manner that could distract attention from the matter. Sometimes she paused to explain, addressing the convicts, "We (not you) have felt . . .", "We are convinced . . .". The women were perfectly silent, with their eyes fixed upon her . . . and the children sat quite still the whole time.'[12]

Elizabeth helped many others besides those in prisons and planned a training establishment for women to learn nursing. Although coming from a wealthy family, Elizabeth was reduced to poverty towards the end of her life because of the mishandling of her husband's financial affairs by others. The resulting bankruptcy in 1845 was considered a disgrace in Quaker circles and he was expelled from the Society. The couple found this very upsetting and together with the strain of travelling abroad and at home Elizabeth became ill and before long she died.

Martyrdom continues abroad

While hymns were being penned, novels written and social wrongs righted in Britain elsewhere women and men continued to die for their faith. Christianity had begun to spread into **Korea** from 1777 onwards, but by 1800 the authorities started to consider the influence it was having in their country and found this disturbing. **Persecution** of the Christians had begun in 1801 and many of the three hundred people who were put to death at this time were women, including the sister of one Paul Ni Tsiong-hoi who was himself put to death in 1827 at the age of thirty-six.

A similar scenario took place in Madagascar a little later. **Mary Rafaravavy** and **Rafavavy Rasalama** became Christians in Madagascar, after two missionaries had arrived there in 1817 bringing the faith and schooling to the island. By 1836, the missionaries had to withdraw because of opposition from the authorities, leaving a group of about fifty Christians behind.

Mary, who was a daughter of a court dignitary, was the first to arrange prayer meetings in her home. She was arrested in July 1836 and condemned to death, but escaped execution because the soldiers guarding her panicked when a fire broke out and she escaped. Mary thought of herself as being like the Pilgrim in *The Pilgrim's Progress* which was popular reading amongst the Christians in her country. She remembered Christian crossing the valley of the shadow of death and how it is often through numerous tribulations that Christians enter the Kingdom of heaven.

In 1837 Rafavavy was put to death and her martyrdom 'became the symbol of unswerving and edifying determination'.[13] Whenever people like Rafavavy died for their faith, (in her case either by being burned alive or scalded to death), throughout Christian history the Church has grown through the witness of their martyrdom. Despite the greater persecution of 1849, the Christians increased four-fold and by the 1860s the church was fully accepted in Madagascar.

The difficulties of being a missionary

The missionaries who took Christianity out to these far flung places included women as well as men. Often they were the

wives of missionaries, who were as much involved in converting the native inhabitants of a country as their husbands, and
sometimes through their easier relationship with the womenfolk were more successful. It is fashionable to criticise the
methods of these nineteenth-century missionaries nowadays,
but they were working in the Lord's service as they thought
best and bringing the Good News of Salvation to those who
knew it not.

Margaret Cargill was born in Aberdeen in 1815. Her
father died there while she was still young, but although poor,
her mother ensured that her children were well educated. At
the age of seventeen she met and married a student, David
Cargill, who was training for missionary work with the Wesleyan Methodists. On their wedding day, they set sail for the
Friendly Islands, to which they felt they had been called.
Margaret was very ill on the journey, but they continued
until they reached Nukualofa in the Friendly Islands. There
they were well received by the king, but after a few days they
were asked to move on to the island of Vavua where they
were to remain for three years, before moving to Fiji.

The Fijians at this time were cannibals and while welcoming
strangers initially, their welcome was sometimes short-lived!
The Cargills travelled by boat together with another couple,
the Crosses, and an interpreter, amidst much prayer for their
safety. They were received by the Fijians and Margaret made
the care of the women and children her special work. Always
before them in their work, were the words 'Lo, I am with you
always, *even* unto the end of the world'. Margaret died in 1840
following the illness and death of her sixth child, worn out by
childbearing and her missionary work. But from her shining
life a light had begun to shine in the darkness that was Fiji.

Elsewhere other lights were also shining in the darkness,
and one of these lights was **'Deborah' Bowen Thompson**.
From her childhood, Deborah's faith was evident in her
unselfishness and devotion to others. She became interested in
ancient monuments, and when the Rosetta Stone was discovered in Egypt, she became very involved in studying Egyptian
and Eastern antiquities. Deborah met her husband, who was
a doctor appointed to run the British Syrian Hospital in
Damascus, in 1843. They went to live in Antioch where
Deborah began to help educate the women of the area. When

the Crimean war broke out Dr Thompson felt it was his duty to offer his services but soon after he arrived he became sick himself and died shortly after.

Deborah returned to England where she helped many of the widows of soldiers who had died in the Indian Mutiny of 1857 but in 1860, after the Druses massacred all the Christian Maronite men in Syria between the ages of seven and seventy, Deborah began to involve herself in caring for those who were now left destitute. Eleven thousand Christians had been put to death and three thousand homes burned to the ground. Four thousand Christians also died of starvation as a result of the massacre and there were twenty thousand widows and orphans. Syria at that time included the Lebanon where religious persecution still continues today.

Deborah travelled to Beirut where she founded a refuge for thirty women and sixteen children. She received a great deal of help from the people of Britain, and her friends there formed the 'Society for the Social and Religious Improvement of Syrian Women.' Commenting on the filth, the wailing and the misery of these poor, sad people, she wrote that they had 'no idea of the truth as it is in Christ Jesus, for their souls were filled with revenge. When, however their Christian teachers unfolded to them the Good News of our Saviour, they would sit at their feet in rapt attention and exclaim, "We never heard such words. We are women. Does it mean for us?"' Eagerly these women and children, including many besides those in the refuge, began to learn more of the joy of the Christian Gospel. Sometimes the memories of the massacre were too much for the women but gradually their lives began to improve.

Deborah started schools and began workshops for the women to find employment. Work always began with a Bible reading, prayer and a hymn. She arranged for Arabic Bibles to be sent out from the British and Foreign Bible Society and other educational materials also came from Britain.

In 1861 a school was founded and was visited by the Prince of Wales and this soon included not only Christian children but Druse children as well. Even some of the older widows who had never known how to read came to learn. For many of these women it was the first time that they had realized that the Gospel message was meant for them as well as the men. Deborah not only opened the schools in Beirut but also in many of the villages round about, including some particularly for the women and girls.

Deborah returned home again in 1869 after her health had given way and died that year but even to the last her faith sustained her as on her death-bed she proclaimed 'Glory be to the Father, the Son and the Holy Ghost. Jesus! Jesus! Rest! Arise! Amen!'

Marie Regina Gobat and her husband were also in the Near East at the time of the massacre of the Maronites in 1860. Born in 1813, Marie lived in Benggen, Switzerland until she was married at the age of twenty-one to Samuel Gobat, a missionary who served in Ethiopia, then called Abyssinia. Shortly after their marriage the young couple set sail for Egypt on their way back to Ethiopia where she began to learn Amharic, the language of the Ethiopians. The journey from Cairo to Ethiopia took many months during which time Samuel became very sick and their first child was born.

Both Marie and Samuel became ill again after their arrival in Ethiopia and decided that it would be best to return to Europe. Their journey back was not to be easy. None of the family were well and the boat journey up the Red Sea took twice as long as expected so that they ran short of food. Then they had to cross an empty desert during which time their baby sickened and died.

Marie and Samuel then remained in Cairo for a time where their second child was born, a son they called Benoni after the son of Jacob's wife Rachel [Genesis 35.18 – She called his name Benoni (i.e. Son of my sorrow)]. Eventually they arrived back in Switzerland much to the surprise of many of their friends who had thought they were dead. They remained there for about two years and then went to Malta where Samuel had been appointed to teach in a Protestant College. From Malta, Samuel was called to be Bishop of Jerusalem and in 1846 he was consecrated in London and set sail for Alexandria once more. They travelled on to Jaffa where they received a warm welcome on their way to Jerusalem.

Once she was settled there Marie began her work amongst the women and children teaching them about Christianity. After thirty-two years her schools had fourteen hundred children in them, each one of whom Marie knew by name. Much of this education was paid for by Marie herself. When the Druses began their massacre of the Maronite Christians, the Gobats found that they, too, were in some danger. The Druses eventually drew back from attacking Jerusalem but the strain had made Samuel ill once again. Five years later the Gobats had to face starvation after a famine hit the country they loved. During all this time Marie and her husband showed their love for the people and she was able to share their sorrows, comfort them and bring them happiness when they were down-hearted. Marie was a great strength and support to her husband and the wider family of his flock.

In 1878, the Gobats returned to Switzerland where Samuel once again became ill. He managed to return to Jerusalem but he died there soon after Easter the following year. Marie herself became ill with the strain of grief and bereavement and, although she longed to continue her work in Jerusalem praying that God would spare her to serve him further, she died only twelve weeks after her husband. Many of those at her funeral felt that in losing Marie they had lost their own mother, one who was also a mother to Israel.

Mary Louisa Whately also spent much of her time in the eastern mediterranean. Born in Halesworth in Suffolk in 1824 where her father was rector, she moved at the age of three to Oxford. At the age of seven Mary moved again, this time to Dublin when her father became Archbishop there.

Mary was a bright child and was soon able to help her father in the poor school which he opened, often taking the children food to share. When she was twenty the great famine broke out in Ireland and many hundreds were dying whilst others emigrated to escape. Mary continued to help those struck down by poverty and death but the famine was followed by the Crimean war when many Irishmen who went to fight died in Russia. Mary's work of consolation continued among those who once again were grieving for the loss of their bread winners, this time to the ravages of war.

Eventually Mary left Ireland and set out with a friend to Cairo, where she stayed for a while before visiting the Holy Land and Lebanon. She returned home but her mother and sister both died during her visit and she became ill herself. This made her decide to return to Egypt to help the women and children there, feeling that God was calling her to this task. There were at that time no schools for any but the Copts, and Mary felt called to do something for the poorer Muslim children. She knew that it would be uphill work, but began with prayer and the search for a suitable house.

The house which she and her cousin decided upon was not yet finished but they managed to arrange it so that they could open their school. They appointed an Arabic woman as teacher then went out into the streets to find some young girls who were otherwise denied any education. When the two women asked the mothers if they would allow their daughters to come to learn to read and sew, the mothers replied that girls don't read and they don't need to learn. The mothers were very wary of a stranger wanting to educate the young girls. Eventually they got a few promises and on the first day, nine pupils actually started at the school. The girls were all Muslims and were taught the Old Testament, reading, needlework and singing. The second day brought another five girls and so the school grew. After a while Mary had to return home but sent another teacher to take her place through the Society for Promoting Female Education in the East.

After two years, Mary returned to find the school closed so she reopened it and soon it was again full of eager children. She was able to obtain help from some Coptic girls in teaching embroidery and eventually, with the aid of a Muslim teacher, opened a school for boys as well.

After her father died in 1863 Mary had to return briefly to Dublin but was soon back in Cairo. The Prince of Wales visited her there and helped her in her plans to enlarge the school. Mary's work amongst the poor was welcomed and she began to visit some of the villages along the Nile taking copies of the New Testament with her. Many of the village women were eager to know more of the Gospel which they had heard about through friends. But Mary was beginning to weaken. On one of these visits to the village in 1890 she became ill and was taken back to Cairo. Shortly afterwards she died, having brought the Gospel and education to many of the women of Egypt and their children.

Anna Hinderer was also called to be a missionary in this fruitful period. Born Anna Martin at Hempnall in Norfolk in 1827, her mother died when Anna was only five years after which she was brought up by relations in Lowestoft, and then by a Revd and Mrs Cunningham. By the time Anna was fourteen she had become a Sunday School teacher and started her own ragged Sunday School. Within a few years, she had over two hundred children attending but by then her thoughts were turning to missionary work.

In 1852 she married David Hinderer, a German missionary at Yaruba about sixty miles north of Lagos in Nigeria, who had been ordained by the Archbishop of Canterbury as part of the work of the Church Missionary Society. The climate was not good for Europeans and soon after she arrived Anna became ill. The young couple moved to Ibadan where they lived in a mud house managing to convert the local people and build both church and mission buildings, including a school which Anna ran.

Anna continued to get recurring attacks of the fever which had affected her health in Yaruba and after a tribal war in 1860 they had to return to Britain because of her illness. Although she went back again to Nigeria briefly, she had to return to England where she died in 1870, secure in the knowledge that she had done her best to bring Jesus to the people of Ibadan, and that she had left the church there in good hands. **Mary Smith** also went to Africa as the wife of a missionary, once again not only supporting her husband in his work but also witnessing herself to the love which she had for Our Lord.

Born around 1800 in Dunkinfeld in Scotland, Mary was the daughter of a nonconformist and attended a Moravian school. She later helped with teaching children and worship at a chapel in Ashton-under-Lyne from where she went to join her future husband, Robert Moffat in South Africa in 1819.

Mary had to make the long journey on her own, travelling by ship from the Isle of Wight to the Cape. She went in the knowledge that God was calling her to serve beside her husband in his missionary work with the Africans. 'She had bidden adieu to a home with all its comforts and delights, and entered upon a time of hardships, toil, shame and reproach for her Master's sake.'[14]

Mary enjoyed her life in Africa and wrote many descriptive letters home. Towards the end of 1820 she gave birth to a daughter, Mary, later to become the wife of David Livingstone. The baby's nurse was one of two children saved by

Mary Moffat from certain death, as they were to be buried with their dead mother by their relatives according to local custom. The Moffats were to encounter a great deal of violence and theft amongst the people of Africa but the difficulties they faced brought them closer to the native people amongst whom they worked.

Robert endeavoured to translate the New Testament and some hymns into the local language, and Mary continued in her caring for the people and in prayer. In 1838, the family returned home for a visit which lasted four years. They were greeted on their return by David Livingstone, who married their eldest daughter and helped them in their work for a while. Mary's work with her husband was very fruitful, and she defended her decision to remain in Africa in a letter to a friend, writing 'I will go on God's errand even though I am the means of saving only one lost soul', but in her work she brought not one but many to know the Christian Gospel. Although their daughter Mary died while she was still young, the Moffats continued with their work in Africa.

By 1871, they felt a need to return to England, and it was with great sadness and reluctance that the African villagers said goodbye. Mary caught a chill in the Christmas of that year, and died shortly after. Robert was the first to acknowledge how much she had been with him in his work in God's service. As he heard of her death, he said 'For fifty-three years I have had her to pray for me'. A fitting acknowledgement of the work that sustains many clerics, and is often not recognized.

Women writers of the nineteenth century

While the more adventurous women were offering their lives in the service of Christ on the mission field, others were continuing the literary and musical heritage of Jane Austen and Harriet Auber.

Elizabeth Barrett Browning was one woman whose faith shone throughout her life, a life which was never very easy. Elizabeth was born in 1806 near Durham but her family moved to Herefordshire when she was very young. Although always very frail Elizabeth was bright and enjoyed sharing her brothers' education, particularly Greek and Philosophy.

She loved writing from an early age and published some poetry while still in her teens.

Elizabeth's mother died when Elizabeth herself was only twenty and the family then moved first to London and later to Torquay by which time Elizabeth's health had deteriorated and her spine had become damaged. While the family were at Torquay her favourite brother and a friend were drowned after which shock Elizabeth retired to a darkened room for a year as a helpless invalid.

The family returned to London where Elizabeth remained an invalid, virtually imprisoned by her father who did nothing to encourage any hope for an improvement in her health. In 1845, when Elizabeth was nearly forty, her cousin brought a friend, Robert Browning, to meet her and they fell in love despite the opposition of her father. In the September of the following year Elizabeth walked out of her father's house and was married to Robert in Marylebone. She left her family home finally a few days later to travel to Italy with her husband and a maid. Elizabeth lived happily with her husband in the warm sun where their son was later born.

Much of her poetry was written during this happy period when she was able to reflect her vision of God in nature, humanity, human love and motherhood. Her meditations on her own experience of life gave rise to writings which reflected the love she saw surrounding her. 'Earth's crammed with heaven and every common bush afire with God.' She valued the place of Christianity in the Arts, writing, 'We want the touch of Christ's hand upon our literature as it touched other dead things; we want the sense of the saturation of Christ's blood upon the souls of our poets, that it may cry through them . . . expounding agony into renovation.'[15]

Even though she was often very ill, and it was not easy at the time for a woman to have works published, Elizabeth showed a determination and spirituality which inspired her to overcome these difficulties and return them with love. Despite her frailty Elizabeth had fifteen very happy years of marriage.

In 1853, the Congregationalists of North America opened their ordained ministry to women and one of the better known women writers of this period was **Harriet Beecher Stowe**, the author of *Uncle Tom's Cabin*, herself the wife of a Congregationalist Old Testament minister and a lay theologian.

Of those with a gift for writing popular hymns which have stood the test of time and fashion one who stands out is **Cecil Frances Alexander**. Frances Humphreys was born in 1818 and married William Alexander when she was twenty-two. He eventually became Bishop of Derry, Archbishop of Armagh and finally Primate of all Ireland.

Before she was married Fanny wrote tracts with her friend, the Lady Harriet Howard, and also published books of poetry. She was influenced by the Oxford Movement and John Keble wrote the preface to her *Hymns for Little Children* written in 1848. This volume is believed to have been written when some children complained about the Church's Catechism being dull. Many of her best known hymns are in this volume, where they were placed in sections on Baptism, The Apostles' prayer, The ten commandments and the Lord's prayer. Her hymns include 'Once in royal David's city', 'All things bright and beautiful', 'Jesus calls us! O'er the tumult', 'Do no sinful action' and 'There is a green hill far away'. This last hymn is believed to have had its first line inspired by a hill outside the city of Londonderry where she lived, a city surrounded by a wall which thus reminded her of Jerusalem. Frances died in 1895 having contributed in many ways to the life of the Church.

Caroline Maria was born in 1817, the daughter of the Revd and Hon. B. W. **Noel** and like many of the women of this period she started writing when she was still young. Caroline wrote her first hymn when she was seventeen but gave up writing when she was twenty until, over twenty years later, she took it up again. It was during these later years that she wrote her best known hymn, 'At the Name of Jesus'. She died when she was about sixty.

Although **Catherine Winkworth** did not write any original hymns as far as it is known, she did translate a large number including 'Praise to the Lord, the Almighty, the King of creation', 'Christ the Lord is risen again' and 'Now thank we all our God'. Catherine lived from 1827 to 1878. Another favourite hymn, 'Thine for ever! God of Love', was written by **M. F. Maude** who lived from 1820 to 1913.

Anna Letitia Waring was born in the same year, the daughter of a Quaker mill owner at Plas-y-Felin, near Neath, but when she was twenty she was baptized into the Church of

England. Her best known hymn 'In heavenly love abiding' demonstrates how much her faith and love for God shone through her life and all that she wrote. Anna died at the age of ninety.

1820 must have been a good year for women hymn-writers to be born, for it was in that year in New York that another author of some of the best known hymns of this period was born. **Frances Jane Crosby** was ninety-five when she died but when she was only six weeks old she was blinded when poultices which were too hot were put on her eyes. Fanny wrote her first hymn when she was eight and seven years later she went to the Institution for the Blind. In 1844, she published her first book of poems and became a teacher three years later, constantly working to obtain more understanding for blind people.

In 1850 Fanny became converted after a revival meeting at a Methodist Church and eight years later she married a teacher of music, Alexander van Alstyne. It was then that she began to write most of her hymns, particularly the more personal ones. Among her best known hymns are 'Safe in the arms of Jesus', 'To God be the Glory', 'Tell me the story of Jesus' and 'Blessed Assurance, Jesus is mine'. 'Safe in the arms of Jesus' was written after a music composer provided her with a tune to which he needed some words and she wrote it in less than half an hour.

Fanny provided many hymns for Moody and Sankey's hymn book and spoke often about her writing. She had an excellent memory and could recite the first four books of the Old Testament and the Gospels from memory. At the age of sixty, Fanny began to work at the Bowery Mission which was a social and evangelical mission in a deprived area of New York.

Charlotte Mary Yonge was also a daughter of this creative age, born in 1823 and brought up in a family where religion was very much part of life. Charlotte was high spirited and excitable, noisy and with a vivid imagination which created for her a family of ten boys and eleven girls, who were actually her dolls. This ability to use her imagination meant that she was able to make up stories easily.

Charlotte not only wrote many novels but also various educational and religious text-books on such subjects as history,

nature study, the classics, poetry and civic studies, besides the
Bible and church history. She was prepared for confirmation
by John Keble, who was, at the time, vicar of the parish
where she lived, and he was responsible for developing her
religious outlook.

Charlotte was particularly concerned with encouraging the
religious education of women of all classes and the spread of
foreign missions. With the proceeds of *Heir of Redcliffe*, she had
built a missionary ship for New Zealand. Other royalties were
used for missionary work, building schools and for a scholarship for a Winchester High School pupil to attend either an
Oxford or a Cambridge College. Charlotte died in 1901.

Clewer and other religious communities

The opening up of boundaries for women in the missionary
and literary fields, did not mean that they were being accepted
in every part of the Church. While Protestantism had abol-
ished monasticism, it did not open the way for any other
ministry for women within a similar religious setting. However
in the early part of the nineteenth century, groups of women
gathered together to give the caring service which those
women living in convents in earlier centuries had given.
Inspired by the Oxford Movement, in England, and encouraged by Dr Pusey, they began to be called nuns in 1842.
'Why should not God call women as well as men to a life of
devotion?' he asked.

Among those involved in setting up communities under
Pusey's encouragement was **Lydia** (or Priscilla) **Sellon**. She
founded the Devonport sisterhood and another community at
Ascot Priory (which maintained a convalescent home in con-
junction with Guy's Hospital) besides running 'a college for
sailor boys, an orphanage, an industrial school for girls and a
lodging house for destitute women.'[16] She also established a
branch of the Devonport Sisterhood in Honolulu and encouraged the growth of the Society of the Love of Jesus, a company
formed in 1853 for intercessory prayer which provided a
continual chain of prayer, night and day.

Following the establishment of these sisterhoods, other
women began to form similar communities often with particular social concerns. **Harriet Monsell** was a widow of forty

when she was appointed by the vicar of Clewer to be the first Mother of the Clewer home for young women in trouble in 1851. After a while the vicar, Canon Carter, suggested that the home should be run as a sisterhood to be the Community of St John the Baptist. Harriet became the superior at Clewer where she developed helping these women and others in the neighbourhood on both a practical as well as a spiritual level. Eventually the community's work spread and when Harriet became ill, she moved to the community's house at Folkestone where she died in 1883. Harriet was loved dearly by her community, but also kept in close touch with her family. A friend writes of her: 'Often have I seen the Mother attracting to her side some Sister of a younger Community than her own, who listened to her loving counsels; her clear-sightedness into character enabling her to discover at once just what counsel was needed, and her full heart of love making it not only acceptable but very sweet.'[17]

Kaiserwerth and nursing

In Germany, an order of deaconesses was founded by Theodor Fliedner in Kaiserwerth in 1836, although he insisted that the women should have men to lead them. Dr Fleidner had been influenced by Elizabeth Fry and he originally intended that the order should work amongst discharged female prisoners. Amalie Sieveking formed a group of nursing sisters in Hamburg in 1832 separately from Fliedner, with women in charge. The monastic orders in the Roman Catholic Church at this time also began to flourish and people like Florence Nightingale (see p. 178) were influenced by the sisters of St Vincent de Paul and other communities. Florence, together with several others, began to encourage the work of women in nursing, particularly within the religious communities.

Among those involved in nursing at this time was **Agnes Jones**. Born in Cambridge in 1832 to an Irish army family, Agnes spent much of her childhood abroad before her family settled down on the shores of Lough Swilly, in Ireland. There Agnes became involved in caring for the sick and when her family moved to Europe after her father's death Agnes visited the Deaconess Institute at Kaiserworth where she longed to stay in order to train as a nurse. However she remained with her family instead using her nursing gifts to care for both her mother and the poor who lived nearby.

After seven years Agnes returned to Kaiserworth where she learnt more about nursing before returning to St Thomas's Hospital in London where she finished her training. She was still unable to use her nursing skills apart from caring for some sick relatives, until in 1864 when she was asked by a Mr Rathbone to become the Superintendent of a work house hospital and help with workhouse reform. He wanted to provide nursing care for the inmates of the workhouse and was prepared to do this at his own expense. With forty or fifty nurses Agnes began her work among the fifteen hundred people in the workhouse, a number which increased rapidly after the cotton famine. During the long hours she worked Agnes continually witnessed to her Christian faith.

Florence Nightingale wrote of her: 'In less than three years, she reduced one of the most disorderly hospital populations in the world to something like Christian discipline. . . . She converted a Vestry to the conviction as well as the humanity of nursing pauper sick by trained nurses . . . disarming all opposition so that Roman Catholic and Unitarian, High Church and Low Church all rose up and called her blessed.'[18] Agnes died of typhoid in 1868.

The difficulties which Agnes experienced in following that vocation to which she felt she was called were shared by many other women of her time as indeed they had been in earlier centuries and continue to be today. The patience with which such women as **Florence Nightingale** bore their trials is an example to all. Her story demonstrates the machinations of some men unable to accept the vocations of some women to serve God in new ways.

Florence was called after the city in which she was born in 1820. She was an attractive and intelligent young girl who was not enamoured with the thought of a life of 'domestic bliss' and was delighted when on 7 February 1837, she felt she had been called by God to serve Him in a different way. She did not know how this was to be but waited to find out with the same patience which she needed later in Crimea. Meanwhile she travelled abroad with her family for two years returning to her birthplace where she soon began to discover social injustices. On her return to Britain she was presented at court and marriage was generally thought to be her next step – by everyone but her.

Meanwhile Florence was becoming more aware of the poverty which existed around her and the conditions in the hospitals to which the poor were taken. They were crowded and cold and the windows were kept shut to keep the heat in so that there was no fresh air and the mouldy walls streamed with moisture. Patients were not washed and linen was often unchanged from one patient to the next. More often than not the nurses were prostitutes and there was little respect for them.

This situation was accepted as normal even by the Christians in the society in which Florence moved, just as many of us ignore the misery that some of our communities have to live in today. However Florence did meet some other concerned Christians including Lord Ashley, later to become the Earl of Shaftesbury. Eventually, she decided that she wanted to train as a nurse and would study for three months from home. Her parents were shocked and forced her to give up the idea but this made Florence ill. She recovered after friends took her abroad for a holiday but after returning home she became ill again so the friends arranged for her to spend two weeks at the Kaiserwerth Institute where she spent the time working hard. Despite this hard work she recovered rapidly and, as she was by then over thirty, Florence knew it was now time to leave her family possibly in order to enter a convent.

However her father gave her a private income and when she was thirty-three, Florence became superintendent of the Institution for the Care of Sick Gentlewomen in Distressed Circumstances. There she set about organizing matters so that every patient had the best treatment possible regardless of circumstances, and soon the Institute was running smoothly. Florence began to be bored and looked around for something more demanding to do.

The Crimean war was just starting and reports were being sent back by *The Times* correspondent of the terrible conditions in the British hospitals out there. British women were not allowed to nurse the soldiers because of the immoral reputation nurses had, despite the French having Sisters of Charity as nurses in their hospitals. However the British Secretary for War was Sidney Herbert, a friend of Florence, and he asked her to take a party of her nurses out there. She took fourteen trained nurses and another twenty-four nuns, both Anglican and Roman Catholic.

When they arrived in November 1854 Florence and her group were left with hardly anywhere to sleep and the Army Medical authorities made it clear that her group were not welcome. The army had always managed without women, and would not allow them to help. Florence was determined not to go against orders and her nurses remained in their rooms sorting bandages. Men were dying in the wards and the drainage system was so badly blocked that often even those who had come into hospital only mildly ill were dying from sickness brought on in the hospital. Many patients also died from starvation because of the poor rationing of food. Florence began to cook food for those who had difficulty eating and the women were allowed to scrub floors on the grounds that this was women's work anyway. They were even allowed to wash clothes and this helped reduce the cross infection and vermin. Often Florence bought supplies for the hospital out of her own money sending to Constantinople for things that she knew the stores were lacking.

The hospitals continued to remain overcrowded and when Florence arranged to have a new hospital built with her own money to replace one which had burned down, this antagonized the Army Medical Department even more. Florence was by this time caring for the soldiers in a way that they had never known before and she began to provide teaching facilities for the many who were illiterate. Although many of the officers could never be reconciled to her work, the soldiers loved their lady who walked the wards at night with her lamp.

The war ended in 1856 and Florence returned home worn out by the opposition she had received and the sheer hard work of caring for the sick under terrible conditions. She felt a failure because she had not overcome the opposition and soldiers whose health could have improved with proper care had remained sick. She was hardly aware that to the British people she was a heroine because their sons and husbands had been treated as human beings. She tried to evade any publicity on her return, preferring to travel to her family home in the north unrecognized rather than face the welcome back she could have received. Although money was sent and a Nightingale fund was set up to train nurses, Florence continued to be thwarted in her desire to have the Army Medical department investigated. Even though a report was written it was in danger of being ignored but eventually the issue was brought before the government and discussed. Florence continued to press for an improvement in the welfare of the ordinary soldier and many of the facilities which exist for them nowadays result from her influence.

In 1859 Florence wrote a book on the running of hospitals called *Notes on Hospitals* which gave instructions on cleanliness and advocating fresh air and sunshine. She used the money from her fund to start a nursing school at St Thomas's Hospital in London, again despite opposition from some doctors who thought that nurses were fit only to scrub floors. She continued to press for an improvement in public health standards and treatment for the poor including those in workhouses. (Also see Agnes Jones p. 177) In 1871, after researching why so many babies died she wrote *Introductory notes on Lying-in Institutions*.

All this time Florence was a semi-invalid and after 1896 she remained in her bedroom, having established through her work many schools of nursing and a great rise in the standards of medical care. She received the Order of Merit in 1907 and died three years later. Although on occasions she was frequently attacked, even for such matters as using Roman Catholic nuns as well as Anglican, Florence was described by one clergyman as belonging to that rare sect, the sect of the Good Samaritan. During her lifetime she always showed a Christian care for others, an example which achieved a change not only in the care given in hospitals but in the role of women in the late nineteenth century.

The social care movement and education

Whilst such women as Harriet, Agnes and Florence were working amongst the sick and those needing moral support, others were using their influence to develop social caring in different ways. **Angela Georgina Burdett-Coutts** was born in 1814 and by 1837 had become the wealthiest heiress in England. Throughout her life Angela was to put her wealth to

God's service, becoming known as the greatest philanthropist of her time and described by the Prince of Wales as a most remarkable woman, second only to his mother, Queen Victoria.

Angela endowed many educational and ecclesiastical establishments, supporting the Ragged School movement as well as two scholarships for Geology at Oxford and the Bishoprics of Cape Town and Adelaide. She was particularly interested in science but her gifts were used for many purposes. She was one of the founders of the Society for the Prevention of Cruelty to Animals and also helped to found the Society for the Prevention of Cruelty to Children. She was not only a close friend of David Livingstone, General Gordon and Charles Dickens but also encouraged Henry Irving to develop his talent.

In 1871 Angela was made Baroness Burdett-Coutts and the following year she became the first woman to receive the Freedom of the City of London. Some years later, at the age of fifty-seven, she married a man of thirty and she lived until she was ninety-one.

Angela cared deeply about the Establishment of the Church of England, and many of her gifts to the Church were given only so long as 'the Church remains the Protestant Church of England as now by law established under the Supremacy of the Crown, being Protestant'. Should the Church of England become disestablished the monies given were to be used 'to promote the principle of the Protestant Reformation, civil liberty and social well-being'.[19]

Angela also encouraged 'schemes for employment, housing, nursing, health-visiting, the building of public fountains and the provision of recreation grounds'. She provided funds for libraries, famine relief in Ireland and many other needy causes including much housing in Bethnal Green in London.

The role of women in education at this time was spearheaded by **Frances Mary Buss** and **Dorothea Beale**. Well known for having built up the Cheltenham Ladies College and the North London Collegiate School, these two ladies were instrumental in the development of secondary education for girls in Britain. About Miss Beale, it has been said that 'religion was the informing spirit of all her life and work. . . . It was an inspiration in itself to hear her read prayers'.[20]

Other women besides these two were demanding a place for the female sex in the halls of education. One who continued the fight to obtain proper recognition for her studies was **Elizabeth Blackwell** who was born in Bristol in 1821, the daughter of a political reformer who was a member of the Congregational church. The family moved to America in 1832 after business difficulties but shortly after arriving there Elizabeth's father died and the family were left penniless. When she was eighteen Elizabeth and her brothers and sisters opened a boarding school to bring in some money. By that time they were members of the Episcopalian church and belonged to the anti-slavery movement.

Elizabeth moved to Kentucky to become the head of a school but could not bear to watch the degradation of the slaves so she soon returned home. She attempted to study medicine but was continually thwarted in this by those who considered her to be nothing more than 'a pretty little thing of the female gender' and that medicine was not a suitable subject for a young Christian woman to think of studying. A mystical experience together with this unreasonable opposition challenged her to continue fighting to be allowed to study. 'A brilliant light of hope and peace filled my soul. At once, I knew not how, the terror fled away. . . . A deep conviction came to me that my life was accepted by God. . . . This unusual experiment at the outset of my medical career has had a lasting and marked effect on my whole life. To me it was a revealed experience of Truth, a direct vision of the great reality of spiritual existence, as irresistible as it is incommunicable. I shall be grateful to the last day of my life for this great gift of faith.'[21]

Elizabeth continued her attempts with a deepening of that purpose which she must inevitably seek to accomplish. Eventually she found a small medical college which would accept her and she qualified from there in 1849 as a Doctor of Medicine. She then moved to Paris to continue her studies but had to give up her ambition to be a surgeon after an accident to her eye and so returned to St Bartholomew's in London.

Elizabeth went back to America in 1851 to open a college for women and in 1857 opened a hospital to be run by women but returned again to England in 1869 to become Professor of Gynaecology at the London School of Medicine. Her life was devoted to helping the poorest women and children and inspired Elizabeth Garrett Anderson to do the same for women and medicine in Britain as she had done in America.

Elizabeth Garrett Anderson, or Lizzie as she was known, was born in 1836 and was a great friend of Emily Davies, the founder of Girton College, Cambridge, who was six years her senior. When Lizzie went to a lecture which Elizabeth Blackwell was giving in London, Emily persuaded her to introduce herself to Dr Elizabeth who had already been impressed with the young girl's attentiveness during the lecture. However life was not easy for Lizzie for 'in the mid-nineteenth century society as a whole felt not just prejudice but loathing amounting to hatred and fear of women pursuing the same studies as men.'[22]

The male students often made life difficult for Lizzie particularly because she was so bright and their opposition grew when Lizzie came top in a Viva. Eventually she moved from the Middlesex Hospital where she had been studying to St Andrew's University and there, after early difficulties, Lizzie was able to settle down. In 1865 she became a doctor, having taken her MD degree in Paris, because London University would not allow a women to graduate as a doctor. Eventually Lizzie was to become accepted partly through the way she faced up to the cholera epidemic of 1866 and she too had a hospital named after her. She became Mayor of Aldeburgh in 1908, nine years before she died, and was the first woman to be a mayor.

Emily Davies supported Lizzie all through this difficult period and when she gave a paper at the National Association for the Promotion of Social Science, the title of it was *Medicine as a Profession for Women*. Although Emily asked a man to read her paper on this occasion, the next time she spoke she gave the paper herself. At the Association Emily first met F. D. Maurice who impressed both the young women, but even he was against the idea of women studying. Emily began to collect information about why men did not approve of women studying and found reasons which were in fact very little different from those which Dorothea Erxleben had also come across over one hundred years earlier in Prussia.

In 1862 a paper was read at the Association about the possibility of university degrees for women and this was considered a cause for great mirth. This gave Emily the idea to attempt to get the Local Examination Boards to include girls as well as boys in their examinations. After some frustrating time fighting for this Emily and her friends were given six weeks in which to prove her case by producing candidates suitable for a trial examination by Cambridge Local Examination Board. In fact ninety-one girls entered, of whom twenty-five were from Frances Buss' school. Of this number, only six failed, much to the delight of all who had supported the idea although all the girls had done badly in mathematics.

Despite this success, at another meeting of the Association in 1864, many people including the then Archbishop of York spoke about how unsuitable it was for universities to be examining girls. Canon Norris suggested that 'unmarried men do not know how to examine girls; celibate Fellows of colleges, living in the semi-monastic atmosphere of the university, know only that girls are brought up in some private, mysterious way to be as unlike men as possible.' In March of the following year the Cambridge Senate agreed to allow girls to take annual Local Examinations.

In 1866 Emily was asked to give evidence about girls' schools before a Royal Commission looking into conditions in schools. That they should be willing to look at girls' schools was a tremendous breakthrough and, at Emily's suggestion, Frances Buss joined her. Emily continued her fight for London University to allow women to sit their examinations, but to no avail. She also became passively involved in the Suffrage movement and was beginning to think about the possibility of a college for women, perhaps in Cambridge, an idea which received great support from her friend Lizzie.

Having found a suitable property in which to house the college in nearby Hitchin, Emily then found difficulty finding students because families were not prepared to allow their daughters to be subject to the strain of studying. In the event, ten young women were successful in the entrance examination for the college which opened its doors in October 1869. In fact five pupils arrived for the first day and settled down to being the first women to study in a women's college.

In 1870 both Emily and Lizzie were elected on to the School Board in London and Lizzie was persuaded to take the chair, a triumph indeed. Two years later Emily became

Mistress of her college, first in Hitchin and then at Girton and she resigned from the Board. The difficulties about setting up a women's college were to continue, especially when Dr Maudsley attempted to suggest that menstruation afflicted a young woman by so taking away her strength that she was not able to study without damaging her health.

Although Emily had a strong faith herself she did not wish to impose religion on her students, leaving them to sort out their place of worship for themselves. Girton continued to expand although Emily did not remain Mistress for long. She insisted that standards remain high and constantly fought for the students there to be treated as equals in the University with the men. Whilst Jemima Clough (see below) allowed her students to take the Local examinations, Emily knew that the standard of entry to her college was set at a higher level. Through the popular success of the lower standards demanded at the Ladies' Lectures which Jemima organized, the growth of Newnham Hall was initially faster than that of Girton. However throughout her life Emily was not one to lower her standards to please others and this meant that for some while Girton had higher educational standards than Newnham.

Emily died in 1921, after spending much of the last part of her life working for the suffragette movement, but her rival at Newnham, Jemima Clough had died just before the turn of the century. **Anne Jemima Clough** had been born in Liverpool in 1820, the daughter of a cotton business man, and began work by teaching at Sunday School and in the Welsh National School. Her free afternoons would be spent taking workhouse girls out into the country for walks. Although she became short of money when her father's business failed she continued trying to obtain an education for girls as good as that for boys.

Jemima began to be involved with Josephine Butler in organizing lectures for women in the north of England and in 1871 she was asked to take charge of a Hall at Cambridge for women who were beginning to attend the lectures there. This developed into Newnham College where she became the founder and first Principal. She took a close and individual interest in all her girls and in one of her addresses to those leaving she offered the advice to 'take the little pleasures of life. Watch the sunsets and the clouds, the shadows in the streets and the misty light over our great cities. These bring joy by the way and thankfulness to our Heavenly Father.'[23]

More hymn-writers

Inspired perhaps by the earlier women hymn-writers a slightly younger group was now adding to the growing list of beautiful and well known hymns in the English speaking world. In 1830 **Christina Georgina Rosetti** was born into a gifted family. Among the talented brothers and sisters of this attractive and gifted young woman were Dante Gabriel Rosetti, who was both poet and painter, and Maria Francesca.

Both Christina and Maria were devout Anglo-Catholics although they were opposed to the Church of Rome which had driven their father out of his native Italy. Offering their gifts on the altar of their faith they gave them back to the One from whom they came. Maria became a Bible class teacher and published *Letters to my Bible-class on Thirty-nine Sundays*. She entered the community of All Saints, Margaret Street, in London and died in 1876, eighteen years before her sister. Christina and Maria were both devoted to God; he was to them as a Heavenly Bridegroom, and their love for him was pure and spiritual. Christina wrote a poem 'The Master is Come and Calleth for Thee' in which the first verse runs:

> '*Who calleth? – Thy Father calleth,*
> *Run, O Daughter, to wait on him:*
> *He Who chasteneth but for a season*
> *Trims thy lamp that it burn not dim.*'

Amongst the beautiful and sensitive hymns which Christina wrote are 'Love came down at Christmas' and 'In the bleak mid-winter'. This last hymn, in particular, expresses a woman's understanding of the worship and love for Jesus as a babe. Christina did have a natural understanding and sympathy with the problems of women especially after working at the St Mary Magdalene Home for Prostitutes at Highgate for ten years. Whilst seeing women in Eve as bearer of children, the source of life, to Christina men became as Adam returning to dust and therefore the symbol of death.

Another hymn writer of this period was **Frances Ridley Havergal** born in 1836 near Bewdley in Worcestershire, the daughter of a musical clergyman who brought Frances up after her mother had died when Frances was twelve. She was close to her mother and continued to remember her throughout her life with the prayer her mother had given her: 'O Lord, prepare me for all that thou art preparing for me'.

Frances went first to school in England and then to a school in Germany, where she met hostility towards her faith for the first time in her life. When she returned to England, having had her faith tested in this way, she committed her life to Jesus. She was confirmed when she was seventeen and had a deep spiritual experience at that time. It was then she wrote one of her better known hymns:

> '*O Thine for ever, what a blessed thing,*
> *To be for ever His, who died for me;*
> *My Saviour, all my life thy praise I'll sing,*
> *Nor cease my song, throughout eternity.*'

After she left school, she helped in the parish, taught in the Sunday schools and raised money for schools. In her teaching she often used verses and hymn tunes she had written and her best known hymn is, of course, 'Take my life and let it be'. This hymn was written when she was visiting Areley House where there were some others staying who were not Christians. She felt asked to pray, 'Lord, give me all in this house', and by the last night all those present had been converted. Frances was so happy that she spent much of the night composing the hymn, which she preferred to have sung to the tune *Patmos*. Among her many other hymns she wrote 'Who is on the Lord's Side?' Frances also became involved in missionary work, the YWCA and temperance movements before she died at the age of forty-three.

Born the same year as Frances, the niece of Charlotte Elliot, **Emily Elizabeth Steele Elliot** wrote the hymn 'Thou didst leave thy throne and thy kingly crown, when Thou camest to earth for me'. She died in 1897. And yet another of these later Victorian hymn writers was **Dorothy Gurney** who lived from 1858 to 1932 and wrote that most beautiful hymn 'O perfect love, all human thoughts transcending'.

In 1848, a young teacher, **Susan** Thomas, married the headmaster of her school, Alfred **Mowbray**. Ten years later, Alfred, a high churchman, opened a bookshop in Oxford to sell religious books and cards. By 1873, the firm had grown and another branch opened in London. Two years later, Alfred Mowbray died leaving Susan in charge of the business. Under her direction the firm flourished, publishing many books and cards and even framing pictures and making other ecclesiastical woodwork.

Susan developed the business with the help of her son, Edwin, but in 1897, he was found dead. By the time she was seventy, Susan felt that she ought to hand the business over to others and in 1903, the firm she had built up after her husband's death became a Limited Company. By then Susan's health was beginning to deteriorate and fifty-three years after helping her husband found the first Mowbray shop, Susan died. The name and publications are a fitting memorial to a remarkable woman.

Over in America, in 1832, **Hannah Whittall Smith** was born into a Quaker family in Philadelphia, USA. She suffered from depression and uncertainty in her faith as a teenager but when she was sixteen she came across the Brethren community and was converted. Soon after she met her husband who had become a Presbyterian at the same time as her own faith developed. In 1867 Hannah was studying the book of Romans and in the words 'we should no longer be slaves to sin' she gained an understanding of the spiritual victory which God has gained for us. The young couple arranged a series of interdenominational meetings to teach about this victory for all Christians. Hannah was also a founder member of the Women's Christian Movement and a member of the suffrage movement in America.

In 1872, because of her husband's poor health, the Smiths had to move to Britain where they continued their meetings. Hannah published her book *The Christian's Secret of a Happy Life* a few years later, this book being one of the inspirations for the founding of the Keswick Convention, an annual 'teach-in' on the holiness of life which continues to attract many people today. 'Faith ... is simply believing in God; and, like sight, it is nothing apart from its object. You might as well shut your eyes and look inside to see whether you have sight, as to look inside to discover whether you have faith. You see something, and thus you know that you have sight; you believe something, and thus know that you have faith.

For as sight is only seeing, so faith is only believing. And as the only necessary thing about sight is that you see the thing as it is, so the only necessary thing about faith is that you believe the thing as it is.'[24]

Hannah died at the age of seventy-nine after an illness about which she writes, 'Once my divine Master sent me on his errands, and I knew his will was good, and was happy in trying to do it. And now he has shut me up to an invalid life, and tells me to sit in my wheeled chair, and to be content to let others do his errands and carry on his work, and I know his will is good just the same, and am happy in trying to accept it'.[25]

Caring and healing

Abroad, **Adelaide Cini** was born in Valetta, Malta in 1838, the thirteenth child in a rich family. Despite her wealth, Adelaide was a very humble person always ready to help others. From an early age she dedicated herself to working amongst wayward girls and helping children from broken homes. She founded a Home for girls to learn how to read, write and become trained for their future lives of wives and mothers.

Adelaide set up the first Trade School in Malta where young girls and women could learn to sew and embroider professionally, using her family home in the village of St Venera. Her interest lay not only with professional training but also with the spiritual and material needs of her pupils. Although she died in 1885, the orphanage which still bears her name is a witness to her great love for God and for his daughters.

The birth of **Marie Bernadette Soubirous** in 1844 was very different from that of Adelaide. Bernadette was the eldest child of a poor miller in Lourdes and was considered slow and delicate but with a pleasant manner. She suffered from asthma, the effects of cholera and poor living conditions. On 11 February 1858 when she was just fourteen she had the first of a series of eighteen visions as she was playing and picking flowers by a shallow cave on the banks of a nearby river. In these visions she saw a very beautiful young woman who showed her a spring of water long forgotten, which immediately began to flow again. This young woman talked with Bernadette, making various requests and eventually identified herself as the Virgin Mary. Although others were sometimes present during these visions, no one else ever saw or heard anything.

The last vision occurred on 16 July 1858 and investigations were then made by both Bernadette's doctor and her priest into what had been happening. Many disbelieved Bernadette, saying she had either been making up the stories or had become insane but she was so insistent about her visions that the Roman Catholic authorities began to look into the matter.

Bernadette's life became very difficult, with some accusing her of being a cheat whilst others began to reverence her as a visionary and a saint allowing her little peace. She was never very well and began to suffer from the constant importuning of those who craved her attention or besieged her with questions. Her patience with others at this time and her simple trust shone through her life but eventually she entered the convent of the Sisters of Charity at Nevers in 1866.

Even there problems arose. She was very ill with asthma but saw her role in life as now to bear suffering through illness. When a church was built near the place of her visions, she was unable to attend the ceremony because of her frailty, for the pressure of people would have been too much for her.

After her death at the age of thirty-five, visitors began to arrive from all over the world to receive healing from the spring which flowed from the cave and there were many cures claimed. Again the Roman Catholic Church began to investigate and found some of these to be false claims, but others were not easily explained and it was recognized that many were true miracles of healing.

The place by the river bank where the young and simple girl had first seen Our Lady became a great place of pilgrimage and Bernadette was canonized in 1933 for her humble simplicity and religious trust in Our Lady and in God.

About the same time as the young Bernadette was declaring her simple faith in the countryside in France, **Mary Townsend** was becoming concerned about the young women of Britain. Mary became aware of the problems which beset many of these young women, particularly those young girls who had left the countryside to obtain domestic employment

in the towns. They were often made to work long hours for
low pay, threatened by being put in the workhouse if they lost
their jobs. So in 1875, Mary founded a society to help these
girls to learn more skills, the Girls' Friendly Society. Besides
continuing this work, the Girls' Friendly Society is now involved in industry, housing schemes and parishes.

Missionary work has always been supported by the Girls'
Friendly Society and among the earlier women to receive this
help from the Society was **Alice Marietta Marval**. Alice was
born in India in 1865 of mixed French and English blood. She
was a lively, bright and strong willed girl who adapted easily
to the constant moves which her parents made in her childhood. She was also thoughtful and compared the beauty of
the unspoilt flowers around her with the squalor of a poor
young Indian girl in the streets. Alice's mother pointed out
that whilst a gardener cared for the flower, the child had no-
one to love her.

This sort of incident no doubt encouraged Alice in her desire
to become a missionary and eventually she went to the Royal
Free Hospital in London to study medicine. While there her
brother died and she gave up her studies for a while before
continuing them in Edinburgh. There she helped to form a
branch of the Society of the Annunciation, which was a religious
guild for women students meeting for the purposes of Bible
Study and talks on spiritual subjects. Alice was very popular at
Edinburgh for her attractive personality and sense of humour.

After graduating Alice went to a hospital in Clapham,
working amongst the most poor and from there she joined Dr
Barnado working in one of his homes for the waifs and strays.

In 1901 Alice was sent out to Cawnpore by the Society for
the Propagation of the Gospel in Foreign Parts and there was
supported by the Girls' Friendly Society for work in a hospital
staffed only by women, to encourage the women to come for
treatment. The hospital had been opened two years before
and her work was with the poorest women and children.
While she was working there, there was an outbreak of the
plague from which many people died.

Alice was kept very busy looking after her patients both
inside the hospital and in the villages nearby. During all this
work she wrote constantly of her experiences asking for prayers
for her patients and teaching them about her faith.

During 1903 the number of plague cases increased, the vast majority of them fatal and Alice continued, busier than ever. In December she was visiting 246 patients in the city, most of them plague cases, and it was not surprising that she became ill herself on New Year's Day. Within a few days Alice had died of the plague which she had bravely fought so often in others.

Missionary work in Asia

Another missionary working out in India at about the same time was **Irene Petrie**. Irene was born in London around 1867 of well-to-do Scottish parents. She was presented at court and travelled in Europe but eventually began helping with Sunday school teaching in the Kensington area of London where she lived. She was an ardent church worker helping to train others in church work.

From her childhood she had been interested in missionary work in India and became involved with the Church Missionary Society Ladies' Union. Eventually in 1891 she decided to become a missionary herself and the following year set sail for Lahore. She lived and worked near the Cathedral in Lahore, working with both Europeans and Eurasians, learning Urdu to help her in her work. She loved the people of Lahore and particularly the Hindus but soon realized that she must move on, this time to Kashmir.

In Kashmir Irene was working with women who had not been allowed to share in their menfolks' religion and had suffered greatly from being dominated by the men. These women rejoiced in the opportunities that the Christian women opened up for them and loved to learn. Often Irene had to defend the women when men tried to oppose their new found opportunities even fighting for them in court at times. She not only taught the women and children but helped in the hospitals as well. The work was very tiring and in 1897, while on a visit to friends in Tibet, she became ill and died, mourned by a great number including her many friends in Srinagar and Kashmir.

While Louisa and Irene were involved in spreading the faith in India, in China another woman was helping her husband in his missionary work. **Louisa** Smyly was born in

1852 in Dublin into a family known for good works and evangelical religion. When she was twenty-four she married the Revd Robert **Stewart** and went with him as both wife and missionary to Foochow in China. She said she wanted to give her life to God to use in whatever way and wherever He pleased.

In China she opened a school to train local women to lead Bible study and this sort of training was taken up by others, particularly the Church of England Zenana Missionary Society. In 1890 the Stewarts moved with their seven children to Kucheng and they were living at a place called Hwasang in the summer of 1895 when the China-Japan war broke out.

In the resulting violence Robert and Louisa and two of their children were killed together with many others by a band of people who were against foreign missions.

Jessie Ransome had been a teacher at Leeds High School for over ten years when she followed a call to serve with the North China Mission in 1896. Having also had some medical training, she went to Peking to work at St Faith's Home, a mission centre for Chinese women and girls. There she had to start by learning Chinese which she found very difficult. After some months she was made a deaconess in the church hoping that before long some of her Chinese sisters would follow along this path. By 1898 her own sister and four Chinese women were admitted as deaconesses and she moved on to a mission-station in the interior where the work was more difficult because of strong opposition to Christianity. Many of the women thought that they would be killed if they became Christians but gradually Jessie won them over with patience and understanding.

Jessie continued teaching her people to read and about Christianity until, at the very end of 1899, one of the missionaries was murdered by the 'Boxers'. Five months later two more missionaries were killed in outlying places. The Chinese Christians were very afraid and the missionaries from abroad had to return to Peking where they were to stay with other foreigners in a state of siege for nine weeks. Many of the people were ill and Jessie helped in the hospital there. Throughout this time Jessie was sustained by her faith. Eventually the siege was relieved and the missionaries returned to their mission houses and began to build up the Church once more among the people. However Jessie was not to continue for very long in this work as she died of dysentery in October 1905.

Missions in Africa

David Livingstone, the explorer and missionary, married the daughter of Mary and Robert Moffat in the early years of the nineteenth century, but it was after hearing about his death in 1874 that **Mary Slessor**, one of the best known missionaries of this period became inspired to go to Africa. Born in 1848, the daughter of a drunken Scottish shoemaker and a strong mother who supported the family on her wages as a weaver, Mary started work herself when she was eleven. She continued to attend school until she was fourteen, when she worked all day, went to evening classes in the evening and spent every Sunday in worship.

Mary's conversion came through a fear of hell after a sermon preached at the local church but this changed into a desire to serve God as a missionary and when she was twenty-six she offered herself to serve in West Africa where she was sent to the unhealthy station of Calabar. From there Mary travelled even further into the interior, apparently fearless of the consequences that could arise. Her earlier experiences with a drunken father stood her in good stead at this point as drunkenness was rife among the peoples and Mary made it her particular care to help the women, particularly any who had given birth to twins who would normally have been left to die.

Mary was not prepared to abide by rules and regulations if they went against human caring even if they were those of the mission station, and knew that loving care and understanding of the local ways was the way to help the people and to bring them to a knowledge of the Lord she loved herself. Rather than imposing her faith from above as so many missionaries attempted to do, Mary lived with the people and shared their lives. Perhaps this is all too often a reflection of how women throughout the ages have brought the message of the Gospel to others, by showing their commitment to them rather than demanding an obedience and commitment from them.

In 1892 Mary, by then known familiarly as the 'Great

White Ma', was made the first Vice-Consul and exercised a loving and considerate justice among the local people. In the courts where she presided women knew that they would receive fair justice, something that could not always be guaranteed elsewhere.

In 1900 Mary went to one of the areas in the country where some of the fiercest Africans were carrying on a slave trade and exploiting their neighbours. There she established a hospital, the Mary Slessor Hospital, which she placed in the hands of other women while she continued her own missionary work. Mary died in 1915 and her name continues to be remembered to this day. Her lifetime's work was to help the poor and afflicted and to bring them to a knowledge of the love of God. In this she was doing the work which Christ had done before her and which many other women and men have done ever since, following his example.

Missionary work in Australia

Her way of loving was no different from other women such as **Daisy Bates** who went as a journalist to Australia in 1899 to investigate charges of cruelty to the aborigines and realised that the missionary ways of the Trappist monks with whom she stayed were those of imposing their faith rather than a sharing with them the love of Christ. While the men tried to bring the natives into the twentieth century, Daisy sat by their bedsides and listened to them. After tending one dying woman for eight weeks, Daisy wrote 'I sat beside her holding her hand. Suddenly she sat up in the firelight searching my face with troubled eyes. "Where am I going?" she cried in fear. In fear.... "My Father is sitting down where you are going, Jeera" I told her, "and as soon as I let go your hand, my Father will catch hold of it. He will take care of you until I come." "Your Father? Then I shall be safe," she said and settled down to sleep. I did not know she was dead until her hand grew cold in mine....

'I could have taught them prayers easily enough but I did not want parrot repetition.... I tried to give them the only Christianity I knew they understood which was nothing but loving kindness and an unfailing trust and example, example always.'[26]

Daisy lived alongside the aboriginal people, being with them in their fears and loving them, fighting against such evils as cannibalism but understanding them in a way that many of the men missionaries never even tried to do. Both Mary Slessor and Daisy Bates found that being a woman was a help in their work, protecting them against the hostility which the white men received and building up a trust with the local people which soon overcame any fear that they might have had in what could have been dangerous situations.

The ministry of women

It was during the Victorian age that changes in social life gave new opportunities to women both at home and abroad. Contraception and education meant they were beginning to feel that they had a place outside the confines of home life. Whilst some Protestant churches had allowed women to be preachers and ministers it was only towards the end of the nineteenth century that women in the more main-stream churches began to ask that their voices should be heard also.

In the Roman Catholic Church women could enter the monastic orders, giving up family life in order to devote themselves to the service of the Church. In Protestant Churches there began to be a decline in the numbers of those willing to offer themselves for ministry. Other professions were beginning to open their doors to women, albeit very slowly. Women were not only asking for the vote but were asking that their vocations to the wider ministry of the Church should be recognized and accepted, even vocations to the priesthood. Thérèse de Lisieux was one who felt so called. Some say that God called her to be a priest in heaven, as men would not allow it on earth for she died before reaching the age at which men may become priests. While the missionary women were bringing people to know the love of God in far away places, in France this young woman was witnessing to her great love for God.

Thérèse was born in 1873 in Alençon in northern France, the daughter of Louis and Zélie **Martin**. Her father was a watchmaker and both her parents had hoped to become members of religious communities. Instead they had married and had nine children of whom five daughters survived, all destined to enter convents. Thérèse's parents were deeply spiritual and this spirituality filled the whole of their lives giving themselves to help others in many ways. When Thérèse was only four her mother died, which must have greatly affected Thérèse who according to her own writings admits to being a very naughty child.

At the age of fifteen Thérèse entered the Carmelite convent of Lisieux in Normandy which had refused her on an earlier occasion. Following this earlier rejection she had been present at a Papal audience during which she begged to be allowed to enter the convent when she became fifteen and this was granted.

Thérèse's life was not spectacular, she lived and prayed in a simple way fighting her pride, obstinacy and moodiness. She also fought and lost a battle against tuberculosis and died at the age of twenty-four. During her lifetime she had written not only about her childhood but also the story of her thoughts and prayers, *The Story of a Soul*, which had a tremendous effect on everyone who read it. In one of her letters Thérèse wrote 'it is enough to realize one's nothingness, and to give ourself wholly, like a child, into the arms of the good God.'[27]

During her lifetime and after many people asked for her intercession prayers were answered and miracles happened. In 1925, twenty-eight years after her death, Thérèse Martin was canonized. Thérèse showed in her life that even the most ordinary person, however obscure or lowly, could become a saint by doing little things in a spirit of love for God. One of her favourite sentences from the Bible was 'Whosoever is little, let him come to Me'.

Many are the women who give their lives in witness to their love for God and for their neighbour. Some become well known but possibly the vast majority are never known outside their immediate family or community. 'Among the unrecorded Saints of the Church of Christ, there are hundreds of names of wives, widows and daughters . . . and of single women, who in obscurity have dedicated their lives and their substance to the promotion of the kingdom of God in our own country and in heathen lands.'[28]

One such saint whose witness was recorded was **Mary Ann Rogers** who married when she was young but was left a widow not many years later with two young children. She obtained work as a stewardess on passenger boats sailing from Southampton to the Channel Isles.

On Maundy Thursday 1899, she was on board the *Stella* which ran aground in fog off Alderney. Mary helped the other women to fix their life belts but became aware that there was one young woman who had not woken from sleep. After helping her Mary was about to enter the lifeboat when she realized that it was too full already and insisted that it go without her. She called out 'Goodbye' and as the boat sailed away Mary lifted her arms to heaven saying 'Lord, have me' as she sank into the water and was drowned. In offering her life in this way Mary was a true example of the many Christians who literally give their life that others might live.

The social Gospel

Some women like **Josephine Butler** gave their lives to helping others but in a different way. Josephine was born in 1828 the daughter of John Gey from Dilston in Northumberland, who brought up his children with a great social awareness and dislike of those who abused their power especially in such ways as the slave trade. Josephine's mother had been educated by the Moravians and was a warm and loving person whose concern for others she shared with her daughter.

Josephine was very aware of her own failure to be as good as she would have wished and longed for a closer communion with God. In later life she wrote 'Now the things which I believe, I had learned direct from God. I never sat at the feet of any man; I never sought light or guidance even from any saint . . . though I dearly loved some such whom I had known – nor on Churches and creeds had I ever leaned.'[29]

She married a clergyman, George Butler, who was first a tutor at Durham University and then moved on to Oxford. A short while later he became the first vice-principal of Cheltenham College and then principal of Liverpool College in 1865.

While they were living in Cheltenham the young couple lost their very much loved daughter through an accident when she fell over the bannisters while rushing to greet her mother who had been staying elsewhere for a short time. The grief and anger felt by Josephine caused her to go and look for someone with a pain deeper than her own. She went to call on a friend who asked her to visit a rescue home for girls that the friend had been caring for but was now too old to manage herself. This was the start of Josephine's caring for those who had been cast out by society because they had been abused by men who took advantage of them, men who were themselves very often the pillars of society.

Josephine felt a deep sympathy and sorrow for her women that they should have become the victims of sin, not only their own but that of others also. She became a dedicated social reformer who campaigned for the rehabilitation of prostitutes. These prostitutes were tolerated although restricted by law but the legislation was discriminatory, punishing the prostitutes only and not their clients. Josephine fought for these women, feeling for each one as an individual, a soul for whom Christ had died. She was stoned, reviled and persecuted for their sake as she continually called on men to give up their own sinful ways, pleading at political meetings for people to vote so that the laws would be repealed for 'they subjected a certain section of the feminine population to slavery and gave State sanction to masculine immorality.'[30]

'Her belief in Christ as the saviour of these and all women was expressed in a letter she wrote to a friend. You remember how sweet and lovely Jesu always was to women, and how He helped their women's diseases, and how respectful He was to them, and loved them and forgave the sins of the most sinful. And He was born of a woman – a woman only – no man had any hand in that!'[31]

'Whilst she was fighting, she was ostracized by many in society, including church-men and women. She never spared herself in the fight for the sick and suffering, the deprived and abused and often spoke out against that form of organization which prevented right being done because it was against the ordered lives which men had created for themselves. Seek men and women first, before any machinery. If you have not got them, seek the breath of that wind which will breathe upon the dry bones, and make them live and spring to their feet. Beware of thinking that organization is the first and most important thing . . . that good statutes, rules, a sound financial basis, a regular income are needful, before you can make any effectual attack on an enemy which is daily and hourly murdering souls and bodies.'[32]

It was after nearly twenty years of hard fighting that the Act of Parliament was repealed in 1883. Josephine always knew throughout this time that God was in control and organised prayer meetings to ensure this including a twelve hour prayer vigil before the actual debate. 'It was a sight I shall never forget. At one meeting there were the poorest, most ragged and miserable women from the slums of Westminster on their knees before the God of Hosts with tears and groans pouring out the burden of their sad hearts. He alone knew what their burden was. There were women who had lost daughters; there were sad-hearted women; and side by side with these poor souls, dear to God as we are, there were ladies of high rank, in their splendid dresses – Christian women of the upper classes kneeling and also weeping. I thank God for this wonderful solidarity of the women of the world before God. Women are called to be a great power in the future, and by this terrible blow which fell upon us forcing us to leave our privacy and bind ourselves together with our less fortunate sisters, we have passed through an education – a noble education.'[33]

Josephine's faith in God, together with her deep spiritual life, gave her the patience to wait on him even when things were at their worst. A great fighter all her life against the wrongs of society, Josephine died in 1907.

The Mothers' Union

Born in the same year as Josephine Butler, **Mary Sumner** helped women to live fuller lives in a different way. Mary was born on New Year's Eve, 1828 at Swinton, near Manchester. Her parents were both rich and well educated and Mary had a very happy childhood being encouraged to join in with all that her brothers did both in schooling and play. When Mary was three, the family moved into the house in Hope End in Herefordshire which had previously belonged to the father of Elizabeth Barrett Browning. Mary had a number of foreign governesses and her father taught her mathematics. She was also very musically gifted and was brought up as a devout Christian.

When Mary was eighteen while on holiday in Rome she met George Sumner, the youngest son of the Bishop of Winchester, who was soon to be ordained and the two immediately fell in love. George became curate at Crawley and the following year, after George was priested, they married and began what was to be a long and happy partnership. Shortly after their wedding, George's mother died and the young couple moved into Farnham Castle where George became his father's chaplain. In 1851 George was given the living of Old Arlesford where their home is now used as a Diocesan Retreat House.

Mary was like every other new young mother in her awareness of how little she knew about caring for her children and bringing them up in the Christian faith. As Rector's wife she visited the sick, taught in the Sunday school and even arranged meetings for men in the rectory on Sunday evenings when Evensong was at the daughter church. There she led Bible studies and encouraged the men to share in the caring for their children. 'But all the while she dreamed of the day when women all over the world could be bound together, working towards the same ends, living by the same beliefs, warm in a sense of unity of purpose.'[34]

In 1876, after her children had grown up and left home and soon after her daughter had given birth to her own first baby, Mary held a meeting for the mothers of Old Arlesford at the rectory. Mary lost her nerve when the mothers arrived and had to ask her husband to take the meeting. The next week the mothers returned and Mary overcame her nerves. The mothers began to meet regularly and membership cards were printed with the words: 'Remember that your children are given up, body and soul to Jesus Christ in Holy Baptism and that your duty is to train them for His service'.

In 1885 Mary and her husband moved to Winchester following his appointment as Canon of the Cathedral. Later that year the Church Congress met in Portsmouth and Bishop Ernest Wilberforce, who was a friend of the Sumners, was to be the principal speaker at a meeting about women. The Bishop realized that he had little to tell the women present from his own experience and as Mary was sitting close by he asked her to speak herself. She was reluctant to do so as it was not usual for a woman to speak at a public meeting but the Bishop encouraged her.

Mary spoke of the role that she felt women could play in

raising the moral character of the country and the opportunities that Christian mothers had for bringing up children in faith and prayer. 'She told the audience that wives and mothers had tremendous work to do for their homes; their husband, their children. All women, no matter what class, what age, could unite in prayer for the home and to try to work for God.'[35]

'She suggested that the mothers form a mothers' union, based on prayer, and the following day the Winchester Diocesan Mothers' Union was set up with Mary as its President. Soon it was expanding through the dioceses and within two years seventeen other dioceses were involved. By 1888 the Mothers' Union Journal was being printed with articles that all could read and understand. Eight years later a headquarters had been established in London and the Mothers' Union moved into the present house, named after its founder, in 1925.

'Mary and her husband, now Bishop of Guildford, celebrated their diamond wedding in 1908 but George was to die the following year. In 1916, when she was approaching her nineties, Mary resigned as Diocesan President of Winchester. She continued to speak at meetings for another two or three years and she died peacefully at Winchester in 1921.

'Mary wrote the following prayer and probably used it every day:
All this day, O Lord, let me touch as many lives as possible for thee; and every life I touch, do thou by thy Spirit quicken, whether through the word I speak, the prayer I breathe, or the life I live. Amen.'

The wife of another cleric who was also active in helping women in a different way was **Henrietta Octavia Barnett** whose husband was vicar of Whitechapel and later Canon of both Bristol and Westminster. He saw in Henrietta an ability which was greater than his own and gave her every support. Together with Octavia Hill, Henrietta began to help the poor through good housing management and she also founded the Children's Country Holiday fund to encourage town children to learn something about the country. Working with her husband, who became the warden, she encouraged the setting up of Toynbee Hall, supported by Cambridge University students, about which she was later to comment, 'It must not be forgotten that at that time men, young men, intellectual men, had but recently joined the ranks of the philanthropists, the care of the poor, the children and the handicapped had hitherto been left to women.'

A contemporary book describes Henrietta in the following way: 'The names of the offices she holds show something of the range of her activities. She is Vice-president of the National Association for the Welfare of the Feeble-minded and Director of the Garden Suburb Company, and has been Vice-president of the National Union of Women-Workers and Hon. Secretary for the Hampstead Heath Extension Council, while she was on the committee which founded the Whitechapel art Exhibition, and has been a promoter of Homes for Workhouse Girls. As a lecturer on Poor Law and on questions of Social Reform, Mrs Barnett is thorough, interesting and convincing. The very hearty reception she met with at the recent Church Congress (1907), when she spoke on the Ethics of the Poor Law, shows the importance attributed to her views on the scientific treatment of poverty by those Churchpeople who are most anxious for the extension of the Church's usefulness and most desirous that religion shall dignify and direct all of social political as well as of individual life.'[36] A truly formidable woman!

The Woman's Bible and poetry

That women could lead Bible studies as well as men was no longer being disputed as it had been in Susannah Wesley's day, but it was not until 1895–8 that **Elizabeth Cody Stanton** produced a woman's interpretation of the Bible called *The Woman's Bible*. Elizabeth was an American who had been involved in the suffragette movement and had also attacked the legal position of married women in America.

Although the contribution that women were able to give in the service of their Lord was becoming more acceptable in some circles, discrimination against women continued to exist as it still does a century later.

One who was to experience this discrimination in later life was **Alice Meynell** who as Alice Thompson was a very bright young girl born in Barnes in 1847 but living much of her childhood in Italy where her father rented a house. By the time she was fifteen the family had settled in Bonchurch on the Isle of Wight and there she was confirmed into the Church of England, the start of a spiritual pilgrimage which was to take her into the Roman Catholic Church.

Her frustrations at the restrictions placed upon her as a young woman are spelt out in a piece from her diary written in 1865: 'Answer O World, man-governed, man-directed, answer for the sanity of your laws and your morals. Of all the crying evils in this depraved earth, aye, of all the sins of which the cry must surely come to Heaven, the greatest, judged by all the laws of God and of Humanity is the miserable selfishness of men that keeps women from work.'

In 1868, whilst with her mother in Malvern, Alice became a Roman Catholic. For her it was the path of submission, self-discipline and moral guidance that she needed. Her bondage to the Church was not that of slavery but of voluntary obedience. She became very close to the priest who had received her into the Roman Catholic Church after their friendship deepened through correspondence exchanged between them, but in 1877 she married Wilfrid Meynell.

Both the Meynells were already involved in writing by this time and Wilfrid became the Editor of the *Weekly Register*, a Roman Catholic ecclesiastical periodical. Alice wrote much poetry and also contributed to papers and journals besides doing book-reviews and translation work. The writers Francis Thompson, George Meredith and Coventry Patmore were all great admirers of her and became close friends of the family. At times she would help Francis in various ways including writing to him on such matters as his difficulty in reconciling belief in a merciful God with belief in Hell.

She continued to uphold the woman's point of view when in 1912 she supported the suffragettes and was prepared to write to *The Times* in order to support the idea of women and men doctors working together in response to a letter deploring this. Discussion took place in 1913 as to who would be the next Poet Laureate after Alfred Austin and Alice's name was frequently mentioned, but in the end Robert Bridges was chosen. Alice was to bring up seven children in a close and loving family. She was admired by many who knew her, not least for her deep faith which shows itself in the following verse from her poem 'Christ in the Universe':

'*Of His earth-visiting feet*
None knows the secret, cherished, perilous,
The terrible, shamefast, frightened, whispered, sweet,
Heart-shattering secret of His way with us.'

The fight against poverty

Alice died at the age of seventy-five having led a comfortable life, but though many lived in comfort there was much poverty about even in Europe and there were many in the churches who fought against this poverty, helping wherever possible to alleviate it. Amongst these was **Ersilia** Bragaglia, an Italian women who married a minister, Riccardo **Santi**, in Bologna. After their marriage they both began work for the American Methodist Church in Naples.

Living near the little church which was in a very poor part of Naples, the Santis shared what little they had with those who came to the church. Ersilia helped to teach at the church where love was preached on Sundays and practised throughout the week as the church became a social centre for the neighbourhood.

On one of his birthdays Riccardo was out visiting when he came across two small children begging him to buy matches from them. They explained that their father was dead and that they slept with their mother in the railway tunnel at Naples Station. Riccardo immediately knew he had to take them home where Ersilia reluctantly welcomed them because she had barely enough food for two and they would have to share a bed with their own children. These two children were the start of many with whom they shared their home and when Vesuvius erupted in 1906 Ersilia kept open house and table to all who asked for food and shelter. Ersilia was gifted musically and spent much time teaching her enlarged family to sing and play the piano.

Although she was herself a Methodist, Ersilia's doors were open to anyone who knocked regardless of church, faith, or situation in society. Her outlook was ecumenical long before ecumenism became fashionable. She was an example of one who serves Christ however costly that service may be, however disruptive to family life in the greater interests of the whole Christian family.

While Ersilia was helping all who came to her in Italy, others were giving similar help elsewhere. Not least in this work of proclaiming the Gospel in word and deed were the members of the Salvation Army. One of the best known women in the Salvation Army was **Catherine Booth**, the wife of William Booth, the leader of the Salvation Army. Born in 1829 Catherine was an excellent preacher who drew the crowds to listen partly because she was a woman. Her husband appreciated her gifts and valued what she had to give in their joint ministry. Her own thoughts on women in ministry were very positive. Not only did she silence criticism of women becoming officers in the Army by saying that souls have no sex but she also wrote: 'Who can tell what God can do by any man or woman, however timid, however faint, if only fully given up to him.'[37]

Referring to Mary Magdalene's call to tell the message of the Resurrection to the disciples Catherine declared, 'Oh, glorious privilege, to be allowed to herald the glad tidings of a Saviour risen! How could it be that our Lord chose a woman to this honour? Well, one reason might be that the male disciples were all missing at the time. They all forsook him and fled. But woman was there, as she had ever been, ready to minister to her risen, as to her dying, Lord. . . . But, surely, if the dignity of our Lord or his message were likely to be imperilled by committing this sacred trust to a woman, he who was guarded by legions of angels could have commanded another messenger; but, as if intent on doing her honour, and rewarding her unwavering fidelity, he reveals himself first to her; and, as an evidence that he had taken out of the way the curse under which she had so long groaned, nailing it to his cross, he makes her who had been first in the transgression first also in the glorious knowledge of complete redemption.'[38]

Catherine supported Josephine Butler, a great friend, in her fight to help the prostitutes and against the trafficking of young girls. When she died of cancer in 1890 the Salvation Army celebrated the release of their 'Mother' to heaven with a great funeral in which all wore white. Though Catherine and William helped to establish the Salvation Army, in the example of a lesser known life the story of many a Hallelujah Lassie can be told.

Born in the Welsh valleys in 1836, the daughter of a

blacksmith, **Pamela Shepherd** was soon caught up in the terrible events which were to affect Welsh politics for many decades. The miners and ironworkers were rioting against the harsh conditions which many of their employers were imposing on them and Pamela's father was himself involved in the Chartist Riots. In 1842 he was asked by his neighbours to speak for them at a select committee in Westminster and three years later he was forced to move to London permanently to obtain work as he was now considered a trouble-maker back in the valleys.

Although Pamela's father did find work much of the money he earned went on drink and Pamela herself no longer went to school but worked as a child nurse. Although a native Welsh speaker she had by now become used to speaking English, but she still longed for the hills and countryside of Wales and the time when her father was a respectable blacksmith instead of a drunken shipworker.

In 1860 Pamela married and within a year a baby was on the way, but by then her husband was in prison for drunkenness. Life in the poorer parts of London was very harsh in those times, as people were starving and often in debt. There was a great deal of violence and drunkeness and many took their own lives. During the cholera epidemic of 1866, many thousands died despite the hard work of such people as Lizzie Garrett Anderson. Pamela tried to keep going by taking in washing but life was by no means easy especially as her husband had now left her. She began drinking herself and one day decided there was no future for her anymore and that the only thing left was to take her own life. Rather than leave her two small daughters behind to suffer she took them with her to the river where, with irons in her pocket, she intended holding the two little ones as together they sank in the dirty waters. Despite a lingering faith which told her this was wrong she was resolute that death was preferable to the life before her.

Suddenly a friendly voice called out from a house she was passing. It was a woman she knew from earlier days who invited her in to a warm kitchen where, with food and drink to strengthen her, Pamela shared her despair and stayed there. She soon found work again and one day called in at a place where members of the Christian Mission were talking of the need to offer oneself into God's hands. Eventually, in 1868,

Pamela came to realize that Jesus had indeed died for her and it was not long after that, that Pamela actually began to work for Catherine Booth.

By 1876 Pamela had become hallkeeper and cook at the Headquarters of the Mission in Whitechapel and assisted with the services. Two years later the Christian Mission changed its name to The Salvation Army. Meanwhile its mission work had been spreading and had reached Wales where several of the Army sisters were achieving success in bringing the Gospel to the valley people. Who better to send to join them but someone who was a Welsh speaker herself?

By then Pamela's family had grown and in 1878 she and her daughters made their way by train to the village of Talywain near Pontypool. Never before had a woman spoken to a crowd of drunken men in the streets of Aberdare. They were hostile towards this woman from London until suddenly she astounded them by defiantly challenging them in Welsh. By telling her own story of how she was saved from the squalor and decadence of drink and poverty by turning to Jesus she gradually won the people of the valleys round and they began to come to her meetings. Soon not only Pamela but also her daughter, Kate, were preaching and crowds were gathering to hear the 'Hallelujah Lassies' as they came to be known. They encouraged those who had been brought to Christ to tell their own stories. Despite a law having been passed ten years before, to stop women working in coal mines Kate managed to arrange to visit a mine so that she could see what conditions were really like for the men to whom she preached.

By 1879 the crowds listening to Kate had increased to several thousand and there was a religious revival beginning in the valleys with numbers attending churches and chapels increasing week by week. Amongst those who came to know Kate was one **Florence** Soper, born in 1861 and the daughter of a doctor in Blaina, who later married Bramwell **Booth**, the son of William and Catherine in 1882. In 1904 she was to write to a newspaper the following letter: 'As to my views on the part that women should play in the revival and in church work generally, I can only say in few words that women ought always to be well to the front in things pertaining to God and his Kingdom. In nothing has the influence of the

Saviour been more quickly felt by the world at large than in the new standard of womanhood which his influence has raised up.

'Woman, as the world knows her since Christ came and set her free, is a totally different being from the woman of old. Her influence, her position, her example, her responsibilities have all changed.

'There is a fitness about this, in view of the fact that woman was unquestionably ahead of man in her service and love when Jesus was on earth. Women played a great part in most of the important events of His life. When in his direst straits, the men forsook him and fled, the women were faithful. So far as we know, no woman who once joined Him forsook Him or drew back. In the Salvation Army, the principle is maintained that woman has an equal share with man in the service of God. "There is neither male nor female in Christ Jesus." '[39] In these thoughts Florence was reflecting the stance of her mother-in-law.

The Salvation Army has always been at the forefront of those Christian organizations who used women to do the work of Christ and there is no doubt that it was women like Mother Shepherd, as Pamela was known, and her daughter, Kate, who were greatly instrumental in bringing the Revival to the Welsh Valleys. This is ironic when women deacons of the Church in Wales are still struggling a century later to be accepted as equals even to their male equivalents in the diaconate.

The women continued in their work in South Wales but it was not always easy. Despite the effect of the Revival on crime sometimes even the police turned against them and occasionally they were imprisoned for holding meetings in the street. Pamela herself moved on to Gloucester and then to Portsmouth but she eventually returned to the Welsh valleys and died in Aberdare, where she had begun her mission, at the grand old age of ninety-four. All Aberdare turned out to watch as Mother Shepherd's body was escorted through the streets from her cottage to the largest chapel in the town with six police officers acting as bearers. Pamela did not possess great learning, 'but was full of the grace of God. From God's grace emerged the grace of willingness, the grace of loyalty, the grace of fidelity and the grace of perseverance.'[40]

Pamela's story is an example of the difficult life that many who are called to serve God have to undergo before they rejoice in the sure knowledge that they can freely bring others to know God's forgiving Love. Her life reflects that of many women who have served in the Salvation Army and elsewhere, for the greater glory of God and for love of their neighbour.

The fight against abuse

The exploitation and abuse of women and young girls has been present throughout the ages and those martyrs who died rather than lose their virginity to rapists and pillagers in the early days of the Christian Church were only the forerunners of those women who knew the love of God and the gift of eternal life would bring them greater joys than they would ever receive in their mortal lives. **Maria Goretti** was one such martyr who was canonized as a martyr for her purity.

Maria was born in Ancona, Italy in 1890 but her family moved after a while to live in the same house as her fathers' partner near Anzio. The partner had a son who found Maria very attractive and when she was only twelve he tried to attack her, threatening her if she refused his lustful desires. She managed to escape but by that time he had stabbed her fourteen times and she died the next day after expressing her forgiveness.

Another young girl who died in a similarly tragic way was **Laura Vicuna** who was born in Chile in 1891 to a rich and influential family. After civil war broke out, Laura's father died because of the difficult circumstances to which they were reduced. Her mother then decided to try crossing the border into Argentina, where she thought life might be happier for her and her two small daughters. There she met a man who attracted her because he was very wealthy, despite the fact that he drank heavily and had a violent temper. She agreed to become mistress of his estate thinking that this would provide a suitable home for her two daughters.

Laura and her sister were sent to a boarding school run by the Salesian Sisters where Laura joyfully came to learn more about the God she loved. She began to realize that the treatment her mother received and the way she lived her life was very wrong and tried to influence her to move away.

However her mother was happy enough with the life she was leading as mistress of the estate and would not leave.

Eventually the owner of the estate began to show an interest in Laura who was beginning to grow into a beautiful young girl. He tried to get Laura on her own but she managed to evade him. He then decided to throw a party hoping to obtain her favours by choosing her to be his partner at the dancing but Laura refused and in his fury he turned her out of the house and whipped her mother in front of his guests.

Laura returned to school where after catching a cold she became very ill. Her mother took this opportunity to escape from the house where she now realized she was no more than a slave and went to care for her sick daughter. They found a small cottage in which to live where Laura's mother continued to nurse her sick daughter and there Laura told her mother about God's love for her.

One night the estate owner discovered where they were and bursting in on them said he was going to stay the night. Laura, who was still only thirteen, summoned up all her energy to tell him to go but he struck out at her with his whip beating her until she lay in a crumpled heap on the floor. She lived only long enough to forgive him and to tell her mother how much she rejoiced that she was now going home to be with both her heavenly Father as well as her earthly one. The two women received Communion together, Laura happy in the knowledge that she had given her own life to save her mother and bring her back to God.

And so with the stories of these two young girls the history of women in the Christian Church continues both to progress and yet to repeat itself. The eighteenth and nineteenth centuries were indeed times of development for women when their voices were beginning to be heard and their spirituality to make itself known in some of the most beautiful hymns and writing of that period. Perhaps one of the greatest advances of that time was in the spread of the social gospel in which women took a large part. There were many wrongs to be righted and abuses of power to be acknowledged.

Despite this 'the social gospel had its blind spots (at the beginning of the nineteenth century). The problems of black America hardly ever found notice by its leaders. . . . While Christians, and, sometimes, restless critics of Christianity, were working for women's rights and women's suffrage, which came to be assured through a Constitutional Amendment in 1917, the social gospel males not only did not speak up for women's rights. Many of them advocated the Victorian Home model of domesticity which called for women to stay at home and make their contribution to America and Christianity through domestic faithfulness.'[41]

The period described in this chapter was a very fruitful one generally for Christian women. In a report on the ministry of women by an eminent committee appointed by the Archbishop of Canterbury written in 1919 this contribution was recognized and valued. 'In a very large proportion of the parishes of England and Wales, during the last seventy years, under the different heads of district-visiting, Sunday-school teaching, Church music, parochial clubs, missionary societies, study circles, rescue and preventive agencies, besides the larger organisations represented by the Sisterhoods and the Deaconess Institutions, by The Girls' Friendly Society and the Mothers' Union, an extraordinary amount of good work has been quietly and unostentatiously, voluntarily and gratuitously, achieved by women.'[42]

At long last women were beginning to break out of the stereotype models into which men had set them, those of being mothers, virgins (preferably as members of religious orders), or whores. It could perhaps be said that it was this period which saw the growing possibility of women re-entering the holy orders of the Church from which they had been excluded for so long.

CHAPTER EIGHT

The Resurrection of Womanhood

'He is the Lord of lords and King of kings, and those with him are called and chosen and faithful.' (Revelation 17.14 RSV)

So THIS history of the contributions of women to the life of the Church and the service of God arrives in the present period, the last century of the second millenium, a century which has probably seen more change in the way of living than any previous period. As the millenium draws to a close so prophecies of the end of the world and the second coming of Christ increase. With the increased likelihood of an environmental or nuclear disaster an urgency arises which adds to the fears and apprehensions of many.

The voice of womanhood is heard more frequently and often stridently, reflecting the frustration of those who see women being treated equally as humans within the secular world while still considered second rate in the life of the Church. But women continue to serve God in whatever roles they are called to, roles which have not changed much over the years. They continue to serve God as martyrs, preachers, writers, in religious communities and as apostles in taking the message of the Gospel to the world around, a world by now both greater in known size and smaller because of its improved communications, so that action in one country increasingly affects and concerns people in many others.

Christian women of the twentieth century have continued their fight against social injustice. In Britain they were often seen in the battle lines of the suffragette movement demanding the right for all people to vote in a so-called democratic country.

After the difficulties of the last century when they asked to be allowed to receive public education, women in Britain were now beginning to take their place in the universities and the first woman lecturer in religion at Oxford University was appointed. Her name was **Evelyn Underhill**, a name well known in Church circles for she also became the first woman to give retreats within the Anglican Church.

The revival of spirituality and mysticism

Born in 1875 Evelyn came from a middle class family and was largely self educated. A great nature lover, she had started to write while she was still young. When she was thirty-two years old she experienced a religious conversion after which her devotion to God through Christian worship, prayer and mysticism grew enabling her to become spiritual counsellor and retreat conductor to many especially at the Anglican retreat centre at Pleshey, in Essex.

For Evelyn her faith came first in her life, even before family or professional responsibility. It is through Evelyn that many ordinary people have come to know the way of mysticism, the transforming power of God and the acceptance of the weakness of human nature. Because she was a woman, both lay and married, she was able to bring to the ordinary person an understanding of theological and spiritual topics which often the clergy with their narrow experience of life were not. In words which are just as telling now as when she originally spoke them nearly sixty years ago, she tells 'how some people may seem to us to go to God by a moving staircase where they can assist matters a bit by their own efforts, but much more gets done for them and progress does not cease. Some appear to be whisked past us in a lift; whilst we find ourselves on a steep flight of stairs with a bend at the top so that we cannot see how much farther we have to go. But none of this really matters; what matters is the conviction that all are moving towards God, and, in that journey, accompanied, supported, checked and fed by God. Since our dependence on Him is absolute and our desire is that His Will shall be done, this great desire can gradually swallow up, neutralise all our small self-centred desires. When that happens life, inner and outer, becomes one single, various act of adoration and self-giving; one undivided response of the creature to the demand and pressure of Creative Love.'[1]

She had a great ability to 'combine profound insight into
the deepest mysteries of the Faith with a sympathetic understanding of the practical difficulties which Christians must
encounter in their ordinary life. Her aim was simply to allow
Christ's truth and grace to shine more brilliantly into the
hearts and minds of all those who acknowledge him as Saviour
and Lord.'[2] Thus she wrote 'To say day by day "Thy Kingdom
Come" – if these tremendous words really stand for a conviction and desire – does not mean I quite hope that some day
the Kingdom of God will be established and peace and
goodwill prevail. But at present I don't see how it is to be
managed or what I can do about it. On the contrary, it
means, or should mean, "Here am I! Send me!", active costly
collaboration with the Spirit in whom we believe.'[3]

Evelyn's writings renewed an interest in mysticism, particularly in Julian, Teresa and other medieval women mystics,
which grew steadily throughout this century, a movement
which has recently developed even more widely. These women
constantly arose in her writings in such passages as "All the
earth doth worship thee" means what it says. The life, beauty
and meaning of the whole created order, from the tomtits to
the Milky Way, refers back to the Absolute Life and Beauty of
its Creator . . . Thus the old woman of the legend could boil
her potatoes to the greater glory of God; and St Teresa,
taking her turn in the kitchen, found Him very easily among
the pots and pans.'[4]

Evelyn inspired many through her writings, not only those
with whom she came in contact but also the many who
followed in her footsteps both in the universities and in the
mystical quest. She died in 1941 but, as with so many of these
women, her memory continues in the writings and work of
her life.

Dame **Laurentia McClachlan**, Abbess at Stanbrook
Abbey, took part of this renewal in mysticism as she initiated
a study of the great liturgy and music of earlier days researching the Gregorian chant and its use in Britain. In 1915 she
produced a book on plainsong and Stanbrook became renowned for its music under her inspiration.

Another outstanding women preacher from this period,
following in Evelyn's footsteps, was **Maude Royden** who was
born in 1876, the youngest child of a wealthy shipping owner

in Liverpool. Maude was born with dislocated hips and suffered from lameness throughout her life as a result. She went to Oxford where she was a student at Lady Margaret Hall and there she thought about becoming a Roman Catholic. When she left she began working amongst the poor of Liverpool, work which encouraged her to become a socialist and also a supporter of women's suffrage. She refused to believe that the Christ she worshipped would allow the denigration or patronising of women, seeing instead that none of what he said was addressed specifically either to men or to women.

When Maude left Oxford the parish she helped in was run by Hudson Shaw with whom she fell in love despite his being married. The relationship did not develop physically until after the wife died in 1944 when Hudson Shaw and Maude were married. Hudson Shaw encouraged Maude to lecture and address congregations and she became a pacifist and suffragette. She also became more involved with the Church and by 1915 realized that women would want to be priested. To the consternation of many she became a pulpit assistant with the Congregationalists and commented that 'the Church will never believe that women have a religious message until some of them get, and take, the opportunity to prove that they have. My taking it in a Nonconformist church will ultimately lead, I believe, to other women being given it in the Church of England.'[5]

Many people would come from a long way to hear her preach at the Guildhouse in Kensington for her theology was more concerned with caring for the souls than with doctrine; she had become a 'female shepherd'. A frequent broadcaster on religious topics, Maude died when she was eighty having contributed much to Church and society in so many ways.

Miina Sillanpää was a woman who also contributed much in her own country. She was born in 1866, the seventh out of the nine children of a Finnish farm worker at a time when Finland was part of Russia. She was brought up as a Christian, but could not go to school as she had to work from an early age. She learned to read and write from a peripatetic teacher but went out to work in a textile factory when she was only thirteen. Eventually she moved to Helsinki where she worked as a servant girl until 1899. There she began an employment agency for servant girls and hearing their experiences made her determined to help those who were being exploited.

Together with others she founded a home for them and started a union to fight for better conditions. Neither the work of a housewife nor that of a servant girl was considered to be real work, (Plus ça change . . .!) and many attacked this former servant girl who dared to question this attitude with scripture passages and speeches. She was a member of the Lutheran Church but was often very critical of the conservative faction in the Church who condemned her work as immoral.

By 1906 attitudes towards women were beginning to change in Finland and Finnish women were the first in Europe to have the right to vote. Miina was elected together with twenty other women to the 'unicameral' Parliament and became a Member of Parliament in 1912.

Miina and the other women members of the Social Democrats tried to introduce a bill for the protection of unmarried mothers, for many of the servant girls had become pregnant. It was however another forty years before the first home for unmarried mothers was opened. There are now eight such homes and these 'First Homes' as they are called are a lasting memorial to Miina.

Miina became the first woman minister in Finland with the honorary title of Economic Counsellor and was also called 'the greatest beggar in Finland' but her constant persistence in fighting for a cause that she knew to be right remained an example to all people, both men and women, even after her death in 1952.

The writer of the well known hymn 'Morning has broken', **Eleanor Farjeon**, was born in 1881 and morning did indeed break at that time with the last two decades of the nineteenth century seeing the birth of a number of remarkable Christian women. By the time Eleanor died at the age of eighty-four women were being regarded in quite a different light thanks to the persistence of these women in overcoming many obstacles.

The Suffragettes

One of the most persistent and best known Christian members of the suffragette movement was **Fedora Gadsby** who was born in 1884. Fedora went to France when she was seventeen but returned home a year later to look after her father and three sisters. At that time she helped a great deal with the flowers and altar linen of a church in Kentish Town and was a member of the Catholic Women's League attending their lectures and also studying psychology.

In 1907 she joined the suffragette movement led by Mrs Pankhurst and became fully involved in their meetings, selling their paper, *Votes for Women* and taking part in processions and poster parades where the women would wear poster boards as they paraded about the streets. They were made to walk in the gutter at least fifty feet apart by the police and Fedora took care to obey this because she did not want to break the law in case that would prevent her entering a convent in the future.

Although the Catholic Woman's Suffrage (now St Joan's Alliance) was formed in 1911, Fedora did not join it as she was then about to enter a convent but she always took a great interest in it. She became a Cenacle sister and eventually the Superior of the convent but she always retained a great interest in the rights of women until her death at the age of eighty-seven.

Some Auschwitz martyrs

Known too for her strong views about women's rights as a student **Edith Stein** was to die a martyr not so much for her Christian faith but for her Jewish blood. And yet it was her Christian witness within the darkness of her treatment by those who themselves came from a Christian background which earns her a place as apostle and martyr.

Edith was born in Breslau in 1891, the youngest of a large Jewish timber-working family. Though her father died young her mother, a practising Jew, carried on the timber business with energy and competence. Edith was a very gifted child who had rejected her faith by the time she was fourteen, saying 'I became conscious of prayer and gave up (the Jewish faith) of my own free will'. Edith studied German philology, history and psychology in Breslau, and then philosophy under Husserl in Göttingen. Edith fought hard for equal rights for women earning herself the nickname 'suffragette' among her student friends. She became involved in adult education running further education courses for female workers but in 1915 her studies were interrupted when she joined the Red Cross to train as a nursing auxiliary, working in an isolation hospital. In 1916 she completed her studies with a philosophical dissertation whilst working as assistant to Husserl in Freiburg and giving outstanding introductory lectures to students.

From these years as a student we can discern in the young Edith a passionate thirst for truth, for even her loss of faith did nothing to silence her questions about God. 'Whoever seeks truth, also seeks God, whether he knows it or not.' Meeting with Christian friends and studying the writings of Teresa of Avila led her to become a Christian and she was baptized into the Roman Catholic Church on New Year's day, 1922 at the age of thirty.

She became a teacher in a girls' Grammar School and then in a Dominican teacher training College. In 1932 Edith was appointed lecturer at the German Institute for Scientific studies in Münster but she lost this position the following year because of her Jewish origins. As any public appointment had now been made impossible for her by the coming to power of the National Socialists, she put into effect a plan which she had thought about for a long time; in 1933 she entered the Carmelite order in Cologne. There she became Sister Teresa Benedicta of the Cross.

In the face of Nazi persecution Edith was transferred from Cologne in 1938 and found refuge in Echt in Holland. After the invasion of Holland by the Germans the persecution caught up with her. In revenge for the local protest of the Roman Catholic Church at the Nazi persecution of the Jews in Holland, (Holland has always had a splendid reputation for kindness to its Jewish community) the Nazis arrested numerous Jewish converts to Christianity in July 1942. Among them were Edith and her sister Rosa who was also living in Echt at the Convent gate. They were transported to Auschwitz where Edith inspired many of her fellow victims. Her birthday fell on the Jewish feast of the Atonement, Yom Kippur, and Edith saw in this a sign of providence. As she was taken away by the Nazis she said to her sister 'Come, we will go, for the sake of our people'. She was probably put to death in the gas chambers on 9 August 1942. 'Her martyrdom was a witness to the fundamental decency of human nature in the face of its dark, bestial nature.'[6]

The deep shock felt by Christians at the crime committed against Jews by their fellow men, most of whom were baptized Christians, has led to Christians, new and old, to examine the Jewish roots of their own faith. So we may hope that Edith's parting words may be fulfilled as Jew and Christian, Israelite and German begin to be reconciled.

On 1 May 1987 Edith was beatified by Pope John Paul II in Cologne.

Jane Haining was also to die at Auschwitz for her Jewish connections. Born in Dumfries in 1897, Jane began work at J&P Coates in Paisley to which she travelled daily from Glasgow. She also helped at this time with the local Sunday school and began a missionary library. She became a member of the Jewish Mission Committee and decided then that her work was to be among the Jews. After a while, Jane trained at a college in domestic science and when she was thirty-five, having become fluent in Hungarian, became matron of the popular school, known as the Girls' Home of the Scottish Mission in Budapest where there were many Jewish girls.

Although she was in Scotland in the summer of 1939 when the war broke out she returned to Budapest to help her girls, particularly the influx of Jewish ones who had come from all parts of Europe. She was ordered home in 1940 by her Church but she stayed on because she felt there was no risk. Again ordered to return to Scotland or else to go to Palestine she refused because she felt the children needed her support where she was.

By the spring of 1944, the Nazis had taken possession of Hungary and life for the Jewish community became much harder. They had to wear the Star of David on their clothes and Jane helped her girls to sew this on, weeping as she did so at the cruelty of human beings. That May Jane was taken by the Gestapo to Fö-utca prison where she was charged with working among the Jews, crying as she sewed their Star of David badges on, dismissing an Aryan housekeeper, listening to the BBC, receiving British visitors, visiting British prisoners of war, sending them food parcels and being active in politics. She was taken to Auschwitz where she died in hospital barely two months later.

The work of the Salvation Army continues

Born in 1883 **Catherine Bramwell Booth** lived through two
world wars and lived to be over a hundred years old. Catherine
was the daughter of Bramwell Booth and Florence (née Soper –
see p. 209) and the granddaughter of Catherine and William
Booth, the founders of the Salvation Army. Because of the nature
of the work her parents did in the Army Catherine travelled to
France when she was less than a year old with her mother and no
doubt was in her own way being used in spreading the Gospel
even then. She was soon back in London and by the time she was
in her teens became committed to Army work after terrible times
of doubt and having, as she said, 'met with the Devil'.

After becoming a cadet and then a soldier, in 1914 Catherine was made Major in the Salvation Army, teaching others
how to address meetings and deal with social problems and
getting to know all her cadets personally. In 1924 she went to
headquarters in London to take charge of European affairs as
'Under Secretary for Europe' and then ran the 'Women's
Social Work' section. By 1946 Catherine had become International Secretary for Europe helping also with international
relief work and she retired in 1948 at the age of sixty-five.

Her retirement was busily spent in writing a book about
her grandmother and she received many awards including a
CBE, a Best Speaker of the Year Award and the Humanitarian
of the Year Award by the Variety Clubs International. On
her 100th birthday it was said that 'she had accomplished a
century of service to the Lord whom she loved'.

Marie Rafajova was also a member of the Salvation Army
in the early part of the twentieth century. Born in 1896 in
Brno to a Presbyterian family Marie devoted her life to service
in nursing homes and writing spiritual poetry which not only
declared her own faith but also attracted others to find faith.
Whilst many in the Arts world considered her poetry to be
amongst the best contemporary work, she also served with the
Salvation Army in their social and evangelistic work. Marie's
life was sacrificial, dedicated to the one, true, eternal and
living Saviour. She described the revolution which Jesus
caused in her life in a canticle where 'the eternal Word, that
stood silent at the Earth's cradle and rocked it in cosmic
nebula . . . has addressed me in human voice today'.

The core of Marie's writing was always the love of Christ
for all the suffering people to whom she spoke in words which
both comforted and roused. It bears witness to the gentleness
of her approach to those whom she served – the wretched, the
wrecked and the lost. Her poetry talks to the souls who strive
to return to a life filled with love and human dignity, transformed by a new piety which arouses them from the barren
secularized life in the large metropolis of today.

Marie witnesses to the sacrifice of Jesus Christ, which awak-
ens human hearts to serve and follow Him: 'Speak, my Lord,
speak that I may, under the strokes of Thy words, pour out
the happiness in the gems of tears like a rock in the desert,
and clear up the world ashen with sin.'

The love of her country and her wide understanding and
active participation in the struggles of the age culminate in
the glorification of the work of Christ, the ever living Lord.

Marie wrote poems, letters and stories in Czech and in
Slovak. Her warm heart was filled with resolution and tender
love, showing the discipline of a daily renunciation of the
world in order to grasp the love of Christ. She saw the love of
God our Saviour and His Eternal Word of Truth revealed on
this earth in people, in works and in countries and creation.

A healing path

Helen Waddell also began life as a Presbyterian. Born in
Japan in 1889, the youngest of ten children of a missionary
family, Helen was only three when her mother died. Her
father was open in his faith and had little time for those who
showed sectarian prejudice. He taught the young Helen himself and was obviously an able teacher. Her first memories
included seeing her father walking up and down singing the
psalms in Hebrew, reciting the New Testament in Greek and
the Lord's Prayer in Japanese.

By the time Helen was eight she used to sit in a tree where
she would recite the whole book of Hebrews by heart, at the
same time looking out through the green leaves thinking
about the resurrection of the dead, 'How could a woman have
her dead restored to her?'

After a while her father married again, this time to a cousin
who was not an easy person. Helen drew very close to her

elder sister and her brothers, particularly her young brother Billy with whom she went on adventures at night to the shrine of the goddess of mercy to pray for the gift of a white rabbit, preferably with a pink nose! However when Helen was eleven her father became very ill and he died less than a year later. Helen was very upset and all she could do to relieve her grief was to read and to think.

She went to Victoria College in Belfast where she rebelled against the punitive, small minded, sectarian God that she encountered around her. With great daring she went into the Roman Catholic cathedral one day and made the sign of the cross finding with relief that no thunderbolt struck her down! Helen went on to Queen's University, Belfast, and she had intended continuing her academic life in London, having been offered a research scholarship, but decided to turn it down to look after her stepmother who was by now very ill and very difficult.

The next decade was full of tragedy for Helen, for her favourite brother. Billy, drowned after a lost fight against drugs; another brother George, died of a heart attack a few days after being ordained; and an appointment at Queen's University fell through because it was decided not to appoint a woman when there was a suitable man available. This was a great blow to her as she needed the money.

Helen's sister, Meg, was married with a family and living at Banbridge and Helen would often visit her there, taking presents for the children and telling them stories. Caring for her stepmother made this period particularly difficult but spiritually Helen was moving along a pathway to God. It appeared to her as if she was climbing a steep hill and having come to a soft grassy patch she would walk along it until suddenly she would encounter a valley of dry bones.

After her stepmother died in 1920 Helen went to Oxford where she took the University by storm. In 1923 she was awarded a travelling scholarship and went to Paris where she became immersed in the world of the Middle Ages. She studied the story of Abelard and Heloise and eventually she worked so hard that she finished up ill in hospital where she felt the experience of actually being Heloise as an old abbess, entering into the mind of the woman who had never ceased to love Peter Abelard.

Helen was a celebrity now, mixing with politicians and royalty, but she also became a more humble person in herself. She began to use the money she received from her studies of Heloise and Abelard to help others, buying a house for orphaned children in Primrose Hill in London. Helen also helped her elder brother who suffered from drink problems but she sent him money only out of a sense of duty rather than from the generosity of her nature with which she gave plentifully to beggars.

Helen's final years were a time of consolidation in her faith. She saw death as being a gateway to life and beyond death was the love which called to her to follow and which she felt she had so often failed to do in this life. She would look at the Crucifix, her eyes filling with tears as she gazed on Christ crucified. It was about this time that she wrote in a letter to her sister 'I believe that cry, "Let this cup pass from me" was the last knife-edge pinnacle of human dread of anguish at Calvary . . . I think we harp far too much on Christ's Godhead, make things too easy for him that way. I believe in the Incarnation, but I believe that it was a real incarnation – that the temptations to short cuts in the wilderness were real temptations, that he was in a sense walking in the world with bandaged eyes, like the rest of us, and that he had to spend those long nights praying, to feel for the hand of God to guide him.'[7]

Helen died in 1965 after a life following a path which had not been easy but she had trodden it with her eyes directed towards God and feeling for his hand. He was the God whom she had come to love – not the God she had encountered in her childhood in Belfast but a warm and loving God who was generous to her as she was in her turn warm and loving in her generosity to others.

Born the same year as Helen, **Dorothy Kerin** grew up a happy child with her sister and three brothers until her father died when she was twelve. The shock of his death made her ill and when she was fifteen she went into hospital with diptheria. She had still not fully recovered when she returned home after convalescence and remained an invalid having by then contracted tuberculosis. By the end of 1911 her condition had worsened and she became unconscious and blind due to the tubercular meningitis from which she was now suffering. On

18 February 1912 the family, expecting her death at any moment, were gathered round her bed. As they watched and prayed Dorothy suddenly announced that she had heard a voice telling her that her sufferings were now over and she must get up and walk.

Despite the fact that she had eaten no solid food for several weeks Dorothy got up and walked to her stepfather's room and soon after sat down to a meal of cold beef, pickled walnuts and coffee. Her condition increased dramatically and in the morning Dorothy, who the previous day had been wasting away, greeted her doctor as a plump and smiling girl. Many people, including other doctors, were witness to this miracle.

Dorothy felt that her own restoration to health was in order to take a message of healing to the world. She was filled with a Christ-like love which transformed her and God's healing love poured out from her. Dorothy wrote 'In my restoration to health, I have been entrusted with a message to the whole world, a promise of healing to the sick, comfort to the sorrowing and faith to the faithless. This message is for everybody as soon as they are ready to accept it and have the desire.'[8]

As with other women mystics, Dorothy experienced many physical and psychological disorders such as headaches, stomach disorders and even depression but there were also many signs of God's favour too. In December 1915 she received the wounds of the Stigmata, to which several were witnesses, including the Bishop of South Tokyo. Dorothy often had visions including seeing the Holy Family at Bethlehem and at other times was very aware of the presence of the devil. One Good Friday she spent the whole day in prayer in chapel during which time she experienced the whole of the Passion.

Dorothy lived with Dr and Mrs Langford-James for several years in a period of withdrawal from the world. She then went to live in Ealing with her mother and younger brother where an opportunity arose to rent a house which she could open as a home of healing. She saw it as a place where she could 'harbour the weary in spirit; shelter the sheep that had temporarily lost their way from the fold of faith; and it could be a place of rest for those convalescing.'[9] Every time Dorothy made a purchase she did it in faith with little money to hand. From the time that Dorothy first opened the doors of her

Home of Healing in Ealing, many miracles of healing occurred there.

During the Second World War Dorothy adopted nine babies who were always well cared for. In 1946 they all moved to Speldhurst in Kent and there a new chapel was built. The house at Speldhurst became a Nursing Home when Dorothy moved to Burrswood in nearby Groombridge two years later. In 1959 Dorothy had a vision of a church standing in what was then the rose garden and, with her usual obedience to what she felt was the will of God, she arranged for the building of the Church of Christ the Healer. Although many healings took place in that church, Dorothy also visited many who were sick and asked for healing. She also travelled to Europe and America to give talks about her work. There is no doubt that it was the work of this remarkable woman as an instrument of God which helped to revive the ministry of healing in this century, a ministry which continues to be much needed. Dorothy died in 1963 but the ministry which she initiated still continues as does the Burrswood Home of Healing.

Helping the young

Born the same year as Helen and Dorothy, **Olave** married Robert **Baden-Powell** in 1908 soon after he had started the scouting movement. When girls began to join their brothers in the scouts the Guiding movement was formed and eventually Olave became the World Chief Guide. She shared her birthday with her husband and this day, the 22 February, is remembered by Guides as Thinking Day, a day when Guides think of other members of their world wide movement. Olave died in 1977 after a lifetime of inspiration to many young girls.

Only a couple of years younger than these remarkable British women, two other women grew up elsewhere, one in Alsace, the other in Russia. **Suzanne de Dietrich** was born in Niederbronn into a family of industrialists and became both an engineer and a theologian. She played an important role both internationally and nationally in both youth movements and ecumenical matters, contributing much to the renewal of Bible study. Suzanne was a true pioneer and also displayed extraordinary courage in overcoming her own frailty towards the end of her life.

Earlier this century it was rare for a woman to do well as a student of engineering but, in order to join her family firm, Suzanne began a four year course in 1909 throughout which she shone. However after she had finished her course the war intervened to give a new direction to her life to the benefit of the Church.

Suzanne was among the pioneers in Bible scholarship and the ecumenical movement. Whilst studying engineering in Switzerland Suzanne had met groups of Christian students dedicated to being Christian witnesses at their universities. In 1914 when there was general mobilization it seemed natural to ask her to ensure the continuity of the French Federation of Christian Associations of Students. Throughout the war years and until the thirties she continued this work, at the same time developing her vocation in interpreting the Bible. The service of young people was a major factor in her life for nothing was more important to her in educating them for active life than for them to enter a living relationship with the Word of God, so offering a demanding and liberating challenge for the lives of both individuals and nations.

Suzanne continued to carry the personal responsibility for the French Federation in the Second World War and between 1935 and 1946 she also worked as Secretary of the world-wide Federation of Christian Associations of Students.

The second area of her life was in La Cimade, an ecumenical mutual aid service. In 1939 Suzanne visited those people of Alsace-Lorraine who had been evacuated to south west France. There she found them confused and living in poor conditions so she organised the protestant youth movement and set up 'la Cimade – Comité intermouvement d'aide aux évacués'. La Cimade increased its work and in 1940 also began to help the Jews in the southern areas. In later years Suzanne spent much time in the spiritual support of this work. In this way she encouraged the young in helping victims, an action which had always been at the heart of her life and on which she based her faith.

The third area of her work was when, together with other members of the Universal Students' Federation, she became involved in the start of international ecumenism which developed mainly through the Student Christian Movement. An important stage in the founding of the Assembly of the World Council of Churches in 1948, the World Assembly of Christian Youth met in Amsterdam in 1939 on the very eve of war. Suzanne encouraged reconciliation not only between Protestants and Orthodox but also arranged a series of retreats in her home which included theologians from Roman Catholic and Anglican churches as well. Suzanne became the first assistant director of the Ecumenical institute at Bossey, near Geneva which was founded in 1946. Pastor Visser't Hooft, secretary general of the World Council of Churches which set it up, saw in Suzanne the unique talent required for this post, for youngsters from all over the world would be sent by their churches to be trained in the ecumenism which was then, and always would be, her vocation. Suzanne was ninety when she died after a long and valuable life spent helping others.

Russian women bearing the cross

Mother Maria Skobtsova was also born in 1891 and as Elisabeth Yurienva Pilenko, daughter of a family of landowners, she grew up in the south of Russia. She had been married twice, divorced and become the mother of three children before becoming an emigree Russian-Orthodox nun living in France after the communist take-over. After the death of her father while she was still young, Lisa had lost her faith but still wanted to dedicate herself to the service of the poor. She married at eighteen, separated from her husband, became converted and then a Jesuit. She began to be involved in politics, becoming the first woman mayor of her hometown of Anapa in 1917. She married again and had two children. The family eventually moved to France in 1922 where they lived in poverty and in 1926 the youngest daughter died and the couple separated. Shortly after this Lisa rediscovered her faith and began to be involved with Orthodox Russian students and other emigrés in Northern France.

Lisa made her profession in March 1932, when she was given the name Marie after Mary of Egypt. As Mary lived a life of penitence in the desert, so Marie was asked to go and act and speak in the desert of human hearts. Marie's desert was to be in the sufferings of those around her. She saw Christ suffering with the poor and the unfortunate in their poverty and wretchedness and united herself with that love of Christ which helps by its own suffering to alleviate their pain.

In 1934 Mother Maria started a house where many people could come for food and a bed and where others met including a group of Orthodox who founded Orthodox Action in 1935. With Maria as its first president its aims were to serve men and women as the image and likeness of God, the temple of the Holy Spirit, the incorruptible icon of God. The house also became a spiritual centre for those who lived nearby. Maria also 'spent her time in caring for the inmates of prisons and mental hospitals, living in great poverty, sharing all the privations of the downtrodden and outcasts and confirming their own precious identity in her witness.'[10] She wrote, 'I am ready to pay for eternal life with the death of my earthly body and the agony of my soul, attached to this earth. In my faith I die to the life of the present world.'

Following the German occupation she dedicated herself to helping the Jews and in due course she was arrested by the Nazis and sent to a concentration camp. Shortly after her arrest she wrote, 'I am your message, Lord. Throw me like a blazing torch into the night, that all may see and understand what it means to be your disciple.' The strength of her faith gave courage to all those around her for, although continually in pain herself, she never complained. It was probable that she died a martyr's death in the gas chambers in April 1945 after changing places with a young Jewish mother.

About the same time as Maria made her profession in France another young Russian woman was bearing her cross. **Iulia** had been born into an aristocratic family in St Petersburg and married a Russian Diplomat, Nicholas de **Beausobre**, who was shot by the Bolsheviks in 1933. Iulia was herself sent to prison and then to a concentration camp, but English friends paid a ransome for her release in 1934. She came to England determined to let the West know what was happening in Russia and wrote a book called *A Woman Who Could Not Die*. This book bears witness to the sufferings of millions who were unable to speak for themselves.

Iulia rooted her faith in the traditions of the Orthodox Church, the Bible and the Eastern fathers, whilst her philosophy comes from such writers as Dostoevsky. She realised after she began to live in England that she could only share the treasures of Orthodoxy here if she could interpret its message to those around her.

Iulia's sufferings under the Bolsheviks were an inspiration to her faith, seeing suffering itself as part of the redeeming compassion of Christ. Even though she was frequently close to death, she continued to live and bear witness to her faith and the understanding of that faith which she had received from the Orthodox Church. 'Her spiritual insights have a direction and lucidity as well as a profound sureness which contrast vividly with the gropings of many contemporary writings on religion.'[11]

She writes about vocations for women: 'Life now is an invitation to women to find vocations other than marriage. But once you have set yourself to follow the will of God you must not expect to find a "pattern" in your life, though sometimes later on you can look back and see glimpses of how the pattern fitted together. Remember that the pattern of God's purpose and of one's life are all the time criss-crossing.'[12]

Writing in 1955 on how to follow the will of God, she says 'One must wait in stillness . . . This is not easy, and it is specially difficult in these days when everyone is in a hurry and wants to know what you are going to do and when. But you must wait in stillness from day to day, sometimes from hour to hour. And then the things that are meant to happen will happen.'[13]

'It is important to realize that in our progression along the way of Christian advancement, the Church has placed the Massacre of the Innocents immediately after the birth of the Redeemer of Mankind. *Their* massacre is an essential step in *our* (adult) spiritual advancement, because mankind is an inseparable wholeness in the divine mind. And the entombed bodies of the massacred innocents are the essential purifying substance of God's beautiful earth, polluted by those innocents' ancestors and their own surviving contemporaries.

'The first intimation of this came to me as I knelt by my son's grave, (he was barely four months old at the time of his death from unavoidable starvation.)'[14]

When Iulia was waiting in hospital for her papers to come through in Russia, she met an old nun, Feodosiya, who was dying and who gave her great comfort. Feodosiya told Iulia how her joy was infinite because others kept burning on the altars of their hearts the flame that was tortured from theirs. 'If only some of them keep it burning, we will find it in our prayers, in our sleep and in our flight away from our tormented bodies. It will shine to us as a glowing beacon of light in the numbing darkness and we shall be comforted and Christ will rejoice. . . . We only ask that they should see the light that bears our burden with us.'[15]

Helping the Jews

Women were born to suffer and the first half of this century was a time of great suffering for many, both men and women. **Corrie ten Boom** was born in 1892 and until she was in her mid-forties, nothing much unusual had happened to her. She lived then in old Haarlem with her father and elder sister, having never married. In Holland in 1939, people were aware of the rise of Hitlerism but it was only at the outbreak of war that any danger began to be felt. With the occupation came persecution of the Jews so Corrie and her family, who were Christians, began helping their Jewish neighbours. At this time, Corrie prayed 'Lord Jesus, I offer myself for Your people. In any way. Any place. Any time.' It was a prayer that was to have a tremendous effect on Corrie's life.

The ten Boom's had a secret room upstairs in which they hid their Jewish friends but eventually this became known to the Gestapo and they arrested Corrie and her family. Imprisoned first of all in Holland, she and her sister were moved to Germany after a while and there Betsie, Corrie's sister, often supported those around with her faith. 'If people can be taught to hate,' she said 'they can be taught to love. We must find the way, you and I, no matter how long it takes . . .' They always offered as many prayers for their enemies as for their friends.

When they arrived in Germany they were sent to the concentration camp at Ravensbruck. With them they took a Bible and 'a knowledge of the power of Him whose story it was'. The awareness of His power remained with them constantly as the study of the Bible brought answers to their questions. 'Rejoice always, pray constantly, give thanks in all

circumstances; for this is the will of God in Christ Jesus.'
Somehow they managed to retain their Bible, despite searches.
Gradually, they began to build up a group around them of
others who would worship together, Roman Catholics, Luther-
ans, Eastern Orthodox. The Word would be read in Dutch
from the Bible, then would be passed around the women
prisoners in French, Polish, Russian, Czech and back into
Dutch. The atmosphere of the prison life began to change as
prisoners began to help each other but the prisoners continued
to be treated harshly by the prison staff.

Although Betsie became ill they continued to pray together
for all in the camp – guards as well as prisoners. They prayed
for the healing of Germany, of Europe, of the world. At times
they sensed a change in the attitude of the guards, whose
harshness became softened. Eventually Betsie's struggle ended,
her life on this earth was no more. Corrie's last view of her
sister was that of a face filled with the happiness, joy and
peace that comes when a Christian meets her maker. A few
days later Corrie was given her release. On New Year's Eve
1944 she left Ravensbruck prison.

Corrie returned to Haarlem where, after the liberation, she
was asked to help run a home for those who had returned
damaged from time spent in the prison camps. But her compassion remained for those who had been guilty. Corrie opened
her own home to those Dutch collaborators who were now
suffering for the wrongs they had done. Gradually, this compassion began to spread and healing began to take place.

Some time later Corrie was to meet one of her own jailers at
a church service. He held out his hand to her but she could
not bring herself to respond. She breathed a silent prayer.
'Jesus, I cannot forgive him. Give me your forgiveness.' A
current seemed to pass through her to the man who had
caused her so much pain in prison and she felt a great surge of
love for him. Jesus had told her to love her enemies and given
her the strength to do so.

New openings

One who also worked to bring peoples of differing ideas
together was **Constance Padwick** who was attracted to the
Arabic way of life after visiting the Holy Land. Constance

wanted to view Islam through Christian eyes and made a
particular study of *Awrad* and *Ahzad*, the Sufi manuals of
prayer, spending much time acquiring and studying them.
Ten years later, in 1961, she published them in a book,
Muslim Devotions. Besides devoting herself to the study of
Muslim spirituality, Constance also wrote Arabic School text-
books and biographies of other Middle Eastern Christians.
She died at the age of eighty and from her Muslim translations
come an epitaph: 'Lord, it is enough for me of honour that I
should be your servant: it is enough for me of grace that you
should be my Lord.'

Another writer from that period, **Dorothy L. Sayers** was
born in 1893. A bright child who went to Oxford University
before beginning her writing and translating career, she wrote
many detective novels but also won fame when her play, *A
Man Born to be King*, was broadcast on the radio in 1941–42.

Among her other writings *Are Women Human?* was published
in 1971, fourteen years after her death. In this she suggests
that 'Perhaps it is no wonder that the women were first at the
cradle and last at the cross. They had never known a man like
this man – there never had been such another. A prophet and
teacher who never nagged at them, never flattered or coaxed
or patronised, who never made arch jokes about them, never
treated them either as 'The women, God help us!' or 'The
ladies, God bless them!'; . . . who praised without condescen-
sion; who took their questions and arguments seriously; . . .
who never urged them to be feminine or jeered at them for
being female; who had no axe to grind and no uneasy male
dignity to defend; who took them as he found them. . . . There
is no act, no sermon, no parable in the whole Gospel that
borrows its pungency from female perversity; nobody could
possibly guess from the words and deeds of Jesus that there
was anything "funny" about woman's nature.'[16]

Mission work continues

While Dorothy was writing in Britain, the interest in missionary work continued and women were at the forefront of this
work. In 1897 **Mary Harrison**, the great niece of Cecil
Frances Alexander, was born and when she was twenty-two
she went to visit an uncle in Calcutta for eighteen months.

After her return to England she became bursar for the Student Christian Movement and in 1930 she was asked to go with the Universities' Mission to Central Africa to be a diocesan treasurer in Masasi, Tanganyika. She was responsible for much of the administration there for the next thirty years. In 1950 she wrote a history of the work of women in Masasi over the past half century, her response to one Canon Porter who had said, 'I hear they are going to send us out some lady workers to Masasi. I can't think what for: we have done very well without them for the last twenty years.'

When Mary retired she moved back to England to help the Mission in London. When UMCA merged with SPG, Mary stayed on. She was not a supporter of the ordination of women despite her great support for women generally. She was very firmly catholic in her Anglicanism and towards the end of her life lived in a convent. She died at the age of ninety-two.

A year younger than Mary, **Carol Graham** also went abroad but in her case it was India which beckoned. Arriving there at the time of the Raj in the 1930s she did not live the normal missionary life for she felt that it was too removed from the Indians and that the future lay in an Indian ministry and an Indian liturgy. She went into the villages barefoot wearing a sari, learnt the language and ate Indian food. When independence came to India she became a deaconess and taught the Indians how to lead in their own churches.

After the founding of the Church of South India, in which she was instrumental, there were difficult times when financial support was withdrawn even by the Mothers' Union. However Carol and her Sisterhood survived and shared in the poverty of those around them. Carol left India in 1960 so that an Indian could lead the Sisterhood and died in 1989, the same year as Mary Harrison.

Peace, justice and the home

Dorothy Day was a year younger than Carol and became a Roman Catholic when she was twenty-three after separating from her husband. She dedicated her life to the cause of peace and justice, a dedication which stemmed from her compassion for the poor and which gave her the strength and the power to act courageously. From her own difficulties in trying to bring up a child as a single working mother, and despite opposition from many Church authorities, Dorothy founded the Catholic Worker Movement. Her belief was that every act of love added to the balance of love in the world and every strong and courageous act changes the world for good. Dorothy gained an inner freedom from her Christian belief, seeing the Church as the Body of Christ with a duty to care for all and this belief enabled her to bear criticism and rejection because she knew that she was accountable only to God. She died in 1980 after a lifetime of fighting for those causes close to her heart.

Dorothy wrote how women can help to bring peace even through their own work at home. Giving the example of St Thérèse who did all for the love of God, she wrote, 'She began with working for peace in her own heart, and willing to love where love was difficult, and so she grew in love, and increased the sum total of love in the world, not to speak of peace.'

'Paper work, cleaning the house, cooking the meals, dealing with the innumerable visitors who come all through the day, answering the 'phone, keeping patience and acting intelligently, which is to find some meaning in all these encounters – these things too are the work of peace, and often seem like a very little way.'[17]

Carryl Houselander also wrote about women and the way they look after their homes. Born in 1901, she had deep mystical experiences while she was still young including an ability to discern the presence of Christ in other people. She too was Roman Catholic and wrote much spiritual prose and poetry.

Describing the place of prayer in our lives, she writes, 'There should be, even in the busiest day, a few moments when we can close our eyes and let God possess us. He is always present, always giving us life, always round us and in us, like the air we breathe; there should be moments at least when we become more conscious of his presence; when we become conscious of it as the only reality, the only thing that will last for ever.'[18] Carryl later continues, 'Christ asks for a home in your soul, where he can be at rest with you, where he can talk easily to you, where you and he, alone and together, can laugh and be silent and be delighted with one another.'[19]

Carryl died when she was only fifty-three but she is immortalised in her writings from which ordinary people are able to relate their own lives to God and so deepen their spirituality.

Yvonne Darbre was one who saw that women also had a part to play in life beyond the home. Born in 1902, Yvonne gave the first sign of her vocation at the age of eight when she could no longer hide her indignation that in French grammar the masculine is always superior to the feminine. All her life she struggled for those causes which were dear to her and like Dorothy Day she was sustained by her strong faith despite rebuffs and setbacks. Yvonne was courageous and although she rejoiced if she was expressing the ideas of the majority, often saying aloud what many were thinking to themselves, she did not waver if her opinions were in the minority or were disturbing to others. Although a good speaker herself she despised oratory for its own sake and just wanted people to commit themselves to what was right. She spoke fearlessly for the development of the laity, for the place of women in the Church, for the search for an authentic and bold ecumenism. Too much caution angered her – she was a woman of passion.

Yvonne was a faithful woman, her friendships were permanent, her commitments were irrevocable. She knew how to mobilise people's energies, even in the most difficult situations, because her fidelity and her tenacity were creative. She was also a witness to charity in the greater sense of the word, in caring for individuals not only by simple action at local level but at the same time with a perception of global problems. This is why she struggled with all her might – both at home and on an international scale – for social progress, relaxation of economic rules and human rights to make a world fit for all.

In the sixties this commitment led her to create a mutual aid organization to help women in developing countries to receive training and to allow them to be aware of their value and dignity. With Marie-Jeanne Perrenoud she also founded the French-speaking Swiss (Romand) Ecumenical Group which has for years offered the women of Romande a place where together they can live out a firm ecumenism within an awareness and respect for traditional diversity.

Yvonne died in 1990 at the age of eighty-eight but shortly before her death, she confided, 'I have never had the time to become an old lady, life is far too exciting for that; as a Christian I do not only have a duty to seek the salvation of my soul, I must also help others when the signs of the times demand it.' These signs of the times led her above all to commit herself tirelessly to the cause of women. 'They are all my sisters',[20] she used to say.

In 1909 in France a baby girl, Simone, was born into a Jewish family. Although never strictly a Christian, **Simone Weil** became very drawn to the Catholic Church but felt unable to accept baptism. Despite this she was able to write, 'I knew quite well that my conception of life was Christian. That is why it never occurred to me that I could enter the Christian community. I had the idea that I was born inside.'[21]

Her father was an affluent doctor in Paris, her mother was gifted and energetic and her brother was a brilliant mathematician. Simone too was very gifted and her study of philosophy led her to an empathy with the poor and underprivileged. Even when she was a small child she refused to wear warm socks because the poor children had none. This relationship with those who were without was to be her philosophy throughout her life and eventually resulted in her death.

Simone became involved in left wing politics and joined the International Brigade in the Spanish Civil War. While in Portugal she visited a small village on its patronal feast day. The poignancy of the music of the Portuguese women as they went singing round the fishing boats reminded her how much Christianity is the religion of the slaves. She had previously identified herself with slaves and she wrote how as slaves could not help but belong to Christianity, she too must belong.

In 1937 in the chapel of Santa Maria degli Angeli in Assissi where Saint Francis often used to pray 'something stronger than I was compelled me for the first time in my life to go down on my knees'[22] she wrote in her book, *Waiting for God*. The following Easter, despite many terrible headaches, whilst following the liturgy of Holy Week she rose above her pain 'to find a pure and perfect joy in the unimaginable beauty of the chanting and the words. This experience enabled me by analogy to get a better understanding of the possibility of loving divine love in the midst of affliction ... There was a young English Catholic there from whom I gained my first idea of the supernatural power of the Sacraments because of the truly angelic radiance with which he seemed to be clothed after going to Communion.'[23]

Simone went to Marseilles at the outbreak of war where she studied Greek and Hindu philosophy whilst doing agricultural work. She found difficulty in seeing Christianity as the only way to God but also wrote, 'I never wondered whether Jesus was or was not the Incarnation of God; but in fact I was incapable of thinking of him, without thinking of him as God.'[24] 'She decided to learn the Lord's prayer in Greek and went through it each morning with absolute attention . . . The effect of this practice is extraordinary and surprises me every time . . . Sometimes during this recitation or at other moments, Christ is present with me in person, but this presence is infinitely more real, more moving, more clear than on that first occasion when he took possession of me.'[25] She remained outside the Church despite her experiences partly so that she might show others the way in.

Simone was persuaded to leave France for England where she worked for the Free French Government. However she always suffered from severe headaches and poor health and eventually contracted tuberculosis. Her illnesses were accentuated by her refusal to eat more than the amount that her fellow French had in their rations and in 1943, largely due to this starvation rationing, she died of tuberculosis. Throughout her life she had remained at the side of those who were without – yet she was closer to God than many a baptized Christian.

Martyrdom in the service of God comes in many ways and although self-imposed in Simone's case it was still witnessing to her love for God and for her brothers and sisters. Even as Blandina and others had died for this love in the early centuries so their sisters were to continue to witness to their love for God through dying in following their call to serve right up until the present day. **Alice Domon** and **Léonie Duquet**, two French nuns who disappeared in Argentina in 1977 were among those who can be counted as martyrs for their disappearance means they would have suffered detention, and probably torture and death.

Alice came from a devout French farming family who lived near the Swiss border and two of her sisters were also nuns.

Alice became a member of the Toulouse Institute of the Sisters of Foreign Missions and went to Argentina in 1967. She began her work there with mentally retarded children and went on to work in the shanty towns where she lived for five years in the same poverty as the inhabitants. She spent half of her time working as a servant like them, and cared for the community during the rest of her time.

In 1973 Alice moved to the country where she encountered the exploitation of the peasantry. She returned to Buenos Aires in 1977 to help a young peasant woman who had been abducted, imprisoned and tortured. There she became involved with the mothers of many of those who had been detained sharing their suffering as they sought for news of their children. A meeting for these mothers was arranged on 8 December that same year and afterwards thirteen women including Alice were taken away by the authorities. Two days later Léonie was also taken away, apparently because Alice had used her home as her address.

Alice was admired not only for her simplicity, humility and good humour but also because of her immense respect for her neighbour. She never judged but guided others towards a better understanding. She went to help the people and to share in the good and evil of their lives. Two days before she was abducted, she had asked for a blessing from an elderly and very poor grandmother she knew, a blessing which she herself could well have pronounced but preferred to ask for, yet another example of the humility which ruled her life.

The mission to China

Gladys Aylward shared with Alice the gifts of simplicity, humility and a determination to spread the Gospel amongst those with whom she felt called to live whatever the cost. Gladys was born in North London in 1902, the eldest child of two very ordinary Londoners, and went to work at the age of fourteen in a shop known as a Penny Bazaar which sold nothing costing more than a penny. Moving on from there she eventually found work as a parlourmaid in the West End of London until one evening she found herself attending a service where the preaching compelled her to listen to God's call to his service. A few days later she gave her life to God but it was not for some time that Gladys felt a compulsion to go to China and went to study at The China Inland Mission. Studying was not her strong point, however, and she found herself unable to learn Chinese so, after failing her exams, she had to leave. Disappointed Gladys returned to work, first among the down-and-outs in Swansea and then back in domestic service where once again she offered her life to God.

Placing her hands on her Bible and the few coins she owned she prayed 'Oh, God! Here's me. Here's my Bible, here's my money! Use us, God! Use us!'[26] God's response came immediately with a gift of a few shillings from her mistress which was the first of her savings to be put aside for her fare to China.

Her journey there in 1932 was horrific, travelling through Germany and Russia where there was fighting and she was even imprisoned for a while. After leaving prison she went to a port in eastern Russia where she was nearly raped and from there escaped to Japan. From Japan Gladys travelled to China by boat arriving there only a month and a day after she left London although it must have seemed like a thousand years at times. She had gone to join Jeannie Lawson, an elderly missionary in a country part of China, and there Gladys began again to learn Chinese this time by working among the people.

When Jeannie died Gladys began work for the Chinese government by talking with the women who continued to bind their daughter's feet. This habit had developed because men liked women with small feet to prevent them running away but the government decided to ban this cruel practice. Gladys took this opportunity to spread the Gospel among the women with whom she talked, telling the stories in ways they would understand 'so that they saw the patient young Peasant nailed to a cross, hanging there in the blazing heat of the north China sun, the flies buzzing about his head, two criminals shrieking on crosses beside him.'[27]

Destroying her British passport Gladys became a naturalised Chinese and when war with the Japanese broke out in 1937 she helped many as the Japanese advanced across China. In 1940 she set off across the mountains with about a hundred children to help them escape from the advancing Japanese. Her faith was tested when on reaching the Yellow river it appeared that, as with Moses and the Red Sea, there was no way across. But just in time a Chinese officer arrived to open the way by arranging a boat to ferry them across. The city they were making for was full so they moved on until they reached another town where Gladys collapsed delirious. Recovering slowly, she continued with her missionary work with frequent periods of illness until after the war when the Communists began to take over in China.

In 1949 Gladys returned to Britain where she was invited to speak about her experiences as a missionary and she often startled her audiences as she challenged them to respond to God's call to help. She also worked amongst the Chinese in Britain, some of whom she had met before they left China, but the call to return continued – not to China this time, for by then it was in the hands of the Communists, but to Taiwan where the Nationalists were fighting to retain the China that they knew and loved. She returned there in 1957 and it was thirteen years later after a short illness that Gladys Aylward died, a 'cockney sparrow' who had had nothing to offer but a deep determination to follow the call of God.

It was this same war in China which gave the opportunity for the first Anglican woman to become ordained priest for under these conditions it was often difficult to celebrate Holy Communion either for want of bread or wine or an ordained minister. The Japanese had occupied Hong Kong and the nearest bishop, Bishop Hall, was four hundred miles away in territory occupied by the Japanese. He had no means of getting the sacraments to his people but there was a deaconess, **Florence Li Tim Oi**, living and working in Macao and Bishop Hall took the decision to ordain her as priest.

To get to her ordination, Florence had to go by foot and bicycle over two mountain ranges. She even sheltered one night in a police outpost knowing that if the Japanese found her she would be shot. On 25 January St Paul's Day, 1944 Florence and Bishop Hall arrived at their meeting place at Shin Hing, the Lake of the Seven Stars within half an hour of each other. Apart from the local Anglicans there were also members of other churches there. After the service Florence then had to journey back the four hundred miles to her congregation.

After the war she stopped exercising her priesthood but still suffered persecution under the Communists and particularly during the cultural revolution in China, when she was imprisoned with other church leaders in a factory. After the end of the cultural revolution, through the influence of those who had been imprisoned with her, she once again began to exercise her ministry. Florence celebrated the fortieth anniversary of her ordination in Westminster Abbey in 1984 and died eight years later at the age of eighty-five. In 1971 the next Bishop of Hong Kong ordained another Anglican woman to the priesthood.

The ordination of women

The ordaining of women as ministers spread throughout other Protestant churches and in Scandinavia **Ingrid Bjerkås** who was born in 1901 was the first woman to become a minister in the Church of Norway when she was appointed to serve in Berg and Torsken in the north of Norway just before her sixtieth birthday. In all she had to travel to seventeen different places, each one up to six hours' journey away by boat from other parts. Although the climate was harsh, the warmth of her congregation compensated and she continued there until 1965. A year later she wrote about her vocation in a book, describing the struggles involved for her as the first woman to become a minister.

Ingrid was convinced of the reality of God from the time in 1940 when Norway became an occupied country. During the war she helped and later taught in the local Sunday school. For her, the experience of knowing God's love was one which she just had to share, and today the Church of Norway has over ninety woman ministers.

The beauty of words

Women throughout the world were by now beginning to express their faith and love for God more openly and one who was widely known for her words which were described as gems of spiritual wisdom was **Antoinette van Pinxteren** who was born in 1917 in the Netherlands.

Antoinette, Sister Francesco, was a great philosopher who asked such questions as 'Aren't we the guardian of each other's opportunities for life?' thus demonstrating the responsibility we all have to care for each other and at the same time respecting the way of life of others, neither imposing ourselves nor being authoritarian. Antoinette believes that we need to live in just such a way, our minds being open to listen not only to our own hearts but also to each other. She finds God increasingly present when we truly come to know others.

Antoinette's experience of God is expressed in an ever growing richness of images. 'As soon as I try to put God into an image, I am unfair to him.' She suggests that we ought to try to be the image of God ourselves. One picture describes God as like the root stock of the water lily, 'there, in the dark depths of the water is the umbilical cord through which I live and that unites me with Him, the source of life.'

Antoinette spent her life searching for a God who had already found her. Her life, was not without struggle, loneliness and lack of understanding but she rejoiced in the knowledge that God had given her many more sisters than just those in her own convent. When asked about death, her response was that in death 'I will return to my origin in the womb of God. Where then can there be any fear?'[28] She returned to this womb in 1988.

Perhaps not a philosopher, but certainly one whose spirituality pervaded all her writings, **Elizabeth Goudge** was born towards the beginning of the twentieth century in Wells, where her father was first vice-principal, then principal, of the Theological College. Her mother had wanted to train as a doctor but had married instead and became an invalid following the birth of Elizabeth shortly after a cycling accident. As a result Elizabeth was an only child, very much cherished and perhaps a little spoilt. She began writing as a small child using the experiences she had gained from observing all that went on around her in her family and the homes she came to know and love. With a mother who was a storyteller and a father who was an academic cleric, Elizabeth brought into her writings a charm and Christian belief which make them attractive and sparkling without having to resort to the vulgarity and sexual explicitness which is the hallmark of much modern writing.

Her mother's family came from Guernsey and the joy with which she visited her grandparents and entered the life of being an Islander is expressed in *Green Dolphin Country* some of which is set in that island. Elizabeth and her parents moved to Ely while she was still young and it was in Ely during the war, when her father took over a parish while the Theological College was closed, that she first came into contact with the poor and old of the town. The poverty she met there impressed itself on Elizabeth and caused her nightmares afterwards.

Going to school in the New Forest area brought her new material which was later used in the Damerosehay novels but it was during a school holiday, whilst caring for her Guernsey grandfather who was staying at Ely and was a non-believer, that she realized the despair that comes to those who are facing death without faith. 'When my grandfather said that all that he was, all that he knew, was going into nothingness I felt at first furious, and then incredulous. What he said was a lie. . . . If all this love and struggle and knowledge was to go to waste then not only must God be so crazy that he could not exist but the universe also was crazy and pointless.'[29]

In the 1920s Elizabeth's parents moved to Oxford where her father was Regius Professor and there she met many interesting people, but her mother's health could not tolerate the city life and she had to move to Hampshire. This constant ill health led to Elizabeth pondering on the meaning of suffering from which she concludes that 'God and the suffering caused by sin are inseparably united, and will be so until sin ends . . . it is hard to doubt the love of a God who is ready to suffer and to die for us . . . when we suffer we must be as close to God as we are to the pain.'[30] She sees how so often those who have worked through suffering are also the ones who show the face of God in the world.

Elizabeth was a very sensitive person whose mother had psychic powers which she steadfastly refused to use. Both were aware of the presence of ghostly forms at times and these Elizabeth considered to be a fragment of life left behind like a cast off shell in a place where intense pain or joy has been experienced. Throughout her life, as is reflected in her writings, the love of God shines through bringing good out of evil. She describes the human soul as being drawn towards God but not compelled. 'Love can draw the little animal up and up, perhaps fighting all the way, to the point where he is aware of the presence of the sun and feels its warmth embrace him.'[31]

The beauty of the poor

Perhaps the best known Christian woman of this century is
Mother Teresa whose work and love for God is known
throughout the world. Teresa was born of Albanian parents in
Skopje, Yugoslavia in 1910 as a simple peasant girl called
Agnes. She became a member of the Sodality, a lay Catholic
body, where she heard about the Bengal mission field from
letters sent home by a Jesuit working there. Teresa asked to
be able to join in this work and was sent to the Loreto nuns in
Ireland who had a mission in Darjeeling where she spent her
novitiate. For some years she taught in a school in Calcutta
and was in charge of the Daughters of St Anne, an Indian
religious order attached to the Loreto Sisters. During this time
Teresa realized that her work was to be amongst the people
who lived in the poorest parts of the city.

In 1946, Teresa requested permission from her Superior to
live outside the cloister and work in the slums of Calcutta.
'She (was) a nun, rather slightly built, with a few rupees in
her pocket; not particularly clever, or particularly gifted in
the arts of persuasion. Just with this Christian love shining
about her; in her heart and on her lips. Just prepared to
follow her Lord, and in accordance with his instructions
regard every derelict left to die in the streets as him; to hear in
the cry of every abandoned child, even in the squeak of the
discarded foetus, the cry of the Bethlehem child; to recognize
in every leper's stumps the hands which once touched sightless
eyes and made them see, rested on distracted heads and made
them calm, brought back health to sick and twisted limbs.'[32]
Two years later she changed her habit to a white sari with a
blue border and cross on the shoulder.

After a few months in Patna where she received nursing
training she returned to Calcutta to live with the Little Sisters
of the Poor. In 1950 the new order of the Missionaries of
Charity began in Calcutta and from there spread throughout
India. Thirteen years later the Missionary Brothers of Charity
was formed as a branch and the work was spreading throughout the world. In 1971, Mother Teresa was awarded the Pope
John XXIII Peace Prize by Pope Paul VI.

Her faith and love for God and for his children can best be
expressed through her own words. 'Let there be no pride or

vanity in the work. The work is God's work, the poor are God's poor. Put yourself completely under the influence of Jesus, so that he may think his thoughts in your mind, do his work through your hands, for you will be all-powerful with him who strengthens you.'[33]

'God loves a cheerful giver. He gives most who gives with joy. The best way to show our gratitude to God and the people is to accept everything with joy. A joyful heart is the normal result of a heart burning with love.'[34]

'Dearest Lord, may I see you today and every day in the person of your sick, and, whilst nursing them, minister unto you. Though you hide yourself behind the unattractive disguise of the irritable, the exacting, the unreasonable, may I still recognize you and say: "Jesus, my patient, how sweet it is to serve you." '[35]

'Smile five times a day at someone you do not really wish to smile at at all.'[36]

Many are the smiling faces of women who are, like Mother Teresa, still serving God in this world often far away from their native lands. **M. Mercedes (Josefine) Schwödiauer** who was born in 1913 in Kleinraming Steyr, Austria, the fifth of a family of ten children, also served God in India but has now returned to Vienna where she advises her community on Indian projects.

When M. Mercedes was twenty she met Br Paul Sonntag and he encouraged her to join the 'Queen of Heaven' community which aimed to bring the Gospel of Christ to India. She joined the novitiate in 1934 and then trained as a nurse before going out to India in 1939 just before the war started. She began working in a state hospital at Benares in Utar Pradesh although at first she was treated as an enemy alien. She eventually became matron of the hospital and often helped as a midwife with the more difficult births.

M. Mercedes was Regional Superior to her order in India from 1950–1959, encouraging Indian vocations and opening several mission stations. She was even offered Indian citizenship and in 1964 became Superior General, moving back to Vienna for her term of office. In Vienna she served on a number of different committees especially those concerned with justice and third world issues.

Throughout all her work M. Mercedes has been guided by

a deep faith, a lively sense of humour and a generous and
loving warmth. She has created an atmosphere of joyous
confidence which has attracted not only Christians but Hindu
and Muslim as well.

The triumph of Love

Across the world in New York **Madeleine L'Engle** was born
in 1919. Madeleine received part of her education in Europe
and then began working in the theatre where she met her
husband and eventually began to write. Although she and her
husband gave up their acting and writing after a while
Madeleine began to write again, this time writing books for
children with a Christian message. Whatever the story-line,
the spiritual truths of Christianity and the struggle against
evil are always demonstrated in her writings.

A young girl whose struggle for life against cancer was a
witness to her faith was **Jocelyn Hutton** born in 1962.
Jocelyn was born in Winnipeg in Canada, the daughter of a
minister and his wife. She was a lively child, a member of a
dance company with a strong faith. In 1979 her leg began to
hurt and this was diagnosed as cancer of the hip. Her right leg
was amputated but the cancer had spread so Jocelyn asked
God for His guidance and the strength to follow His will. She
remained in great pain but shone with the joy of knowing
God was with her.

Jocelyn told a friend 'I've prayed to God for guidance and
help, and I've finally realized that God gave me my life to
live, so I'm going to live every day I've got left.' Happily
witnessing to her trust in God, she supported her classmates,
talked to other youngsters and even appeared on television to
share what she had learned through her sufferings. She was an
example of the ordinary person who shows that they are
members of the great fellowship of saints through their sharing
in the sufferings of this world and her light continues to shine
even after her death in 1980.

Of those who live now it is difficult to decide who should be
included and who left out. There are so many women who are
contributing in their own way in God's service and to the
work of the Church. Many have suffered a great deal, often at
the hands of the Church authorities. Others have given their

lives for God. Whilst there are well known women such as Mother Teresa, there are others who, though less well known, have been loved as much by those who were privileged enough to know them. Jocelyn Hutton and **Emma Hawkins** can be counted amongst these.

Born in 1964, Emma made a commitment to Christ when she was sixteen, but because she suffered from cystic fibrosis she realized that she would not be able to offer herself to work in God's service in the way she had hoped. However a year later, by now very ill, she became aware of the presence of God. On 1 July 1988 Emma was ordained deacon together with her husband, John, and together they went to serve in a parish in Birmingham.

'Her illness was an essential part of her ministry. Her faith in bearing it, her sharing in the Passion through it, and her offering herself to God and to others . . .'[37] She was greatly loved both in her parish and the diocese having a special rapport with the young and the women. Her own experience of life and the nearness of death added a depth to her preaching and as she approached death her attitude of giving glory and praise to God witnessed to the faith of the young woman whose life until her death in 1990 was one long expression of great joy and thanksgiving to God.

The same year as Emma was born, **Helen Roseveare** was a missionary doctor on the Congo. This was the time of the violent Simba rebellion and massacres and Helen was forty-one. Beaten and raped by the soldiers, Helen was asked to declare that the President was saviour of the world. She refused even though a gun was held to her head. She was put in front of a firing squad but instead of shooting her, the guards started arguing. So Helen escaped execution and was sent to prison where she helped those of her fellow prisoners needing medical attention even though she was under constant threat of violence herself. Throughout these ordeals, as in the whole of her work, her faith sustained her and she constantly gave thanks for prayers answered.

Christianity shines in the Eastern darkness

Violence continues throughout the world as the powers of Satan use every available method to overcome God's kingdom.

Many a Christian woman is suffering from the violence and evil which affects her nation, her neighbourhood or perhaps just her family. It is often very difficult, as difficult as ever, to bear witness to a loving God when there is so much evil and pain. One who managed to do just this is **Solina Chy** who came from a middle class home in Cambodia, (Kampuchea). In 1975 the Khmer Rouge gained power in her country and they hoped that this would bring peace to this unstable part of the world. Instead came chaos, with everyone being ordered to leave the towns and go into the country for three days. Many people were killed or died, Solina's own mother among them, and the family had all their belongings taken from them.

Solina herself was sent into the fields with very little food to do hard labour. In 1977 she was put in prison with her feet in stocks and there the Khmer Rouge tried to marry her against her will. 'I suffered from mosquito bites, lice, hunger and threats to my life. I was given electric shocks, plastic bags over my head to make me faint and bayonets held against my temples. Accused of being a CIA agent I was beaten. I lay on the floor unable to move, my body bruised and swollen. Tears started to fall, my heart stirred with hurt, hatred, bitterness, self pity, anger and revenge. I felt there must be a God who was alive, watching over me who saw my tears.'[38]

After two horrific years, she was freed when the Vietnamese caused the Khmer Rouge to flee. She was re-united with her family and they escaped to Thailand where they were placed in refugee camps. The conditions there were very bad and Solina spent many days and nights in tears. One day she sought solace with a friend who asked her to translate what someone from a mission group was saying. A week later Solina heard the Gospel Story from another mission worker and she learned how Jesus had died even though he had done no wrong and he had risen from the dead.

The story touched a chord in her heart and she became converted to follow the God who even forgave his enemies. Hatred and bitterness became replaced with a deep love and when Solina moved with her family to Canada Solina trained with the mission group, Youth with a Mission. Eventually Solina was able to return for a short trip to Thailand to visit the refugees and take with her the message of the Gospel for others like herself.

Another person to commit her life in the fight against the evil which affected those she loved is **Jackie Pullinger** who was born in 1944. Jackie was sure from early on that she wanted to be a missionary, but knew little about God. At music college she avoided the Christian Union members but then joined a group of people who met in a flat to drink coffee and discuss the Bible. At these meetings, Jackie found that Christians were no different from other people and with this group she learnt not to be embarrassed by the discussions about God and the Bible. It was then that she realized that she had either to accept Jesus and all that he said about himself or to reject the whole of Christianity. With a slight reluctance she decided to accept Him, an acceptance which opened up a new way of life to her.

Earlier in her life she had wanted to be a missionary but no missionary society would have her as she was too young and had no qualifications. Now once again she thought about being a missionary so she turned to God and asked Him what he wanted for her. 'Go' she heard God say to her 'and I will lead you'. So it was that in 1966 Jackie did just that, taking a boat which was sailing to China and praying hard all the while that God would show her when to leave the boat. Eventually she found herself disembarking at Hong Kong and being drawn towards the walled city of Kowloon.

The walled city is a haven for criminals with no running water, no light and little living space. It is a place where many turn to drugs such as opium and heroin to escape the realities of life. In order to pay for their drugs it is often necessary for the addict to steal, run protection rackets, or be involved with drug selling or prostitution. Jackie tried to tell those involved about the love of Jesus but was making no impact. Eventually she opened a youth group in the centre of the city and there demonstrated the practical love of Christ by taking a personal interest in the people who came and by showing them she cared. Prayer was always at the heart of her work and her gift of the healing power of the Holy Spirit brought many painlessly through what was otherwise the horror of drug withdrawal. Many were also healed of deep emotional hurts and shared with others the joy of knowing the transforming love of Christ.

Jackie's work has grown since she first arrived in Hong

Kong and there are now three large institutes where those who were drug addicts, prisoners and prostitutes can grow into a deeper love with Jesus who has truly saved them from the darkness and degradation in which they were living. Jackie's work continues as does that of many others, as long as such cities of darkness continue to exist. Perhaps it was because she was a woman that she was able to do what she did despite the danger that might have appeared to be present in such a haven of vice.

Whilst Jackie fought the darkness of drugs and vice in Hong Kong, **Lucy Ching** has been bringing light to the blind there. Lucy was born into a middle class Chinese family a few years before the Second World War started and became blind after an eye infection when she was very young. As a young blind girl, there was little future ahead of her and many girls like her eventually finished up as prostitutes. Lucy was very bright and became attracted by stories from the Bible and hymns which she heard from her brother who attended school. She joined a church much against her parent's wishes as they still worshipped their ancestors, but for Lucy her Christian faith was the guiding force in her life from then on. When she was eight, she learnt how to read using Braille with the help of her amah, Ah Wor, and eventually managed to find a teacher who would admit her to a school. There she did so well that when her family were forced to flee to Hong Kong in 1949, after the revolution in China, she was able to study further and eventually received a scholarship to go to America. She returned to Hong Kong to help other blind children and later received the MBE and other awards for her work with blind people in Asia. In 1989, she resigned from her work in Hong Kong and returned to the USA in order to have more freedom.

On 9 April 1992 she received an honorary doctorate in Social Science and continues to live in America with the servant who gave her such support all through her life. Lucy fought against the attitude which could have reduced her and many like her to become *Mang Mui*, blind slaves, because of the evils of ignorance and fear. By overcoming those evils she brought new life to many.

The call to repentance

Today's evil is no different from earlier ages in being all too often watered and fed by human wickedness and it was an urgent call to repentance of that wickedness which came through a Japanese nun, **Agnes Katsuko Sasagawa**.

Agnes is a nun in a small convent in Yuzawadai, Akita. On 12 June 1973 she was alone in the convent chapel when a brilliant light appeared to shine from the tabernacle and Sr Agnes prostrated herself before it. She then returned to her cell, fearful of what had happened and hoping to try to ignore it but the following day the same thing happened. On the third day, the tabernacle appeared to be on fire and surrounded by angels in adoration. The Bishop, who was visiting the convent at that time, counselled Agnes to keep quiet about the happenings but also to trust that God would reveal his will.

Towards the end of June an angel appeared to Agnes and recited the Rosary with her adding a prayer which turned out to be the Japanese translation of the Fatima prayer, a prayer unknown to Agnes at that time. The next day Agnes found a wound in her hand and later she became deaf. On 5 July the statue of the Virgin Mary was surrounded by a brilliant light and a voice spoke to Agnes asking her to pray in reparation for the sins of men and for the clergy and to continue to listen to and obey her superior. When Agnes went to examine the statue there was a wound in the hand from which blood flowed down to the fingertip. Other sisters and the Bishop also witnessed this.

On 3 August Our Lady again spoke to Agnes, warning of God's anger at the sin of mankind, his postponement of chastisement at the intercession of His Son whose suffering and death had been offered for our redemption and through Mary's prayers also. A third message came on 13 October, the anniversary of Fatima, and this message revealed the coming of a great catastrophe if people did not repent. 'If men do not repent and better themselves, the Father will inflict a terrible punishment on all humanity. . . . Fire will fall from the sky and will wipe out a great part of humanity, the good as well as the bad, sparing neither priest nor faithful. The survivors will find themselves so desolate they will envy the dead.'[39]

Bishop John Shojiro Ito of Niigata witnessed the flow of blood and also the tears which flowed from the eyes of the statue over a period of six years between 1975 and 1981 and which were filmed by a television film crew on 8 September 1981.

The struggle against evil in Chile

Evil speaks through human beings and the resulting suffering often becomes unspeakable. **Sheila Cassidy** felt called to serve God, little realising the suffering and torture this would entail.

Born in 1937 in Lincolshire, Sheila emigrated to Australia with her family but returned to Oxford to complete her medical studies. There she met a Chilean who was to change her life for when the medical world in Britain seemed too demanding, Sheila decided to join her friend in Chile. After the military coup in 1973, many people were taken prisoner, tortured and killed, whilst others just disappeared, including some known to the two women.

Although her friend died, Sheila, who had lapsed somewhat in the practise of her faith, remained in Chile and began to become involved with some of the missionary communities working among the poor in Chile. Previously her work had been among the middle classes or the wealthier people, but now she began to work more and more with the marginalised. When a friend of hers was taken and tortured one Holy Week, it brought home to her the passion of Jesus in vivid reality. Again she considered her vocation to become a nun and after spending time on retreat decided that her answer must be 'Yes'. A few months after making this decision, Sheila was asked to treat a man with a bullet wound. This was after an attack had been made on a leftist group from which two men and two women had escaped and were being sought. Sheila realised that her patient was one of the fugitives but, as she told one of her torturers later when he asked why she treated the man, he was sick and she was a doctor.

A week later, at the house of a missionary friend, Sheila was arrested and taken to a place where she was told to undress completely, lie on a metal bunk, spreadeagled, and was given electric shock treatment to make her tell through whom she had met the fugitive. Though she tried to protect her contacts at first, eventually the torture forced her to give names. She was then interrogated until she had told all she knew and taken to a detention camp on the outskirts of Santiago. There she tried to pray, offering up her fears and anxieties to God. Later she was given a battered part of a Bible in which were line drawings including one of a naked man buffeted by the storms of life which spoke strongly to her own situation.

Sheila was then brought before a court which placed her in a house of correction before her trial. Before moving there she had spent some time in prayer fighting the urge to cry out to God to be freed rather than making an unconditional offer to accept whatever he sent. From sharing her prison with women who were often thieves, prostitutes or even worse Sheila was told she would be set free and was even allowed to talk freely with the British Consul but instead of being released she was sent again to a detention camp. There she made crosses for the other prisoners and often led them in worship. Two days before Christmas 1975, Sheila was told that she would face further charges.

After a Christmas act of worship in which prisoners, believers and non-believers alike, joined in praise and thanksgiving, the prisoners celebrated as best they could and with great joy. It was with a certain regret at leaving her friends that Sheila learnt the next day that she was going to be released and flown home shortly. Unable to say her farewells to any of her friends outside the prison, she was taken to the airport by a side entrance to avoid the crowds.

Sheila had been called to serve God but not in the way that she had envisaged as an eighteen year old. Like many other women, her calling involved her in much suffering and yet through it she was able to witness to her obedience to God.

Ordination to the priesthood and episcopate

The present chapter ends with the brief stories of five women who, after nearly two milleniums of male leadership within the episcopal churches, have broken through the barriers which declared that though women and men are equal in the eyes of God, and therefore of Christians, their equality does not extend to the ways in which they are allowed to serve God.

The number of women now serving as priests in the Anglican church in America has been growing steadily since the first unofficial ordination in 1975. In almost every case their ministry has been as fruitful as that of their sisters who still remain deacons in many other countries. Breaking into new pastures is not always easy nor has it ever been for many of the women throughout Christian history. **Geralyn Wolf** is one of many who share in the pioneering life of the women ordained in the Anglican Church.

Geralyn entered Divinity School in 1974 staying at a convent during her studies and building up her spiritual life. She was ordained and then in 1981 was appointed vicar of a small, mainly black parish in Philadelphia. Geralyn built up the parish life both spiritually and by extending its ministry to helping the needy. In 1987 she was appointed dean of Christ Church Cathedral in Louisville, Kentucky on the strength of her organizing skills and liturgical expertise coupled with her deep devotion.

Geralyn is one of many American woman priests who could have featured here. She was the first woman to be made dean of a Cathedral but otherwise there are many others whose ministry as priests or deacons have been equally fruitful. They have given themselves in the service of God wherever they have been placed despite frequent opposition and difficulties which very few male clergy experience for any length of time. In Ireland the opening of the priesthood to women came unexpectedly early. **Irene Templeton** and **Kathleen Young** were priested in 1990, the first two women to be so ordained in the British Isles.

Born in Belfast in 1940 Kathleen trained as a physiotherapist and married a distinguished research medic who died from a disease caught as a result of his research not long after their marriage. Kathleen then went to Queen's University, Belfast to read Divinity and there felt called to the ministry. She was ordained deacon in 1988. Irene was born in Belfast a year after Kathleen and studied in both Bristol and Leicester. She became a parish youth worker, deaconess, head of R.E. and education secretary for the Church Missionary Society and in 1983 she married a teacher. She was ordained deacon a year after Kathleen and the same year as **Barbara Harris** was consecrated Suffragan Bishop of Massachusetts, the first woman to be consecrated bishop in the Anglican Church.

The first woman to be consecrated diocesan bishop was **Penelope Jamieson** who was born in 1942. Penny grew up in Buckinghamshire in England and graduated in Linguistics from Edinburgh University. She married a New Zealander and moved to New Zealand in 1965, working first as a teacher and then as a university lecturer. She gained a Ph.D at Victoria University for work with young Tokelau children and then worked for the Council for Educational Research. She had three children herself and became ordained deacon in 1982 and priest a year later.

She was elected Bishop of Dunedin but before accepting the election she travelled to Dunedin because she wanted to see if it 'was of God'. It was on St Peter's Day 1990 that she became consecrated a diocesan bishop.

Many provinces of the Anglican Church have now decided to ordain women to the priesthood and in an historic decision on 11 November 1992, the General Synod of the Church of England voted by a majority of over two thirds in all three houses (bishops, clergy and laity) to ordain women to the priesthood. Several of the Old Catholic Churches in Europe have also agreed to this and it appears that after nearly two thousand years the part that women have played in the spread of the Gospel is being acknowledged on a wider scale.

This point appears to be a good and positive note on which to end the stories of these women of faith. It is a story which will never end while men and women continue to be born and live and die. Penny Jamieson and the deacons waiting to be priested would, I am sure, agree that theirs are not the most exciting or deeply spiritual of lives recorded here, nevertheless for many the decisions to ordain and consecrate women are the culmination of much of the striving for recognition of women's gifts that has been recorded in these pages.

★ ★

Epilogue

'Therefore, as God's chosen people, holy and dearly loved, clothe yourself with compassion, kindness, humility, gentleness and patience. Let the peace of Christ rule in your hearts, since as members of one body you were called to peace. And be thankful. Let the word of Christ dwell in you richly as you teach and admonish one another with all wisdom, and as you sing psalms, hymns and spiritual songs with gratitude in your hearts to God. And whatever you do, whether in word or deed, do it all in the name of the Lord Jesus, giving thanks to God the Father through him.'(Colossians 3.12, 15–17 NIV)

★ ★

IN MANY ways this has been a spiritual journey, travelling through time with so many women who have given so much in their lives. Women have come a long way and yet in some ways they have travelled no distance. As God is both transcendent and immanent, both far away and within us, so has been the journeying of women both far and near. For when the women were called by Jesus to tell their neighbours that they had found the Messiah or to tell their brothers that Jesus was risen, they were doing no less than many women are at long last being allowed to do today. And when the women were sharing in the Passion of Jesus as they stood watching round the Cross, they were sharing the same suffering as the early martyrs and as little Laura Vicuna or even Solina Chy. Being beloved and chosen by God is, in his paradoxical way, not only receiving his love but also receiving his command to love others with his compassionate love which can be so costly.

Women are still standing at the Cross and in the arena, but women are also sharing that love which Jesus poured out to Mary Magdalene as she sat at his feet, to Martha as she continued in her work for him, to the woman with the haemorrhage as he healed her and bade her go in peace and to the woman at the well to whom he entrusted his message.

Deborah Thompson told how the Maronite women exclaimed at the message of the Gospel. 'We never heard such
words. We are women. Does it mean for us?' They had never
realized that the message of the Gospel was not just for men
but was also for women. This is, I believe, why these stories
need to be told and retold.

This book only contains a sample of all that could be told,
of the beautiful and sensitive writings that so many women
have given to tell of their love for God and his love for us. In a
way, therefore, it is only a taste written in the hope that it will
inspire readers to explore further, to find out more about the
lives and writings of these women. Hopefully it will also
encourage many to look further into the inspiration which
moved these women to serve God in this way. It is by
studying their lives that we come to know that great love
behind them, and in turn come to know that Love Himself.

The stories are part of a whole and yet many are also
individual stories in themselves. They tell the history of Christianity from the woman's side but also they are part of our
identity whoever we are, male, female, Christian or non-Christ-
ian. For whatever any of these women have done in the world
has affected the life of the world, just as any action we as
individuals make affects the world for good or bad. Many of
these women were ordinary women who responded to God's
call to serve him. They would deny that they were anybody
special but they were willing to trust in God, to know that he
would give them the strength to do what may have seemed
impossible to them. They listened to God and then followed
his call, knowing that his Love would help them along the
way and could overcome any danger that they could encounter in this life.

Dean Hutton once wrote 'Knowledge, prudence, simplicity,
devotion – a calm, sane and complete dedication to the work
given by God – that is what the Church has taught through
the lives of the Englishwomen of the past'. But it is not just to
Englishwomen that Christians owe their heritage, for women
from all over the world have and still are dedicating their lives
to do God's work in whatever way he calls them. And so
many of their stories will never be told. Stories of ordinary
women who offered themselves in the service of Christ, ordinary women who may have done nothing more than sit at the

fireside and tell their sons and their daughters tales of the God who, out of his great love for humankind, gave his own life so that they might have life more abundantly.

Another man, Gerald Priestland, wrote 'Saints are still around, and in my experience two in every three are women', a tribute to women perhaps sparked off by his knowledge of Mother Teresa. Saints are people who are set aside for God, chosen by him to do his work in the world. The women whose stories are told here were beloved by God, were chosen by him, but then if the reader studies a far greater book than this, he or she will know that so are we all.

Notes

Introduction
1. Alice Kemp-Welch, *Of Six Medieval Women*, p. xv.

Chapter 1
1. Joyce Huggett, *Open to God*, p. 136.

Chapter 2
1. A. R. M. Gordon, *Deacons in the Ministry of the Church*, p. 8.
2. Ruth B. Edwards, *The Case for Women's Ministry*, p. 59.
3. Dean Ryle and Others, *The Ministry of Women*, p. 9.
4. Ruth B. Edwards, *op. cit.*, pp. 58, 70.
5. Labarge M. Wade, *Women in Medieval Life*, p. xiii.

Chapter 3
1. Labarge M. Wade, *op. cit.*, p. xiii.
2. Source unknown.
3. L. Ouspensky & V. Lossky, *The Meaning of Icons*, p. 136.
4. *Ibid*.
5. B. Chenu, C. Prud'homme, F. Quéré, J-C. Thomas, *The Book of Christian Martyrs*, p. 91.
6. *Ibid*, p. 92.
7. *Ibid*.
8. Kallistos Ware, *The Oxford Illustrated History of Christianity*, p. 132.
9. K. Moore, *She for God*, p. 20.
10. Paul Johnson, *A History of Christianity*, p. 109.
11. Benedicta Ward, *Sayings of the Desert Fathers*, p. 234.
12. *Ibid*, p. 230.
13. Benedicta Ward, *Harlots of the Desert*.
14. *Ibid*, p. 33.
15. *Ibid*, p. 34 (Canon of St Mary of Egypt, *Lenten Triodion*, p. 448)

Chapter 4
1. P. Brown, *The Book of Kells*, p. 27.
2. Bede, *A History of the English Church and People*, p. 115.
3. Ecumenical Forum of European Christian Women (EFECW) – Individual writings, translated or adapted by author, collected for the Third Assembly of the EFECW held at York 1990.
4. Bede, *op. cit.*, p. 247.
5. *Ibid*, p. 248.
6. K. Moore, *She for God*, p. 28.
7. Karl Krumbacher, *History of the Byzantine Literature*, (Munich 1897).
8. Coust. Trypanis, *Greek Verse*.
9. J. Alick Bouquet, *A People's Book of Saints*, p. 100.

Chapter 5
1. Labarge M. Wade, *Women in Medieval Life*, p. xiii.
2. Alice Kemp-Welch, *Of Six Medieval Women*, p. 6.
3. EFECW, *op. cit.* (quoted in *Towards Reconciliation*, Summer 1988, source unknown).

4. Donald Attwater, *The Penguin Dictionary of Saints*, p. 109.
5. J. Alick Bouquet, *A People's Book of Saints*, pp. 173–4.
6. *Ibid*, p. 169.
7. Walter H. Capps and Wendy Wright, *Silent Fire*, p. 55.
8. Paul Johnson, *A History of Christianity*, p. 260.
9. Labarge M. Wade, *op. cit.*, p. 108.
10. *Ibid*, p. 127 (from De adventu fratrum in Monumenta Franciscana (RS4) 1, 16).
11. Quoted by Lavina Byrne in *The Hidden Tradition*, p. 119 (from Armstrong and Brady, *Francis and Clare: The Complete Works*, p. 220).
12. *Op. cit.*, p. 230.
13. EFECW.
14. Walter H. Capps and Wendy Wright, *op. cit.*, p. 83.
15. M. G. Steegmann (Trans.), *The Book of Consolations of the Blessed Angela Foligno*, pp. 31–63.
16. Margaret Aston, in *The Christian World*, p. 167.
17. Source unknown.
18. Peter Anson, *The Call of the Desert*, p. 176.
19. Julian of Norwich, *Revelations of Divine Love*, p. 82.
20. *Ibid*, pp. 87–9.
21. *Ibid*, pp. 167, 169–70.
22. *Ibid*, p. 212.
23. Gillian Hawker, *The Mirror of Love*, p. 41.
24. Walter H. Capps and Wendy Wright, *op. cit.*, p. 143.
25. Veronica Zundel, *The Lion Book of Christian Classics*, p. 42.
26. K. Fischer, *Women at the Well*, p. 143.
27. J. J. Delaney and J. E. Tobin, Dictionary of Catholic Biography, p. 220.

Chapter 6
1. Ruth B. Edwards, *The Case for Women's Ministry*, p. 113.
2. *Ibid*, p. 114.
3. J. J. Delaney and J. E. Tobin, Dictionary of Catholic Biography, p. 440.
4. B. Chenu, C. Prud'homme, F. Quéré, J-C. Thomas, *The book of Christian Martyrs*, p. 99.
5. J. B. Dalgairns, An Essay on The Spiritual Life of Medieval England from *The Scale of Perfection* by Walter Hilton, p. xxxix.
6. Walter H. Capps and Wendy Wright, *Silent Fire*, p. 149.
7. *Ibid*, p. 150.
8. *Ibid*, p. 152.
9. *Ibid*, p. 153–55.
10. EFECW, *op. cit.*
11. Quoted by Lavinia Byrne in *The Hidden Tradition*, p. 116 (from *The Collected Works of St Teresa of Avila*, trs K. Kavanagh and O. Rodnguez, Vol 1: The Book of her Life: Spiritual Testimonies and Soliloquies, Washington DC, ICS Pub. 1976).
12. A. Richardson, *Women of the Church of England*, p. 22.
13. K. Moore, *She for God* (from Foxe's *History of Martyrs*), p. 87.
14. Quoted by Lavinia Byrne in *The Hidden Tradition*, p. 114 (from *Francis de Sales, Jane de Chantal. Letters of Spiritual Direction*, pp. 202–3).
15. Françoise Madeleine de Changy, *Love is as Strong as death*.
16. Nicholas Zernov, *The Russians and Their Church*, p. 81.
17. C. R. Boxer, *The Christian Century in Japan*, p. 354.
18. B. Chenu, etc., *op. cit.*, p. 125.
19. *Ibid*, p. 122.
20. *Ibid*.
21. Quoted by Lavinia Byrne, *op. cit.*, p. 142 (from Lucy Menzies' *Maire de L'Incarnation*).
22. Veronica Zundel, *The Lion Book of Christian Classics*, p. 70.
23. A. Richardson, *op. cit.*, p. 116.
24. *Ibid*, p. 138 (but Susannah's words).
25. *Ibid*, p. 142 (but Susannah's words).

Chapter 7
1. EFECW, *op. cit.*

2. *Ibid.*
3. *Ibid.*
4. Helen C. Knight, *Lady Huntington and her Friends*, p. 15.
5. *Ibid*, p. 18.
6. *Ibid*, pp. 19–20.
7. *Ibid*, p. 165.
8. Charles F. Hayward, *Missionary Heroines*.
9. K. Moore, *She for God*, p. 136.
10. A. M. Allchin, *The Furnace and the Fountain*.
11. D. Campbell, *Hymns and Hymn Makers*, p. 72.
12. K. Moore, *op. cit.*, p. 146.
13. B. Chenu, C. Prud'homme, F. Quéré, J-C. Thomas, *The Book of Christian Martyrs*.
14. Charles F. Hayward, *op. cit.*
15. D. Campbell, *op. cit.*, p. 100.
16. K. Moore, *op. cit.*, p. 150.
17. T. T. Carter, *Harriet Monsell*, p. 177.
18. EFECW, *op. cit.*
19. A. Richardson, *Women of the Church of England*, p. 333.
20. *Ibid*, p. 292.
21. K. Moore, *op. cit.*, p. 195.
22. D. Bennet, *Emily Davies and the Liberation of Women 1830–1921*, p. 31.
23. Commentary on Liverpool Cathedral Staircase Windows.
24. Veronica Zundel, *Christian Classics*, pp. 94–5.
25. Quoted by Lavinia Byrne in *The Hidden Tradition*, p. 66 (from *Christian Faith and Practice in the experience of the Society of Friends*, 1960).
26. K. Moore, *op. cit.*, p. 176.
27. *Thérèse of Lisieux, Collected Letters*, p. 292.
28. Dean Ryle and others, *The Ministry of Women*, p. 22.
29. K. Moore, *op. cit.*, p. 182.
30. A. Richardson, *op. cit.*, p. 339.
31. K. Moore, *op. cit.*, p. 183.
32. A. Richardson, *op. cit.*, p. 340.
33. Quoted by Lavinia Byrne, *op. cit.*, p. 53 (from Joseph Williamson, *Josephine Butler – The Forgotten Saint*).
34. Joan Chapman, *Mothers' Union Treasury*, p. 13.
35. *Ibid*, p. 16.
36. A. Richardson, *op. cit.*, pp. 336–7.
37. Catherine Booth, *Papers of Aggressive Christianity*, pp. 13–14.
38. Catherine Booth, *Female Ministry: an Address by Mrs General Booth*, pp. 22–3.
39. Charles Preece, *Women of the Valleys*, p. 121.
40. *Ibid*, p. 172.
41. Martin Marty, *North America, The Oxford Illustrated History of Christianity*, p. 410.
42. Dean Ryle, *op. cit.*, p. 22.

Chapter 8
1. Evelyn Underhill, *The Spiritual Life*, pp. 39–40.
2. L. Roger Roberts, *Light of Christ: Evelyn Underhill*, pp. 4–5.
3. Evelyn Underhill, *op. cit.*, p. 93.
4. *Ibid*, p. 71.
5. Quoted by Lavinia Byrne in *The Hidden Tradition*, p. 135 (from Sheila Fletcher, *Maude Royden: A Life*, p. 162).
6. Martin Israel, *The Pearl of Great Price*, pp. 121–2.
7. Quoted by Lavinia Byrne in *The Hidden Tradition*, p. 40 (from Dame Felicitas Corrigan, *Helen Wadell*, p. 322). (Letter to her sister Meg, Easter Saturday 1942).
8. D. M. Arnold, *Dorothy Kerin, Called by Christ to Heal*, p. 14.
9. *Ibid*, p. 71.
10. Martin Israel, *op. cit.*, p. 121.
11. C. Babington-Smith, *Iulia de Beausobre – A Russian Christian in the West*, back cover.
12. *Ibid*, p. 121.
13. *Ibid*, p. 125.
14. *Ibid*, pp. 182–3.
15. *Ibid*, p. 40.

16. Quoted by Lavinia Byrne in *The Hidden Tradition*, p. 44, (from Dorothy L. Sayers, *Are Women Human?* p. 47).
17. *Op. cit.*, p. 69 (from Dorothy Day, *On Pilgrimage: The Sixties*, N. Y. Curtis Books, 1972, pp. 258–9).
18. *Op. cit.*, p. 118 (from Carryl Houselander, *The Comforting of Christ*, p. 15).
19. *Op. cit.*, p. 119 (from *Ibid*, p. 69).
20. EFECW, *op. cit.*
21. Veronica Zundel, *Christian Classics*, p. 108.
22. Walter H. Capps and Wendy Wright, *Silent Five*, p. 223.
23. *Ibid*, p. 224.
24. *Ibid*, p. 225.
25. *Ibid*, p. 226.
26. Phyllis Thompson, *Gladys Aylward, A London Sparrow*, p. 23.
27. *Ibid*, p. 48.
28. EFECW, *op. cit.*
29. Elizabeth Goudge, *The Joy of the Snow*, p. 153.
30. *Ibid*, p. 202.
31. *Ibid*, p. 265.
32. Malcolm Muggeridge, *Something Beautiful for God*, p. 22.
33. *Ibid*, p. 67.
34. Katherine Spink/Mother Teresa, *In the Silence of the Heart*, p. 68.
35. Malcolm Muggeridge, *op. cit.*, pp. 74–5.
36. Katherine Spink/Mother Teresa, *op. cit.*, p. 85.
37. *Church Times.*
38. Bible Society, *Word in Action* report (1990).
39. People to Lourdes Trust, *Have you heard of Akita?*

Bibliography

Allchin, A. M. *The Furnace and the Fountain*, University of Wales Press

Anson, Peter. *The Call of the Desert*

Armstrong, R. J. OFM Cap & Brady, I.C. OFM, *Francis & Clare: the Complete Works: Classics of Western Spirituality*, London SPCK, 1982

Arnold, D. M. *Dorothy Kerin, Called by Christ to Heal*, K&Sc Ltd, 1965

Aston, Margaret. Popular Religious Movements in the Middle Ages, ex *The Christian World*, Geoffrey Barraclough, Thames & Hudson, 1981

Attwater, Donald. *The Penguin Dictionary of Saints*, Penguin Books, 1965

Babington-Smith, C. *Iulia de Beausobre – A Russian Christian in the West*, DLT 1983

Badeni, J. *The Slender Tree*, T. J. Press Ltd, 1981

BBC, Helen Waddell broadcast, 24.5.1989

Bede's *A History of the English Church and People*, Penguin Classics, 1955

Bennet, D. *Emily Davies and the Liberation of Women 1830–1921*, Andre Deutsch, 1990

Bible Society. *Word in Action*

Booth, Catherine. *Papers of Aggressive Christianity*, The Salvation Army, 1980

Booth, Catherine. *Female Ministry: an Address by Mrs General Booth*, London, Salvation Army Book Dept, 1909

Bouquet, J. Allick. *A People's Book of Saints*, Longmans, 1930

Boxer, C. R. *The Christian Century in Japan*, University of California, 1951

Brown, P. *The Book of Kells*, Thomas and Hudson, 1980

Byrne, L. *The Hidden Tradition*, SPCK, 1991

Campbell, D. *Hymns and Hymn Makers*, A&C Black, R&R Clark, 1903

Capps, Walter H. and Wright, Wendy. *Silent Fire*, Harper Forum Books, 1978

Carter, T. T. *Harriet Monsell*, Masters & Co, London, 1884

Cassidy, Sheila. *Audacity to Believe*, Collins, 1977

Chapman, Joan. *Mothers' Union Treasury*, Hamish Hamilton Ltd, 1970

Chenu, B., Prud'homme C., Quéré F., Thomas J-C., *The book of Christian Martyrs*, SCM Press, 1990

Ching, Lucy. *One of the Lucky Ones*, Souvenir Press Ltd, 1982

Clarke, C. P. S. *Saints and Heroes of the Christian Church*, Mowbray, 1931

Corrigan, Dame Felicitas. *Helen Waddell*, London, Gollancz, 1986

Cragg, K. *Having in Rememberance*, J& MECA, 198?

Dalgairns, J. B. An Essay on The Spiritual Life of Medieval England, from *The Scale of Perfection* by Walter Hilton, Westminister Art and Book Co, 1908

David, R. *Notes on St Illtyd's Church, Llantwit Major*. St Illtyd's Church, (Between 1947 & 1971)

Delaney, J. J. & Tobin, J. E. *Dictionary of Catholic Biography*, Hale, 1961

Donovan, Mary S. *Women Priests in the Episcopal Church*, Forward Movement Publications, 1988

Ecumenical Forum of European Christian Women. Individual writings, translated and adapted where necessary by author, collected for the Third Assembly of EFECW held at York 1990

Edwards, R. B. *The Case for Women's Ministry*, SPCK, 1989

Endo, Shusaku. *Silence*, Quartet, 1978

Fischer, K. *Women at the Well*, Paulist Press, 1988

Fletcher, Sheila. *Maude Royden: A Life*, Basil Blackwell, 1989

Friends, Society of. *Christian Faith and Practice in The Experience of the Society of Friends*, 1960, no. 79

Gordon, A. R. M., Bishop of Portsmouth. *Deacons in the Ministry of the Church*, A Report commissioned by the House of Bishops, Church House Publishing, 1988

Gothic Voices, 'A feather in the breath of God', sequences and hymns by Hildegard of Bingen, directed by Christopher Page. Hyperion Records Ltd, 1982

Goudge, Elizabeth. *The Joy of the Snow*, Hodder & Stoughton, 1974

Green, Victor J. *Saints for all Seasons*, Blandford Books, 1982

Hadden & Stubbs. Catalogue SS. Hib.

Harmelink, B. *Florence Nightingale*, Franklin Watts Ltd, 1969

Hawker, Gillian. *The Mirror of Love*, DLT, 1988

Hayward, Charles F. *Missionary Heroines*, Collins (approx.) 1910

Hood, Morag. *The Peace Of Pocohontas*, BBC Radio documentary, 1989(?)

Houselander, Carryl. *The Comforting of Christ*, London, Sheed & Ward, 1947

Huggett, J. *Open to God*, Hodder & Stoughton, 1989

Hughes, G. *God of Surprises*, DLT, 1985

Hunt, R. and Parsons, M. Obituary notice. *Church Times*, 7 December 1990

Israel, Martin. *The Pearl of Great Price*, SPCK, 1988

Johnson, P. *A History of Christianity*, Penguin Books, 1976

Julian of Norwich. *Revelations of Divine Love*, Tr. Clifford Wolters, Penguin Books, 1966

Kavanagh, K. & Rodriguez, O. (Trans). *The Collected Works of St Teresa of Avila, Vol 1: The Book of her Life, Spiritual Testimonies: Soliloquies*. Washington DC, ICS Publications, 1987

Kemp-Welch, Alice. *Of Six Medieval Women*, Macmillan and Co, 1913

Knight, Helen C. *Lady Huntington and her friends*, Baker 1979, 1853(?)

Krumbacher, Karl. *History of the Byzantine Literature*, München, 1897

Lee, David S. Article about St Tydfil

Liverpool Cathedral Windows commentary

McCutcheon, N. in *The Welsh Churchman*, 1985

Marty Martin. *North America, The Oxford Illustrated History of Christianity*, Guild Publishing, 1990

Menzies, Lucy. *Marie de L'Incarnation*, Oxford, Mowbray, 1928

Merz, Veronica. Notes about M. Parète

Moore, K. *She for God*, Allison and Busby, 1978

Muggeridge, Malcolm. *Something Beautiful for God*, Collins, 1971

Nomura, Yushi. *Desert Wisdom*, Eyre & Spottiswoode, 1982

Ouspensky, L. & Lossky, V. *The meaning of Icons*, St Vladimir's Seminary Press, 1983

People to Lourdes Trust. *Have You Heard of Akita?* 71 Hall Street, Burslem, Stoke on Trent, ST6 4BD.

Peregrina Publishing Co, The 1990 Calendar of Holy Women

Preece, Charles. *Woman of the Valleys*, New Life Publications, 1988

Richardson, A. *Women of the Church of England*, Chapman & Hall, 1908

Richmond, T. 'Mary of Masasi' in *Church Times*, 1989

Roberts, A. C. *So Great a Cloud of Witnesses*, Church in Wales Publications, 1986

Roberts, Roger L. *Light of Christ: Evelyn Underhill*, Mowbray, 1981

Ryle, Dean and others. *The Ministry of Women*, A report written by a Committee appointed by His Grace the Archbishop of Canterbury, SPCK, 1919

The Salesian Sisters, *The Story of Laura*

Sayers, Dorothy L. *Are Women Human?* Eerdmans, 1971

Sheppard, W. J. L. *Great Hymns and their Stories*, Lutterworth, 1923

Sisters of La Retraite. *Catherine de Francheville*, 1990

Southern, Sir R. Address given at Requiem Mass for Devorguilla, 1989, reprinted in *Oxford Today*, 1991

Spink, Kathryn/Mother Teresa. *In the Silence of the Heart*, SPCK 1983

Steegmann, M. G. (Trans) *The Book of Divine Consolations of the Blessed Angela Foligno*, Cooper Square Publications, 1966

Stoney, Fania in *Church Times*, 1990

Thérèse of Lisieux, Collected Letters, Sheed & Ward, 1949

Thompson, Phyllis. *Gladys Aylward, A London Sparrow*, Highland Christian Classics, 1971

Tilby, A. Review of *Maude Royden—A Life by S. Fletcher*, Blackwell, in *Church Times*, 1989

Trypanis, Const. *Greek Verse*, Penguin Books, 1988

Underhill, Evelyn. *The Spiritual Life*, Hodder & Stoughton, 1937

Underhill, Evelyn. *Light of Christ*, Longmans, Green and Co. Ltd, 1944

Wade, Labarge M. *Women in Medieval Life*, Hamish Hamilton, 1986

Ware, Kallistos. Eastern Christendom Ex. *The Oxford Illustrated History of Christianity*, Guild publishing, 1990

Ward, Benedicta SLG. *Harlots of the Desert*, Mowbray, 1987

Ward, Benedicta SLG. *The Sayings of the Desert Fathers*, Mowbray, 1975, 1978

Weil, Simone. *Waiting for God*, Trans. Emma Crauford, NY Harper & Row, 1973

Wells, J. *Oxford and its Colleges*, Methuen & Co. Ltd, 1897, revised 1926

Williams D. in *Church Times*, 1990

Williamson, Joseph. *Josephine Butler—The Forgotten Saint*, The Faith Press, 1977

Worcester Diocese Mothers' Union Bible Studies, 1988

Wright, W. M. & Power, J. F. *Francis de Sales; Jane de Chantal: Letters of Spiritual Direction, Classics of Western Spirituality*, Paulist Press, 1986

Zernov, Nicolas. *The Russians and Their Church*, SPCK, 1964

Zundel, Veronica. *Christian Classics*, Lion Publishing, 1985

Index of
Names of Women of Faith